Date Due

Bayfield			
JUL 4 MAY 11	4		
Blyth			

Essays
In Canadian Criticism
1938-1968

DESMOND PACEY

Essays
In Canadian Criticism
1938-1968

TORONTO
The Ryerson Press

SBN 7700 0289 7

Library of Congress Catalog Card
Number 70-93870

This work has been published with the
help of a grant from the Humanities
Research Council of Canada, using funds
provided by the Canada Council.

Printed and bound in Canada
by The Ryerson Press
Toronto

To George Woodcock
Editor of *Canadian Literature* who
suggested this book

Foreword

THIS book brings together most of the articles on Canadian literature which I have written over the past thirty years. When I began to write on this subject, very little interest was being taken in it, either at home or abroad. Now, fortunately, conditions have changed radically. In Canada, courses in Canadian literature are among the most popular in the undergraduate and graduate curricula of most of our universities; in the United States more and more students and scholars are being attracted to the study of our literature as part of the literature of the English-speaking world; and in the United Kingdom and the other nations of the Commonwealth Canadian literature is increasingly commanding attention as a part of Commonwealth literature.

Although some of these essays express attitudes and opinions to which I no longer subscribe, I have felt it desirable to reprint them almost exactly as they originally appeared.

DESMOND PACEY

University of New Brunswick
Fredericton, N.B.
February, 1969

Contents

Contents

Cosmopolitan literature is, at best, but a poor bubble, though a big one. Creative work has always a fatherland.

There is no fine nationality without literature, and . . . no fine literature without nationality.
                                                   —W. B. YEATS

At Last—
A Canadian Literature*

I T will no doubt come as a surprise to most of my readers to learn that there is someone who has the temerity to believe that the foundations of an essentially national literature in Canada are, if not laid, at least in the process of being laid. For the average Englishman, and even a great number of those who are well above the average in literary erudition, seems to be quite unaware that Canada is either able or anxious to produce anything other than wheat. Let me hasten to assure him that the desire is of long standing, and that it is now in great likelihood of being fulfilled.

Canadian literature, and Canadian culture generally, suffered, during the last century and for the first two decades of this, from the fault of being "derived." It is a fault that all colonial cultures have in common, and it is a fault that is by no means easy to eradicate. For an illustration of this, we have but to pay a visit to the exhibition of Canadian art now on display in the Tate. Quite clearly, the art of the last century can be summed up in the one word "imitative." That is not to dismiss it as entirely valueless as art, but it is to preclude its being in any essential sense considered Canadian. But the persevering critic will notice that, early in this century, a sudden change overcame the pictorial arts in Canada. A national school of painting sprang up, known as "The Group of Seven," which broke the bonds of imitation and painted in a peculiar and distinctive way.

Those interested in Canadian culture have long hoped that an analogous movement would appear in Canadian literature.

---

*Published in *The Cambridge Review*, December 2, 1938.

For the history of literature in Canada in the nineteenth century is the same as the history of painting—it is all "derived," "imitative." If one were to read an anthology of Canadian poetry up to about 1925, he would find himself muttering "Wordsworth," "Tennyson," "Arnold." It makes monotonous reading. A descriptive landscape poem obviously inspired by Wordsworth alternates with a reflective religious poem derived from Matthew Arnold, the only variation being an occasional melting lyric after the lesser manner of Tennyson. Nor did the turn of the century bring relief from the monotony: Bliss Carman, Archibald Lampman, Duncan Campbell Scott—they had talent, but were content to tread the same paths as their predecessors. There are passages of rare beauty in their poetry, but there is nothing that stamps them as distinctly Canadian. One feels a lack of sincerity in their work—they do not see the Canada they describe through their own eyes, but through the eyes of Wordsworth or William Cullen Bryant. It is needless to say that in the process the scene ceases to be Canadian, and becomes a sort of hybrid offspring of Canada and the English Lake Country.

This is tantamount to saying that it was a sentimental poetry. Especially is this true of the women lyricists, even of the best of them, Marjorie Pickthall. What was lacking was nothing more or less than downright honesty. If only some obscure bard, who had read no foreign poetry, would arise and sing of his native land!

But such a phenomenon was most unlikely to occur. For literature in Canada had largely fallen into that most deadly of traps—that of being "a polite accomplishment." At times Canadian poetry was in the hands of hardly a score of people— a vested interest of the select few.

It might have been expected that the Great War would bring a change. And in a measure it did. Robert W. Service, an ambulance attendant in the Canadian army, attracted widespread attention in England, Australia, and America, by his volumes of war verses. Let those who are inclined to scoff, pause to consider that Robert Service did more by his rough rhymes to attract attention to Canada than all the sentimental vapourings of decades. Admittedly the poems were, for the most part, mere doggerel, but they had a rude vigour and an unflinching honesty that had so long been lacking in Canadian poetry.

But such humble efforts could not be expected to initiate a literary revolution. The real hope lay in another, and quite unexpected, quarter. It was said above that what was needed was a "natural poet," one unlearned in the traditions of foreign literature. Paradoxically enough, the man who, we hope, has really laid the foundation of a Canadian poetry, was one who, probably, knew more of foreign poetry than any other in the country—a young professor of English Literature. This was E. J. Pratt, now Head of the Department of English in Victoria College, University of Toronto.

Beginning in the 1920's, Dr. Pratt has produced a body of verse quite unlike any that had appeared previously in Canada. The ruggedness that had been so woefully lacking he supplied in full measure. He brought to his task a first-hand knowledge of the essential Canadian occupations—he had been a member of the crew of Maritime fishing boats, he had helped harvest wheat in the great Canadian prairies. He was also gifted with a keen sense of rhythm, a power of striking imagery, a wealth of humour, and an unsurpassed humanity of temperament. Moreover, his talent seems to increase with the years, and his latest volumes, such as *The Titanic* and *The Fable of the Goats*, reveal, in addition to the qualities enumerated above, a keen sense of social justice and a fine satirical verve.

One name is not, of course, sufficient to constitute a literature. But there are signs that others will follow. Two years ago *The Canadian Poetry Magazine* was founded, and, under the editorship of Dr. Pratt, bids fair to establish, on a firm foundation, the edifice so lately begun. For aspiring poets in Canada have now, what they have hitherto lacked, an organ for expression.

Nor is poetry the only department of literature in which signs of life are evident. The novel, so long entirely neglected, has now a very able and promising practitioner in the person of Mr. Morley Callaghan. His best novels—such as *Such Is My Beloved* and *More Joy in Heaven*—have attracted wide attention in America, where he is considered to rank beside such figures as John Dos Passos and Ernest Hemingway. The establishment of an annual award for the best novel, for which we are indebted to the Governor-General, Lord Tweedsmuir, should prove a great stimulus to potential authors. Last year this award went to Bertram Brooker, a painter turned novelist, whose work showed great promise.

The same stir is evident in the sphere of expository and critical prose. A comparatively young magazine, *The Canadian Forum,* provides a medium for such literary endeavour, and by the quality of its prose and the keenness of its literary acumen has already attracted a considerable following both in Canada and the United States.

An effort is also being made to arouse the Canadian reading public from its apathy. The Canadian Bookmen's Association, newly formed under the direction of Dr. Pelham Edgar, is enrolling all book-lovers under its banner, and by such means as Book Fairs in the cities and provincial towns, and free lectures on literary subjects, is rapidly attracting the attention of the people.

With so much activity, may one not be excused for believing that we are at last to have a Canadian literature?

Frederick Philip Grove*

I, the cosmopolitan, had fitted myself to be the spokesman
of a race—not necessarily a race in the ethnographic sense;
in fact, not at all in that sense; rather in the sense of a
stratum of society which cross-sectioned all races, consisting
of those who, in no matter what climate, at no matter what
time, feel the impulse of starting anew, from the ground
up, to fashion a new world which might serve as the
breeding-place of a civilization to come. These people, the
pioneers, reaffirmed in me my conception of what often
takes the form of a tragic experience: the age old conflict
between human desire and the stubborn resistance of nature:
order must arise out of chaos; the wilderness must be
tamed. No matter where I looked, I failed to see that the
task of recording that struggle of man with nature had ever
adequately been done . . .[1]

THUS does Mr. Grove indicate his central aim as
a writer, and hint at the strange destiny that fitted him, the
erstwhile intimate of the literary salons of Paris, to record the
drama of pioneer life as it unfolded on the prairies of Western
Canada.

Frederick Philip Grove was born in 1872 while his parents
were in transit through Poland. His father was of Anglo-
Swedish stock, his mother Scottish. His parents separated while
he was still an infant, and most of his childhood and youth
were spent travelling about Europe with his mother. In the
course of this travel he came in contact with a brilliant cosmopolitan society of artists and intellectuals, and was encouraged
to read widely in both classical and modern literature.

As a result of his unsettled mode of life, his early formal
education was desultory, but by the fall of 1889 he had secured
the academic standing necessary to enter the University of

*Published in The Manitoba Arts Review, Spring, 1943.
[1]This passage is from Grove's Autobiography, still in manuscript. I wish to
express my gratitude to him for permitting me to read the manuscript and
quote from it. [The autobiography was published in 1947 under the title In
Search of Myself.]

Paris. His entrance was deferred, however, in order to permit him to accompany his uncle on an overland expedition to Siberia. Of the climactic effect of this journey on his future Grove writes:

Life as a student in Paris, life in the various parts of the world through which I was to hurry during the years that followed, paled in my eyes whenever I thought of the steppes; and only when I struck my roots into the west of Canada did I feel at home again. In the steppes, only, so it seemed, life was lived as life pure and simple, as life *qua* life. For here was the staggering fact: these steppes were inhabited; they were peopled by man. Perhaps, in this experience, I must look for the reason why, when shipwrecked in America, I remained in Canada and clung to it with my soul till it had replaced Siberia as the central fact in my adult mentality. Like Siberia, Canada needed to be fought for by the soul: but very few Canadians know it; they think of it as of a Europe enlarged.[2]

Instead of retracing his steps across Russia, he returned to Europe by way of Java, Malaya, India, the Red Sea, and the Mediterranean. In 1890 he entered the University of Paris, devoting himself chiefly to the study of archaeology.

Thanks to connections of his mother, who had died two years previously, Grove enjoyed contacts in Paris with such French writers as André Gide, Henri de Régnier, Jules Renard, Heredia, Mallarmé, and Rimbaud. These contacts, of varying degrees of intimacy, served to confirm in him a desire, early conceived, to be a writer. His first efforts were in French verse, but none were published.

His period of study at Paris was a brief one, and was followed by equally brief periods at the universities of Rome and Munich. He secured no degree—a fact which was later to prove of almost fatal significance. His summer vacations, meanwhile, were spent in travel. In this he was encouraged by his father, who gave no hint of financial stringency. In 1891 he made a voyage to Australia and New Zealand by way of Madagascar and Capetown, and in 1892 to America.

In August, 1892, having travelled across the continent and back, he found himself in Toronto without funds. He cabled

---

[2]*Ibid.*

to his father for assistance. The disconcerting response was that his father had recently died, leaving little but debts. The plight of the twenty-year-old youth was desperate. Having no degree, the professions were closed to him; on the other hand, he had no business or technical training or experience. It was this dilemma which made necessary the successive attempts to make a living by manual labour, and concurrently to come to terms with American civilization, which Grove has graphically described in his best-known book, *A Search for America*.

His first job was as a waiter in a cheap eating-house on Yonge Street, Toronto, and this was followed by jobs as a book-agent, factory-hand, roustabout on a lake steamer, and finally as a hobo following the wheat harvest across the western plains of the United States and Canada. This last phase continued for almost twenty years, and provided Grove with the material for his novels of western life; but this was its only asset. He yearned for a settled home, and for leisure in which to write. Yet there seemed no possible avenue of escape: certainly he could never hope to save enough from his seasonal earnings to establish himself.

Escape came, dramatically and unexpectedly, in 1912. Seated in the waiting-room of Fargo railway station, reading Baudelaire's *Fleurs du Mal,* Grove was accosted by a French-Canadian priest from St. Boniface. Intrigued, doubtless, by the spectacle of such a man reading such a book, the priest drew from Grove the story of his life. The priest's suggestion was that Grove should seek a position as a teacher in the province of Manitoba, and he gave him a letter of introduction to the deputy minister of education.

Grove took the advice, came to Winnipeg (where he took up quarters at a hoboes' hostelry on Main Street North), interviewed the deputy minister in his overalls, and left the office the prospective principal of a high school. For the balance of the school year he was engaged as teacher of the rural school at Haskett, and in the fall, after a summer at Normal, became principal of the Intermediate School at Winkler. He served successively as a teacher at Virden, Gladstone, Falmouth, Eden, and Rapid City, meanwhile acquiring, by extramural study, the bachelor of arts degree of the University of Manitoba. In August, 1914, he married a fellow-teacher at Winkler, and their first child, a daughter, was born in 1915. This girl died in 1927, and the Groves now have a son in his early teens.

It was in 1893, shortly after coming to America, that Grove prepared the first draft of his first novel, *A Search for America*, and by 1912 he had found time, in the intervals of harvesting, to write twelve novels; but it was not until 1925 that a novel of his—*Settlers of the Marsh*—was published. Prior to this, however, he had published two volumes of essays: *Over Prairie Trails* (1922), and *The Turn of the Year* (1923). The publication of these two volumes brought him to the notice of such men as A. L. Phelps, Watson Kirkconnell, Principal Riddell, W. L. Grant, W. J. Alexander, and Carleton Stanley, all of whom urged him to continue writing and promised what aid they could muster in finding publishers. Thus encouraged, he rapidly completed *Settlers of the Marsh*, and rewrote *A Search for America*. The former novel had an unfortunate reception: it was condemned as obscene and banned by most libraries, and this had the effect, rather surprisingly, of killing its sales. *A Search for America*, on the other hand, published in 1927, was a moderate bestseller. Four other novels by Grove have since been published: *Our Daily Bread* (1928), *The Yoke of Life* (1930), *Fruits of the Earth* (1933), and *Two Generations* (1939). A third volume of essays, consisting largely of challenging lectures delivered to Canadian Clubs during a nation-wide tour in 1928, was published in 1929. In 1935 Grove was awarded the Lorne Pierce Gold Medal for his contribution to Canadian literature.

Mr. Grove lived at Rapid City, Manitoba, until 1929, when an offer by the Macmillan Company of Canada to act as a reader took him to Ontario. The depression, however, led to the withdrawal of this offer. For a time he was associated with the firm of Graphic Publishers, in Ottawa, but when this firm broke up he settled on a farm near Simcoe, where he still lives.

He has not found the profession of literature in Canada a very rewarding one, either materially or spiritually, and in two recent articles[3] he has given voice to his disillusionment. In the most recent of these articles, entitled "A Postscript to *A Search for America*", there is an anecdote which focuses his bitterness. Having been forced by sheer financial need to seek

---

[3]*University of Toronto Quarterly*, October, 1940; *Queen's Quarterly*, Autumn, 1942.

seasonal employment in a canning factory last year, Grove encountered an Oxford graduate in similarly reduced circumstances. "What brought you to this?" he enquired of the Oxford man. "Drink!" was the reply. "And you?" "Literature!" said Grove.

He still has several novels in manuscript, awaiting a publisher.

II

It is easy to understand why *A Search for America* has always been Grove's most popular novel. From the standpoint of subject-matter alone it has an enormous advantage over his other books. They are confined almost wholly to a small section of the Canadian rural scene; *A Search for America* ranges swiftly across much of the American continent, from Toronto and New York to the great wheatfields of the midwest. The effect is as of a kaleidoscopic survey of American life as seen through the bewildered but keenly observant eyes of a new immigrant. Nor is it the surface alone that we see: the book takes us behind the scenes, into the kitchens and washrooms of a restaurant, into the headquarters of shady enterprises calculated to trap the "sucker," into the hoboes' camps, and into the bunkhouses of the harvest hands.

In its style and method, too, this book is more immediately attractive. Based as it is on Grove's actual experiences, and written moreover shortly after their occurrence, it has a closeness of observation, a sharpness of impact, a clarity of outline that compel attention. It moves more swiftly than his other novels, which tend to be slow-moving, slightly ponderous in effect. Here is a passage which will convey the pace with which much of the book proceeds:

Behind the counter a casual observer would have seen half-naked maniacs dancing and jumping about in crazy lunacy. In the corridor, waiters were bustling each other, reaching up into the dish-rack, flinging plates on the counter and bellowing orders at the top of their voices. From out of the reeking pit behind me came yelling shouts, repeating every order that was given. Plates full of food were thrown back on trays held by the waiters. The swinging doors in front kept opening and slamming shut in ever-accelerated pulsation. Whoever passed through gave them a vigorous kick. The checker stood on a chair behind his desk, roaring for checks, swinging his arms, jumping like one possessed; but in reality he did nothing but spear the checks on spindles, although he sometimes tried to keep up the pretence of verifying an order which passed out on a tray.[4]

The only clog upon the novel's rapidity is Grove's tendency to generalize, to philosophize, about the events he narrates. One can understand the motivation of these passages: he wished to ensure that his book should be read not simply as entertainment, but as a contribution to the study of the problems of the immigrant. Having chosen to embody his observations in the form of a novel, however, rather than in the form of a sociological treatise, Grove should, one cannot help feeling, have adhered to the laws of the selected medium. He should, in other words, have been willing to allow the narrated events to convey to the reader their general implications. This is not to question the value of these passages as judgments—some of them are undoubtedly shrewd and intelligent comments upon the nature of American civilization; but they are not, at any rate in such abundance, of the proper stuff of fiction. This tendency to authorial comment Grove was never to outgrow, though it becomes steadily less obstructive.

It is to the documentary realism of Zola, and more particularly to such of Zola's Anglo-Saxon disciples as Gissing and Dreiser, that the method and substance of this novel are most nearly related. The determination to tell the truth and the whole truth, no matter how unpleasant; the conception of man as a creature largely in the control of forces other than his own will; the passionate sympathy for the underdog; the patient accuracy and completeness in transcribing material details—all these are here. Particularly in the pages dealing with the restaurant are there descriptions which inescapably remind one of Zola: descriptions of the odour and atmosphere of the kitchen, its dirt and grease. Here is Grove's description of an old man's face, in which the realistic technique is obvious:

It was bony, with the eyes set deep in hollow sockets overarched by bushy, dirty-white eyebrows. His cheekbones were

---

[4]*Op. cit.*, p. 57.

red and warty; the whole face framed by a straggling, grey beard. His lips were thin and dry, his nostrils dilated with exertion.[5]

Even this was not considered by its author to be sufficiently accurate in its detail; there is this further treatment ten pages later:

The cheekbones stood out in high relief, reddened to a carmine tinge by an exceedingly fine network of enlarged surface-veins. Above, they sloped away to temples so hollow that they seemed to form an acute angle with a perfectly flat forehead jutting out over the caves of his eyes like a pent-house. The cheeks too were hollow, as if all the molars in his mouth were gone. Cheek, temples, forehead, were a ghastly white, in strong contrast to the red circles on his cheekbones. Jaws and chin seemed to form a semi-circular ridge under the short, straggling white beard.[6]

From such painstaking accuracy the book derives its strength: it is a full, solid, durable picture of working America at the end of the last century.

It is worth remarking that when Grove came to write seriously he did not employ the techniques of those writers with whom he was friendly in Paris, but followed rather the methods of the preceding generation of French writers.

Of the other five novels, four, dealing with life on the prairies, may be arranged in two pairs, while the fifth, having its setting in Ontario, stands apart. Of the prairie novels, *Settlers of the Marsh* and *The Yoke of Life* form one pair; *Our Daily Bread* and *Fruits of the Earth* the other. The former pair both have their setting in the marshy territory between Gladstone and Falmouth, Manitoba; they both have as a background the efforts of the immigrant settlers of that region to clear the bush and establish permanent farmsteads; and they both have as their central character a young man whose dreams of a bright future are frustrated by a combination of hostile circumstances and his own passion. The latter pair, on the other hand, though retaining the pioneer background, have as their central characters not immigrants but second-generation Canadians of

[5]*Ibid.*, p. 54.
[6]*Ibid.,* p. 64.

Anglo-Saxon extraction, whose aim it is not so much to establish themselves as to establish a tradition that shall live after them. This aim, too, is frustrated.

Settlers of the Marsh is probably Grove's most ambitious undertaking: it is an effort to plumb the very depths of human longing and despair. Niels Lindstedt, the central character, has a dream: that of wresting from the wilderness a permanent homestead in which to marry and rear a family. The land, the house, he secures; but not, until after many years and almost unbearable suffering, the girl. Naive and innocent, but of strong passions, he falls in love first with a girl who, because of certain repugant sexual experiences in the life of her mother, has vowed never to marry. Thwarted by this vow, Niels allows himself in a weak moment to be seduced by a widow of doubtful reputation. He marries this woman, innocent of her past, and after years of hideous incompatibility kills her in a fit of insanity occasioned by the final revelation of her profligacy. Grove, to my mind mistakenly, does not end the story here, but deals with the trial, Niels' conviction to a term of imprisonment, his ultimate release and reunion with the girl of his first choice, who is now a woman of forty and ready to forget her vow.

These last scenes are in the nature of an anticlimax, and seriously weaken the book. It has other weaknesses. It is difficult to believe that Niels should have remained innocent so long of Mrs. Vogel's past; difficult to believe also that she should have consented to marry him, and having done so to submit to his harsh treatment of her. Moreover, the loose episodic structure which, in *A Search for America*, seemed natural and proper, here results in a diffuseness of effect, a kind of scrappiness. Many of the early pages read rather like a rough draft for a novel than the finished product:

Niels cleared his land . . .
Spring came.
He enlarged his stable and built a chicken-house.
    He sold hay . . .
Then breaking and seeding, with propitious weather towards
    the end of April.
He had eighteen acres in crop, six of wheat, four of oats, and
    the rest in barley.[7]

---

[7]*Op. cit.*, p. 120.

Such a scene is not an exception; it is merely one of a long series. We feel the need of a master craftsman, selecting and arranging, building up significant wholes. Render the scene fully, we are moved to protest, or omit it altogether. The sentences trailing off into a row of dots were no doubt intended to be suggestive; actually they are irritating in their unemphatic, inconclusive vagueness.

For all its blemishes, the book is a powerful one, difficult to forget. It contains scenes which, in their capacity to arouse in us the tragic emotions of pity and fear, have seldom been surpassed. Such a scene is that in which Ellen, Niels' first love, reveals to him the sources, in her mother's tragic history as a wife, of her refusal to marry. The novel is memorable also for the insight it gives us into the conditions of pioneer life, for the beauty and accuracy of its descriptions of the Manitoba landscape and climate, and for the creation of characters who live.

Briefer treatment must suffice for *The Yoke of Life.* Len Sterner, its central character, dreams of securing an education, of mastering, indeed, "all human knowledge in all its branches." That the dream proves futile is in part the result of the conditions of pioneer life, in part the result of his falling madly in love with a girl unworthy of him. The book ends with the pair of lovers deliberately going to a joint death in the waters of a northern lake. Again the ending seems to me the weakest part of the book, and this for two reasons. In the first place, it is so similar to the climactic scene of Dreiser's *American Tragedy* that for anyone familiar with the latter novel the association inevitably intrudes itself, thus blurring the impression in the same way that the impression is blurred when two exposures are made on the same section of photographic film. In the second place, this display of adolescent melodramatics does not seem consistent with Len's character. True, we have seen him act wildly on other occasions, but only when feverish or before he had time to think; this double drowning is presented as the deliberate product of days of preparation and planning.

To turn to the second pair of prairie novels: *Our Daily Bread* is the story of John Elliott, a farmer in the Sedgeby district of Saskatchewan, whose dream it is to see his family of ten children settled on farms around him in the patriarchal manner. Instead they all scatter, in most cases meet with misfortune, and he goes to his death a lonely and embittered old man. In its craftsmanship this novel is transitional: it begins hesitantly, awkwardly, in the manner of *Settlers*, but builds up gradually to a compelling intensity over which Grove nevertheless holds strict artistic control. It is in my view the greatest of Grove's novels: greater than *Fruits of the Earth* by virtue of its completeness, than *Settlers of the Marsh* by virtue of its credibility, than *A Search for America* by virtue of its cohesion. The latter half of the book, dealing with the encroaching senility of Elliott and his failure to find comfort with any of his children, is remarkable for its psychological accuracy. One inevitably thinks as one reads, "this is how it feels to be old." The ending of the novel is magnificent. Broken in body and spirit, comfortless, alone, the old man makes his way gropingly back over miles of prairie to his old farmstead to die. There, in the broken-down house, they find him, the house the symbol of the ruin of all his hopes. Once it was the showplace of the district, now:

They were horrified when they saw the house. The windows were broken without exception. The greater part of the floor had been torn up. Black spots on the prairie about the house, covered with charcoal, were evidence of the fact that camp-fires had been lit there, no doubt by travelling harvesters. The room in which the father lay was open to the winds; and everything in it was coated with dust and chaff.[8]

Thus, Grove suggests, does time mock man's dream of permanence.

In style and organization, *Fruits of the Earth* marks a considerable advance over its predecessors. No longer do sentences trail off into a row of dots. More striking still, the story is built up by a series of selected, fully rendered scenes, rather than by scrappy episodes. Very similar in theme to *Our Daily Bread*, as I indicated above, it would have been a better novel than its partner had it been carried to a definite conclusion. It cries out for a tragic finale such as is supplied by John Elliott's death at the end of *Our Daily Bread*, but nothing adequate occurs. We learn from the preface that the germ of the story was the sight of a derelict farmhouse of palatial dimensions; but at the end of the

---

[8]*Op. cit.*, p. 389.

novel, Spalding, though he has suffered much, is far from abandoning his farm.[9]

Two Generations is related to the two novels which we have just considered in that it deals with the conflicting wills and interests of a father and his children, but it has its setting in Ontario and is told from the point of view rather of the younger generation than the older. It is well and solidly constructed, and reveals a keen appreciation of the psychology of childhood, but it has not the power or intensity of the prairie series. One guesses that the relative stability of the Ontario rural scene does not excite Grove's imagination, which seems to thrive best on the stark, the wild, and the forbidding.

The purpose of this article is to assess Grove as a novelist, but passing mention must be made of his three volumes of essays. It may well be that the first two volumes, consisting largely of descriptions of the prairie landscape, will outlive his novels. Grove has a great admiration for Thoreau, and it is of Thoreau that these essays inevitably remind us. There is the same capacity for selfless absorption in the observation of natural phenomena, the same combination of aesthetic and scientific interest and response, the same alternation between the attitude of the practical man and of the philosopher and dreamer. Lacking, however, are Thoreau's brilliant, taut, epigrammatic style and his occasional flashes of mystical insight.

III

As a novelist, Mr. Grove has certain definite limitations. He is not a distinguished stylist. His prose, though capable of occasional felicities, is for the most part pedestrian. His sentences tend to be uniform in length, with insufficient variety in their rhythms. His thought falls naturally into a set of phrases which in time grow stereotyped. Sometimes the style is positively awkward and verbose:

His age, full of enigmatic developments concentrated into a few hours, saturated with what is commonly spread out over years of scarcely preceptible unfolding, was pre-eminently that of the mythic poets who project into nature the procreations of that awe in which they stand of themselves, in the forms of fabulous concrescences of incongruous parts which they harmonize into imaginable wholes.[10]

That is hardly the style of great fiction. When Grove describes nature, however, or a simple farm scene, his prose style often takes on great beauty. It is only just to quote one such passage, from *Fruits of the Earth*:

Perhaps nothing on earth so reflects the Sunday spirit of rest as a large, high and empty barn, with the light entering through the rows of dusty windows above the stalls. The very smell of hay and musty straw contributes to it. The air, pervaded with the slightest taint of ammonia and impelled by the currents which enter through the doors as if it were cooled by them, moves in a leisurely, lazy way. The world of work and worry seems far removed, veiled by a curtain of unreality. Time stands still. The paths which the sunspots trace over floor and walls are deprived of their significance as indicating the flow of hours. The rectangles of brilliant light lie like palpable flakes, their edges curved and curled up by the chaff.[11]

Anyone who is familiar with farming will immediately recognize the truth of that description, and the rhythm of the prose enforces the peace of the scene it describes.

Not only is Mr. Grove limited in point of style; the structure of his novels, especially the early ones, leaves much to be desired. His themes, also, are rather limited, as witness the fact that of the six novels he has so far published, four may be arranged in pairs with very similar themes. Finally, his novels are almost wholly lacking in humour: one would never guess from reading his prairie series that these people could abandon themselves to the wild stamp and fling of the barn-dance.

But if the occasional gaieties of the pioneer life are lacking, little else is. This is Grove's surest passport to immortality, that he has recorded faithfully and accurately the processes by which the farm settlements of western Canada were built up. In *Settlers of the Marsh* we witness the efforts of the immigrant pioneers to clear the bush, break the land, build their rude

---

[10]*The Yoke of Life*, p. 68.
[11]*Op. cit.*, p. 235.

houses and barns, "prove up" their claims, acquire machinery and stock, establish schools. The same struggle as in the background of *The Yoke of Life*; in addition we get an extensive treatment of life in a western lumber camp and glimpses of the city of Winnipeg in the first two decades of this century. In *Our Daily Bread* we see the transition in western agricultural methods as tractors replace horses and automobiles, buggies; we see also the effects of the First World War upon the farmer, and of the alternate booms and depressions which followed in its wake. In *Fruits of the Earth* we witness the growth of a western farm settlement from the arrival of the first settler until it is a thickly settled and properly organized community. with its own municipal institutions and officers. These times are past; and it is Grove's high honour that he alone, in the medium of art, caught them in their passage. Research students of the future will go back to these novels for knowledge of the pioneer era; they are valuable documents in our social history.

The pioneer life, as Grove portrays it, was a grim one, fraught with human suffering. Gradually the settlements took shape, but only at the expense of many individual lives:

How about other settlers here in the bush? There isn't one left out of every five that started. Where are they? They put in three, four years of their lives and then go back to the town to work for wages. New settlers come and take their places; and they, too, leave in their turn. It takes three, four settlers in succession before one can make it a go. Each profits from the labour the last one put in.[12]

For the women especially was it hard. The heavy work, added to the loneliness, broke the spirit of all but the strongest of them. Always with child, they must work none the less; indeed they deliberately over-exert themselves to bring on miscarriages: children are needed to help with the work, but after a certain number they become only extra mouths to feed.

Just as the background of pioneer life is accurately rendered in its grimmer aspects, so is the prairie landscape. The memorable descriptive scenes are those which record the fury of the elements: blizzards, hail and thunderstorms. There is a magnificent storm scene in *Settlers of the Marsh*, too long to quote.

---

[12]*The Yoke of Life*, p. 54.

This briefer description, from *The Yoke of Life*, will suggest how keenly alive are Grove's senses to the subtle changes of mood and shape and colour and atmosphere:

Shortly after dinner there was an indefinable change. No wind sprang up; but the aspen leaves trembled as in the spasm of a sob.

Then, suddenly, things began to develop fast. Huge, vaulted clouds rose into the sky as if from nowhere. Quick little rushes of wind flitted this way and that; and there was a noticeable fall in temperature. A flash of lightning winked over the darkening landscape, followed by an unearthly silence.

Every manifestation of the powers above entered the vast, still dome of the sky as words spoken behind the wings enter a darkened stage. Yet this stage was not dark, but rather lighted with a weird, incomprehensible radiance which made colours and details of form stand out with marvellous brilliance and distinctness and at an enormous distance . . .

A seething, whitish festoon of cloud drew nearer from the northwest, rolling along like a cylindrical, revolving broom. Every now and then it was whitely illumined by a flash which was at last followed by nearer and nearer thunder.

Abruptly, then, with a fierce onslaught of wind which bent the young poplars everywhere to the breaking point, there was a drumming noise which rapidly increased in volume. Everywhere hail rebounded from the ground . . .[13]

The characters who must withstand such onslaughts are portrayed with varying degrees of success. Old men stand out by far the most distinctly. There is an old man in almost every novel, and invariably he steals the show. In *A Search for America* it is the broken-down old waiter, the description of whose face was quoted above; in *Settlers of the Marsh* it is old Sigurdson; in *Our Daily Bread*, John Elliott himself; in *Fruits of the Earth* and *The Yoke of Life* two old schoolteachers, Blaine and Crawford. A sentence from *Fruits of the Earth* makes clear why old men so attract him as a subject: "The decay of the human faculties impressed him as part of the human tragedy inherent in the fundamental conditions of man's life on earth."[14]

---

[13]*Op. cit.*, p. 58-9.
[14]*Op. cit.*, p. 246.

Almost always these old men act as mentor to a young boy, and the accounts of these relationships between youth and age are among the finest things Grove has done. One guesses that these passages are based on personal experience, that as a teacher Grove entered into many such relationships with promising lads. He must have made a very good teacher, for he obviously has a deep understanding of children: next to the old men they are the most real of his characters.

In the sphere of human relationships, Grove seems to me weakest in handling the relations between the sexes. These passages in his novels always seem rather forced and awkward, as if he were bringing himself to deal with something distasteful to him. His characters scarcely ever view sex healthily and normally: either they are burdened with a sense of guilt which makes the very thought of physical union seem evil, or they are shamelessly and vulgarly lustful. Marriages in his novels are the fruit of immature sexual instincts, of physical attraction only, and when this attraction dies from satiety the marriage becomes a yoke.

His view of the frustrations inherent in the sexual lives of his characters accords well, however, with his general view of man's life an earth. All his characters, as we have seen, have a dream, and for all the dream ends in futility. The external forces of environment and circumstance combine with blind internal urges to compass the ruin of man.

The universe he views as a gigantic sand-trap, in which man must defend himself on all sides against a cosmic attack. Environment, time, chance and fate are hostile forces arraigned against him. A blizzard is described as "a merciless force which was slowly numbing them by ceaseless pounding."[15] Man dreams of moulding this environment to his will, but no sooner has he reared his most pretentious structures than wind and weather are at work, slowly but surely wreaking destruction:

He would stand at a corner of his huge house and look closely at brick and mortar. It was five years since the house had been built. Five years only! Yet already little sand grains embedded in the mortar were crumbling away; already the edges of the bricks were being rounded by a process of weathering. When

---

[15]*Settlers of the Marsh*, p. 14.

he bent and looked closely at the ground, near the wall, he saw a thin layer of red dust mixed with those sand grains. The weathering process would go on and on; and what would come of it? Dr. Vanbruik told him of the clay mounds covering the sites of ancient Babylonian cities, loaning him a book or two on excavations. The moment a work of man was finished, nature set to work to take it down again.[16]

All human effort is destined to the same futility. "I don't mind the work," says one of John Elliott's sons-in-law, "but the days go by, and the weeks, and the months, and nothing comes of it."[17]

Men are mere pawns in the hands of vast forces beyond their control. Niels Lindstedt is described as "a leaf borne along in the wind, a prey to things beyond his control, a fragment swept away by torrents."[18] We are told that "Life had him in its grip and played with him; the vastness of the spaces looked calmly on."[19] Over all human endeavour broods the shadow of an inescapable doom:

The moment was coming. It had prepared itself. It was rushing along the lane of time where neither he nor she could escape it. Yes, it was already here. It stood in front of them; and its face was not smiling; it was grimly tragical . . .[20]

But we are doomed not only by external forces. Within us there are born fatal tendencies, beyond the reach of the conscious will, which propel us just as surely to disaster. "He could not help himself; he was he; he could not act or speak except according to laws inherent in him."[21]—thus we read of Niels. And in *Our Daily Bread* Henrietta says:

I supposed I was born under an unlucky star. When my nature was compounded, one ingredient was left out by mistake. Sweetness. Who is to blame? I am I. I can't help myself.[22]

---

[16]*Fruits of the Earth*, p. 160.
[17]*Our Daily Bread*, p. 203.
[18]*Settlers of the Marsh*, p. 78.
[19]*Ibid.*, p. 43.
[20]*Ibid.*, p. 141.
[21]*Ibid.*, p. 248.
[22]*Op. cit.*, p. 200.

Such a philosophy is obviously in the naturalistic tradition, and establishes Grove's kinship with Zola and his school. Of the English novelists, Grove is nearest to Hardy; and of the American, to Dreiser. These affiliations are significant for two reasons. In the first place, they should serve to remind us that Grove came to maturity in the nineties, that he belongs to a generation only slightly younger than Hardy and Zola, and to the same generation as Dreiser and Hamsun. This fact goes far to explain the somewhat old-fashioned air which many people find in his novels, and also the occasional awkwardness of technique. Dreiser's novels, too, seem old-fashioned and awkward today. It is not proper to compare Grove with such writers as Joyce and Woolf and Dos Passos: they are of a more modern generation, with different aims and interests. In the second place, this affiliation is significant because with it, for the first time, the Canadian novel became part of a great movement of world literature.

It was a fortunate chance for Canada, and especially for the west, that brought Grove to our shores. For years he stood alone as a novelist seeking sincerely to record and interpret our life. We are not yet in a position to pass final judgment upon him, for he has work in progress and novels unpublished; but even if he were not to write another line his place of honour in our literary history would be assured. Minor weaknesses his novels have, but above all they are strong and true. If the picture he presents is a grim one, yet the final impression of his life and work is by no means dispiriting. These novels, wrung as they are from Grove's own suffering, are enduring testimony to man's unconquerable hope and his determination to shape truth and beauty from despair.

The Novel in Canada*

THE recent popular success of three Canadian novels has served to arouse a high degree of enthusiasm for the prospects of that branch of our literature. Bruce Hutchison's *Hollow Men*, Gwethalyn Graham's *Earth and High Heaven*, and Hugh MacLennan's *Two Solitudes* have all been chosen by one or other of the large American book-distributing clubs, have maintained high places for a considerable period on the list of best-sellers in the United States, and have been favourably reviewed in leading American magazines. Such a threefold Canadian triumph is, I believe, without precedent, though it is sobering to remind ourselves that novels by Gilbert Parker and Ralph Connor were best-sellers a few decades ago.

My purpose in this article is not to deplore the fact that this enthusiasm has been created, nor to engage in a "debunking" of the three novels named, but rather, by pointing to the difficulties and deficiencies which have characterized the history of Canadian fiction in the past, to restore our critical perspective and to suggest that our enthusiasm should be tempered with caution.

That our fiction has lagged behind our poetry is well known. It is true that we have yet produced no preëminently great poet, but in pioneers like Sangster and Mair, in the Lampman-Scott and Roberts-Carman groups, and in contemporaries such as Pratt, Birney, Livesay and Smith, we have a gallery of poetical figures to whom we can point without embarrassment. In the novel, however, there are no comparable names which would evoke general assent. Of novelists of the last century, there would probably be general approval for the claims of Halibur-

*Published in *Queen's Quarterly*, Autumn, 1945.

22

ton, though *Sam Slick* is rather a series of humorous sketches than a novel proper; and William Kirby would probably also be chosen, though his fame rests upon a single novel, *The Golden Dog*. But who today—apart from professional students of our literary history—remembers Richardson, author of the once famous *Wacousta*, or Mrs. Leprohon, prolific producer of historical romances a century ago? In this century, because our memories are fresher, there are many more names which we might suggest for inclusion, but of them all, how many do we seriously believe to be candidates for fame? Personally, I believe that the novels of Frederick Philip Grove, because of their honest if rather laboured portrayal of the Canadian scene, will be so remembered. Morley Callaghan has written several distinguished novels, but seems, unfortunately, to have deserted the craft in mid-career. Mazo de la Roche, a writer of great gifts, has devoted her career to the romantic portrayal of one thoroughly unrepresentative family. Many others have written one or more novels of promise or distinction, but I think it is fair to say that none of them has yet produced a sufficiently large body of first-rate work to secure a permanent place in our literary history.

What have been the chief deficiencies in Canadian fiction? First of all, too few of our novels have dealt in an adult manner with life as it is lived here and now. In its most obvious aspect, this tendency has taken the form of writing historical romances rather than novels of contemporary life. Almost all Canadian novels written in the nineteenth century—both in English and in French—were historical romances, with Richardson, Mrs. Leprohon, Kirby, and Gilbert Parker as their chief architects. In this century, the tradition of historical romance has been carried on by such novelists as Frederick Niven, Laura Goodman Salverson, T. H. Raddall, and Franklin Davey McDowell. Now it would be foolish to argue that historical novels are valueless, still more so to suggest that in themselves they are pernicious. As Henry James has said, we must grant the novelist his material; what we have a right to criticize is his method of treatment, what he makes of his material. Historical novels can be great novels, as the works of Scott, Thackeray and Tolstoi abundantly prove. Human nature is at least relatively constant, and its strengths and weaknesses can be illuminated as

clearly by a distinguished treatment of the life of the seventeenth century as of the twentieth. Moreover, historical romances frequently give us a more vivid sense of the past than
historical textbooks. But all is not well in the literary atmosphere of a nation which sees something like eighty per cent
of its novelists turning from the present to the past for their
subject-matter. It suggests a weakness either in the writers
themselves or in the society in which they live.

For though it is possible to write great historical novels, the
temptations and difficulties of the form are severe. The temptation in writing historical novels is to desert the ordinary, the
representative, and to try for factitious glamour and false excitement; and this temptation few of our authors have successfully
resisted. The difficulties of the form are many: the securing
of adequate historical detail and the blending of fact and
fiction, to mention but two of the most obvious. All the difficulties stem from this crucial fact, that the writer has deliberately
cut himself off from the richest source of fictional material—
direct observation of the life about him.

But even when our novelists do direct their attention to the
Canadian present, many of them approach their material in as
unrealistic a spirit as the purveyor of the most factitious historical romances. Perhaps next in bulk among our novels are
the edifying books, and of the totally false impression of
Canadian life which they give it is unnecessary to speak. The
same is true of our books for juveniles, by people like L. M.
Montgomery and Norman Duncan, though here the lack of
realism is perhaps more excusable. Most serious is the fact that
even our relatively important novelists tend to approach our
life in a similar spirit. In spite of the flexible style which Mazo
de la Roche has at her command, and her sensitivity to the
beauties of nature, the behaviour of animals, and the souls of
children, the dominant note of her work, from the early
Possession to the latest volume in the Jalna series, is a shallow
romanticism. Even Morley Callaghan, whose best novels (*Such
Is My Beloved*, for example) I greatly admire, is often guilty
of sentimentalism.

What is needed, then, is not merely more novels which treat
the contemporary Canadian scene, but more which treat it in a
realistic and critical spirit. We need to see the festering sores in
our social body, as well as its areas of healthy tissue. Our novel-

ists of the past, with a few honourable exceptions, have been cautious souls, afraid to incur the wrath of the public, and producing either sugar-coated tracts or novels of escape.

In order that this criticism of our national life may be informed as well as passionate, our novelists must subject themselves to intellectual discipline. Our fiction hitherto has been almost devoid of ideas. From how many of our novels would it be possible to extract a coherent and profound philosophy of life? From the novels of Frederick Philip Grove, as I have suggested, such a philosophy may be extracted, though even in his case there is considerable confusion and obscurity; but I am at a loss to suggest any other Canadian novelist of the past or present to whose work such an analysis might be profitably directed. All the great novels of the world, however, have been sustained by a firm philosophical or sociological foundation. We have yet far to go before we can regard our fictional output with any degree of complacency.

A critical awareness of the contemporary scene, and a sustaining philosophy, then, are two wants which our novelists have yet adequately to supply. We miss in them also an adequate awareness of the technical advances made in the art of fiction during the last fifty years. Technically, all our novels cling to the safe paths of the nineteenth century. For all the evidence one finds of it in Canadian fiction, the work of Henry James, James Joyce, André Gide, Marcel Proust, Franz Kafka and other such creative exponents of the novel form, might never have been accomplished. This is strange, especially in view of the influence which the modernist movement has exercised upon recent Canadian poetry. Although we do not want mere imitativeness, the experimental work in other countries cannot be ignored with impunity by our own writers. The Canadian novel is not some delicate exotic flower which will magically bloom only in isolation: it must strike its roots in the great creative achievements of the past, and entwine its branches with the most flourishing growths of the present.

But it is easy to point to the defects of Canadian fiction. A more difficult task is to explain why this branch of our literature has lagged behind our poetical achievement. I propose to offer a tentative answer to this question, conscious of its incompletenesss but hopeful that its formulation may encourage further analysis.

When I put this question recently to a practising writer who has had a measure of success in both media, his answer was that it is easier to write a poem than a novel. The reply was made casually, almost flippantly, but I believe it is of some significance. There is a sense in which it is preposterous to discuss the relative difficulty of works of art. In terms of the creative imagination required, it is just as difficult to write a perfect lyric of ten lines as a novel of ten thousand. But there are other senses, surely, in which such a discussion is not preposterous. In terms of the physical effort required, for example, the novel is obviously a more formidable task.

The fact is that our poetical achievement has been made largely in the form of the short lyric, and it seems to me that there are many ways in which a novel is more difficult to write than a lyric. First of all, a novel demands much more of the writer's time. To give one concrete example: Frederick Philip Grove began to write *A Search for America* in 1893; in its original form it ran to half-a-million words; he revised it seven times; it was finally published over thirty years later, in 1927. I do not think that the most conscientious reviser among our lyric poets could offer a parallel. Now this may seem like a trivial or even irrelevant point, but if it is true, as critics have maintained, that most if not all Canadian writers must have another trade or profession and do their writing in their spare time, then it becomes important. The leisure-time artist, if faced with the alternative of writing novels or lyric poems, can hardly be blamed if he chooses the latter. This would be particularly likely if the writer could expect only a meagre financial return from his novel—and this, though the large sales of the three novels mentioned above may herald a change, has undoubtedly been the prevalent expectation.

The novel also, generally speaking, demands a greater degree of social understanding than the lyric. Most lyrics, certainly most Canadian lyrics, exploit either the landscape, or the poet's personal emotions, or a fusion of the two. I hope it will not be construed as a slight upon lyric poetry if I say that these subjects are relatively accessible and even relatively simple. Most novels, on the other hand, involve a critical examination of a social structure: it is no accident that the English novel began to flourish in the eighteenth century, when a mature society became conscious of itself. It follows that in a country where the landscape is inspiring and society somewhat immature the lyric is much more likely than the novel to be produced. In Canada we have landscapes of exceptional beauty: hence, in poetry, Lampman and his fellows, and in painting, the Group of Seven. Our society, on the other hand, is only just emerging from the pioneer, colonial stage, lacking both the eager experimentation of the United States and the rich traditional features of Old World cultures. In such circumstances it is no wonder that our potential novelists either do not write at all or choose the more glamorous portions of our early history for treatment.

And even should the novelist be sufficiently sensitive to respond to the drama which lurks beneath the rather drab surface of Canadian society, the task which then confronts him is one of unusual difficulty. Let us suppose that he decides to emulate Fielding, and do for contemporary Canada what Fielding did for eigtheenth-century England. First of all, the mere size of the country proves an obstacle. It is given to few men to know this country from coast to coast, especially to know it in the full sense of being intimately acquainted with its various cultural areas. Fielding could divide England into London and the rest—Town and Country—and not fall far short of inclusiveness; it would be a rather inadequate picture of Canada which divided it into Montreal (or Toronto, or Vancouver, or Winnipeg) and the rest. Other contrasts may be suggested: Fielding could rely upon a clearly defined and generally accepted class structure, whereas here such divisions, though they undoubtedly exist, are subtle and tenuous to a degree. England had, and has, one cultural tradition; Canada, two major ones and many minor.

It amounts to this: Canadian society, for all its immaturity—or perhaps because of it—is a peculiarly difficult society to reduce to order. To make generalizations which will apply to all sections of it is almost impossible. It is for this reason that we are not likely to have for some time anything approaching a national novel; the best we can hope for are solid regional studies. But it might be argued that the very diversity and complexity of our society should have proved a challenge to our novelists, both to attempt the herculean task of creating a national novel and the no less important task of interpreting the various regions to one another. Here we encounter two other factors which, I believe, have inhibited the development of Canadian fiction.

For the production of great fiction there is required not merely a developed society but a society which has become conscious of itself. The novels of Fielding and Thackeray, of Turgenev and Tolstoi, of Balzac and Flaubert, were produced when currents of social criticism were flowing strongly in their respective countries. In Canada, however, until recently, the habit of social analysis has been but weakly developed. As a nation, we have been rather apathetic toward broad political and social questions. Although this country has frequently been the scene of agitated social controversies, such controversies have tended to centre rather about immediate *ad hoc* issues—railways, tariffs, conscription, for example—than about more fundamental issues of political and social philosophy. Whether in foreign or domestic policy, our tendency has been to delay action until delay proved no longer possible, and then to improvise a policy on the basis of immediate circumstances rather than on the basis of a clearly reasoned philosophy of government. If this is so, it is not surprising that we have as yet produced no great sociological novels.

Another inhibiting factor is that we have not yet developed a strong national consciousness (though here again there are recent signs of change). This lack is a barrier to the production not only of national novels, but of strong regional ones. A regional consciousness in itself is not sufficient to evoke regional art. Where a merely regional consciousness exists the tendency is towards an inverted, and therefore non-productive, provincialism: the inhabitants of a given region may be assumed to know the nature of their own life, and not to need its representation in art. It is when a strong regional consciousness is supplemented by an equally strong consciousness of the world beyond the region that the need is felt to interpret this region to others.

The great novel, however, will demand not only a profound knowledge and understanding of our national society; it will demand also the assimilation of ideas which transcend the barriers of space and time. We do not demand of lyric poetry that it deal in profound ideas: if we did, our Lampmans and Carmans would fall woefully short; but the novel, because of its greater scope and scale, will omit them at its peril. Responsiveness to international currents of thought, however, is not one of our strong points as a nation. We tend to be suspicious of ideas, to accept them only reluctantly when they have been tried and accepted (and occasionally, in turn, discarded) elsewhere. It is true that we expect the novelist to be in advance of the national average in matters of this kind, but he is one of us, and inevitably shares to some extent our weaknesses.

These, then, seem to me the major reasons why our novels have not matched, in either quantity or quality, our poems: the relative drabness of our society when compared with the beauty of our landscape, the amorphous quality of that society, the weakness of our habits of social analysis, our lack of a strong national consciousness, and our distrust of ideas. It is in the light of these considerations that, as Canadians, we should regard the three novels mentioned at the beginning of this article. There is ground for encouragement, even for temperate enthusiasm, in their appearance, but it does not consist in the fact that they have achieved popularity in the United States. On the other hand, to suggest that because they have attained best-seller status they are therefore poor books seems to me pure snobbishness. The encouraging thing is that in these three books, especially in those by Mr. MacLennan and Miss Graham, and in other recent novels such as Grove's *Master of the Mill*, Sinclair Ross's *As for Me and My House*, and Mrs. Baird's *Waste Heritage*, we have genuine if still striving efforts to wrestle in fiction with the complexities of contemporary Canadian society. None of these novels are great; they are all open to serious criticism in terms of both philosophy and technique; but cumulatively they mark a definite advance. Their joint appearance argues hopefully not only for the maturing of our novels, but also for the maturing of our nation. The end is not yet.

The First Canadian Novel *

THE right of Frances Brooke's *History of Emily Montague* to be regarded as the first Canadian novel might be disputed—not, I believe, on the point of its temporal primacy, but of its Canadianism. Mrs. Brooke spent, it seems, only a little over a year in Canada,[1] and it is highly doubtful whether her novel was written in this country. Under present conditions, these facts would constitute an almost overwhelming obstacle to calling the novel Canadian, in spite of the fact that most of it has a Canadian setting and is concerned with Canadian life. If, however, we bear in mind that at the time of its publication (1769) the English-speaking population of Canada consisted largely of officials whose residence here was more or less temporary, the opposition case loses much of its force. At any rate, not to quibble further about definitions, we are on safe ground in affirming that this was the first novel in English to be devoted predominantly to the portrayal of Canadian life.

From its portrayal of Canadian life the book derives most of its interest and value. It is not a distinguished novel, judged by strict artistic standards: it is significant that the late Professor Saintsbury, whose catholicity of taste and inclusiveness of information concerning English fiction were beyond question, does not even accord it a footnote in his book, *The English*

---

*Published in *The Dalhousie Review*, July, 1946.
[1]For reprints of the extant documents bearing upon the question of the residence of Mrs. Brooke and her husband in Canada, see Frederick Philip Grove's Appendix to a modern reprint of the novel, published in 1931 by Graphic Publishers, Ottawa. All page references in this article are to this edition of the novel.

Novel. Its artistic shortcomings are obvious: the plot is thin, conventional, repetitive, and poorly integrated with the informative sections of the book; the style is generally stilted and monotonous; the characters, with one or two exceptions, are traditional in conception and deficient in life; the whole performance is heavily didactic and sentimental. In spite of these manifest weaknesses, the novel remains of interest and value to us as a social, and to a lesser extent as a literary, document.

That a year's residence in Canada enabled Mrs. Brooke to write with such apparent authenticity of life in the infant colony is proof of her active powers of observation and of an educated literary sensibility. She was indeed a woman of high intelligence, sufficient to win her the friendship of most of the leading writers in the England of her time: Dr. Johnson and his circle, Samuel Richardson, and Fanny Burney.[2] At the age of thirty, in 1755, she was the editor of a weekly magazine, *The Old Maid*—an achievement which would be remarkable even now, and must have seemed spectacular in the eighteenth century. But she was apparently not reconciled to remaining as a spinster writing for spinsters, and in 1756 she married the Reverend John Brooke. This marriage was the means of her coming to Canada. In 1763 Mr. Brooke came to Quebec as a military chaplain, and Mrs. Brooke joined him later in the year. In the meantime Mrs. Brooke had continued to write, and she came to Canada as the author of a volume of poems, a tragedy (which Garrick had declined for Drury Lane), a translation of a French romance, and a novel (*The History of Lady Julia Mandeville*).

In November of 1764 Mrs. Brooke returned to England, taking with her the manuscript of another book, *The Memories of the Marquis de St. Forlaix,* and possibly that of the novel with which we are most concerned, *The History of Emily Montague.* The latter novel was not published until 1769, and this delay suggests that the novel was probably written after her return to England. Dr. Lawrence Burpee, however, inclines to the belief that it was written in Canada, basing his theory

---

[2]*The Dictionary of National Biography* records a contemporary newspaper story to the effect that Dr. Johnson, attending the farewell party preceding Mrs. Brooke's voyage to Canada, insisted upon kissing her in a separate room since he "did not choose to do so before so much company." Fanny Burney wrote of her in her Diary that she was "short and fat" but "well-bred" and "a woman of known understanding."

on the fact that "many of the descriptive passages suggest by their vividness that they must have been written with the scenes before the author's eyes."[3] My own guess, and it can be no more than a guess, is that Mrs. Brooke kept a diary during her Canadian residence, and that she drew heavily upon the diary when writing the novel in England. The credibility of this conjecture is increased when we recall the fashion for travel journals in the late eighteenth century—witness, for example, *The Journal of a Tour in the Hebrides*—and the practice of Smollett and Sterne of incorporating their reminiscences of foreign travel in their novels.

Mrs. Brooke continued writing almost to the end of her life, which came in 1789. The products of these last twenty years were two more novels, two operas and a play (all of which were produced at Covent Garden, the operas with considerable success), and a long elegiac poem devoted to the memory or her friend Mrs. Yates, a leading actress of the period. Mrs. Brooke, it is clear, was a woman of spirit and of varied gifts, and a not unworthy progenitor of the Canadian novel.

To turn now from the author to the book, *The History of Emily Montague* may profitably be analyzed from two points of view: as an embodiment of the literary forces at work in the second half of the eighteenth century, particularly in the field of fiction, and as an early impression of Canadian colonial society on a sensitive and cultivated observer.

The main literary tendencies of a given period may often be more accurately detected in the mediocre work than in a masterpiece, for the masterpiece tends to be in advance of its time, to stake out a claim on the future. In any case, the novel under discussion reveals most of the tendencies of the literary age which we have come to label "pre-Romantic." The cult of sensibility, for instance, practised by such novelists as Sterne and Henry Mackenzie, has an ardent devotee in Mrs. Brooke. Here are some typical passages from her novel:

What a charm, my dear Lucy, is there in sensibility! 'Tis the magnet which attracts all to itself; virtue may command esteem, understanding and talents admiration, beauty a transient desire; but 'tis sensibility alone which can inspire love.

---

[3]See Dr. Burpee's introduction to the Graphic edition of the novel cited above.

I love her with a tenderness of which few of my sex are capable: you have often told me, and you were right, that my heart has all the sensibility of woman.

The same dear affections, the same tender sensibility, the most precious gift of heaven, inform our minds, and make us peculiarly capable of exquisite happiness or misery.

Closely allied with this cult of sensibility is the deliberate exploitation of the sentimental aspects of experience. The Brooke novel is not quite as tearful as Mackenzie's *Man of Feeling,* but it has its abundant quota. In the very first sentence of the novel the young hero proudly recalls "dropping a tender tear at Carisbrook Castle on the memory of the unfortunate Charles the First," and when Mrs. Brooke has a genuinely affecting scene to portray, she approaches it in this manner:

I am not painter enough to describe their meeting; tho' prepared, it was with difficulty we kept my mother from fainting; she pressed him in her arms, she attempted to speak, her voice faltered, tears stole softly down her cheeks . . .

Another indication that the rational pose of the early eighteenth century was now giving way to a more impassioned attitude towards life is provided by the emphasis laid in the novel upon "enthusiasm." Rivers, the hero of the novel, writes to his friend:

You ridicule my enthusiasm, my dear Temple, without considering there is no exertion of the human mind, no effort of the understanding, imagination, or heart, without a spark of this divine fire.

Without enthusiasm, genius, virtue, pleasure, even love itself, languishes: all that refines, adorns, softens, exalts, ennobles life has its source in this animating principle.

I glory in being an enthusiast in everything.

For most of the romantic writers and their precursors, Nature was a favourite object for this enthusiasm. To this rule, Mrs. Brooke was no exception. The Canadian landscape found in her its earliest literary celebrant. "You see here," she wrote, "the *beautiful* which it has in common with Europe, but also the

great sublime to an amazing degree." The wildness of the landscape was, for her romantic taste, an especial attraction: "bold,
picturesque, romantic, Nature reigns here in all her wanton
luxuriance, adorned by a thousand wild graces which mock the
cultivated beauties of Europe." Streaked though her writing
is with romantic hyperbole of this sort, the Nature descriptions
are far from contemptible, and in passages such as the following
she reveals herself to have been an acute and exact observer:

The days are much hotter here than in England, but the
heat is more supportable from the breezes which always spring
up about noon; and the evenings are charming beyond expression. We have much thunder and lightning, but very few
instances of their being fatal: the thunder is more magnificent
and aweful than in Europe, and the lightning brighter and
more beautiful; I have even seen it of a clear pale purple,
resembling the gay tints of the morning.
The verdure is equal to that of England, and in the evening
acquires an unspeakable beauty from the lucid splendor of the
fire-flies sparkling like a thousand little stars on the trees and
on the grass.
There are two very noble falls of water near Quebec, la
Chaudiere and Montmorency: the former is a prodigious sheet
of water, rushing over the wildest rocks, and forming a scene
grotesque, irregular, astonishing: the latter, less wild, less
irregular, but more pleasing and more majestic, falls from an
immense height, down the side of a romantic mountain, into
the river St. Lawrence, opposite the most smiling part of the
islands of Orleans, to the cultivated charms of which it forms
the most striking and agreeable contrast.

And she seized upon what is the essence of the Canadian
landscape, as contrasted with that of Europe: its magnitude of
scale. "Sublimity," she writes, "is the characteristic of the
western world; the loftiness of the mountains, the grandeur of
the lakes and rivers, the majesty of the rocks shaded with a
picturesque variety of beautiful trees and shrubs, and crowned
with the noblest of the offspring of the forest, . . . are as much
beyond the power of fancy as that of description."
In the place which it gives to the description of natural
scenery this novel is, as far as my knowledge extends, unique
among English novels of its period. In most other respects,

however, it is a typical manifestation of the chief methods and purposes then in vogue in fiction. It owes most, perhaps, to Mrs. Brooke's friend, Samuel Richardson. It employs the epistolary method which he had introduced and in which he had been followed by Smollett and Burney; its theme is love and its main substance the detailed and slightly repetitive analysis of the psychological accompaniments and consequences of that emotion; and it is, like Richardson's novels, dominated by a bourgeois moral system in which prudence, caution, and respectability rank very high among the virtues.

As is the case in most eighteenth-century novels, the plot of *Emily Montague* is its weakest feature. Heavy reliance is placed upon chance in general and coincidence in particular, and even the hoary device of the long-lost child intrudes itself. The plot for Mrs. Brooke was obviously little more than a convenient thread upon which to hang natural description, social comment, and moral preachment. The last feature is especially prominent. "I am afraid you will be growing weary of my sermonizing," exclaims one of the characters, and the modern reader promptly echoes a profound Amen. Mrs. Brooke's favourite topic for moral discussion is the institution of marriage. Over and over again we are assured that true love alone is the basis upon which a successful marriage can be founded, and that premarital chastity is a rule binding upon both sexes. She was obviously a determined feminist, out to abolish the "double standard" however many words it might cost her. Indeed her ambitions for her sex went far beyond that, and we find her noting with approval that the Indian squaws have a vote in electing the tribal rulers. "I should be extremely pleased to see it adopted in England," writes her hero, young Rivers, "canvassing for elections would then be the most agreeable thing in the world, and I am sure the ladies would give their votes on much more generous principles than we do."

For the general reader, the most interesting parts of *Emily Montague* are those in which Mrs. Brooke describes and analyzes Canadian society as it existed in the early days after the Conquest. On this subject she is refreshingly frank. Quebec City, she writes, "is like a third- or fourth-rate country town in England; much hospitality, little society; cards, scandal, dancing, and good cheer; all excellent things to pass away a winter evening, and peculiarly adapted to what I am told, and what I begin to feel, of the severity of this climate." What she missed especially was any semblance of cultural interest such as she had been accustomed to in the Johnson circle, and she advances certainly the simplest and one of the most convincing explanations of our cultural poverty: "I no longer wonder the elegant arts are unknown here; the rigour of the climate suspends the very powers of the understanding; what then must become of those of the imagination?" And feminine readers will be interested in this further suggestion as to the degrading influence of the severe climate. One young lady writes thus to her friend in England: "Apropos to age, I am resolved to go home, Lucy; I have found three gray hairs this morning; they tell me 'tis common; this vile climate is at war with beauty, makes one's hair gray, and one's hands red."

But what the young colony lacked in culture and grace it seems to have made up in gaiety:

I begin not to disrelish the winter here; now I am used to the cold, I don't feel it so much: as there is no business done here in the winter, 'tis the season of general dissipation; amusement is the study of everybody, and the pains people take to please themselves contribute to the general pleasure . . . Both our houses and our carriages are uncommonly warm; the clear serene sky, the dry pure air, the little parties of dancing and cards, the good tables we all keep, the driving about on the ice, the abundance of people we see there, for everybody has a carriole, the variety of objects new to a European, keep the spirits in a continual agreeable hurry, that is difficult to describe but very pleasant to feel.

Accounts of social life in the cities of Quebec and Montreal are supplemented by quite detailed discussions of the French peasantry and the Indian natives. Her opinion of the *habitant* was a mixed one: she recognized their virtues of hospitality and devotion, but found them ignorant and lazy. Here are some representative passages embodying her views:

The peasants are ignorant, lazy, dirty, and stupid beyond all belief; but hospitable, courteous, civil; and, what is particularly agreeable, they leave their wives and daughters to do the honours of the house: in which obliging office they acquit themselves with an attention which, amidst every inconvenience apparent (tho' I am told not real) poverty can cause, must please every guest who has a soul inclined to be pleased: for my part I was charmed with them, and eat my homely fare with as much pleasure as if I had been feasting on ortolans in a palace. Their conversation is lively and amusing; all the little knowledge of Canada is confined in the sex; very few, even of the seigneurs, being able to write their own names.

The peasants are in general tall and robust, notwithstanding their excessive indolence; they love war, and hate labour; are brave, hardy, alert in the field, but lazy and inactive at home, in which they resemble the savages, whose manners they seem strongly to have imbibed. The government appears to have encouraged a military spirit all over the colony; though ignorant and stupid to a great degree, these peasants have a strong sense of honour; and though they serve, as I have said, without pay, are never so happy as when called to the field.

Your Lordship asks me what is the general moral character of the Canadians; they are simple and hospitable, yet extremely attentive to interest, where it does not interfere with that laziness which is their governing passion. They are rather devout than virtuous; have religion without morality, and a sense of honour without very strict honesty.

It is evident that thus early in our national development the smug Anglo-Saxon sense of superiority was operating with characteristic efficiency.

This condescension is somewhat modified in Mrs. Brooke's treatment of the Indians by a tendency to regard them as examples of the romantic "noble savage." Early in the novel, she writes of them thus:

I have told you the labours of savage life, but I should observe that they are only temporary, and when urged by the sharp tooth of necessity: their lives are, upon the whole, idle beyond anything we can conceive. If the Epicurean definition of happiness is just, that it consists in indolence of body and tranquillity of mind, the Indians of both sexes are the happiest people on earth; free from all care, they enjoy the present moment, forget the past, and are without solicitude for the future: in summer, stretched out on the verdant turf, they sing, they laugh, they play, they relate stories of their ancient heroes to warm the youth to war; in winter, wrapped in the furs which bounteous nature provides them, they dance, they feast, and despise the rigors of the season, at which the more effeminate Europeans tremble.

Later, however, she seems to have grown rather disillusioned over the Indians, and towards the end of the book, after detailing their treatment of some English captives, she explicitly rejects the noble savage theory in these terms:

Rousseau has taken great pains to prove that the most cultivated nations are the most virtuous: I have all due respect for this philosopher, of whose writings I am an enthusiastic admirer; but I have a still greater respect for truth, which I believe in this instance is not on his side. There is little reason to boast of the virtues of a people who are such brutal slaves to their appetites as to be unable to avoid drinking brandy to an excess scarce to be conceived, whenever it falls in their way, though eternally lamenting the murders and other atrocious crimes of which they are so perpetually guilty when under its influence.

The transparent honesty of such passages as the above constitutes one of Mrs. Brooke's main attractions, and gives added value to her record of early Canadian society. Though her novel had no immediate successors in Canada, and had no discernible influence upon our subsequent fiction, I think that it deserves to be remembered. In spite of its weaknesses, which for the most part are those of its time, it is an effort to deal honestly in fiction with the contemporary Canadian scene. Such efforts have been all too rare in the history of the Canadian novel.

The Poetry of
Duncan Campbell Scott*

THE recent death of Duncan Campbell Scott aroused singularly little excitement in the Canadian public. The Prime Minister, it is true, paid a gracious tribute to his literary achievements; there were a few newspaper and magazine editorials and one or two memorial gatherings; but there was no general sense of loss. Perhaps the fact that Scott has seldom been a subject of critical controversy partly explains the relative obscurity of his reputation.

For Scott was a symbol of dedicated craftsmanship. He resorted to no stunts, either as man or writer, but was content to continue year after year the unspectacular business of seeking the exact words, the appropriate forms, in which to express his vision of life. That vision was one which may well come to be regarded as the distinctive vision of Canadian art, at least in its first major phase. It was a vision of conflict on a titanic scale, of man pitting his resources of courage and endurance against a harsh physical environment. It is basically the same vision that we find in the novels of Frederick Philip Grove, in the paintings of Tom Thomson and Emily Carr, in the poetry of E. J. Pratt, and on a smaller scale in such a poem as A. J. M. Smith's "Lonely Land." In all of these writers and artists we find a conception of Nature as at once frightening and fascinating: frightening because of its capacity to destroy, fascinating because of the intensity of its challenge. And in most of them we find a conception of man as paradoxically puny and mighty at once. Physically, he is incapable of with-

*Published in *The Canadian Forum*, August, 1948.

39

standing the onslaughts of storm and flood; but he has spiritual
resources by which he transcends destruction.

This conception of Nature as wild and threatening sets Scott
apart from the other members of the Group of the Sixties. For
Carman, Nature is always a source of either emotional comfort
or transcendental illumination. Lampman goes to Nature as a
refuge from the harsh realities of a mechanical age. Roberts,
in his animal stories, shows himself aware of the cruelties of
Nature, but in his poetry he almost invariably regards it as
beneficent. All of them characteristically paint Nature in her
moments of calm. But Scott gives us pictures of Nature in
storm, with man withstanding its pressures by virtue either of
an inner moral strength or a supreme outer assurance. An
example is this stanza from "Rapids at Night":

> Here at the roots of the mountains,
> Between the sombre legions of cedars and tamaracks,
> The rapids charge the ravine:
> A little light, cast by foam under starlight,
> Wavers about the shimmering stems of the birches:
> Here rise up the clangorous sounds of battle,
> Immense and mournful.
> Far above curves the great dome of darkness
> Drawn with the limitless lines of the stars and the planets.
> Deep at the core of the tumult,
> Deeper than all the voices that cry at the surface,
> Dwells one fathomless sound,
> Under the hiss and cry, the stroke and the plangent clamour.

There is a touch of reassurance later in this poem, in the
reference to "the great dome of darkness" as "the strong palm
of God, Veined with the ancient laws": above the battle are
the eternal verities. But in "The Eagle Speaks" there is no
such reassurance: man is a puny earth-bound creature which
the exultant eagle can destroy at will. Having killed the man,
the eagle speaks as follows:

> I swirled low over the earth like flame flattened
> By wind, then with a long loop of swiftness
> Rose sheer up into the bubble of the air
> And left him, carrion with his carrion,

For the dull coyotes to scent and overhaul
With snarls and bickerings lower than the dogs.
Rose to the unattempted heights, spurning
The used channels of the air, to the thin reach
Where vapours are unborn and caught the last
Glint of falling light beyond the peak
Of the last mountain, and hung alone serene
Till night, welling up into the void darkened me,—
Poised with the first cold stars.

In those lines, some of the finest Scott ever wrote, we certainly
have clearly expressed the conception of a frightening but
fascinating strength.

The theme of "The Eagle Speaks"—violent death in a wilderness setting—is the dominant theme of Scott's best and most
characteristic poems. In his most famous, and in many ways
his most satisfying, single poem, "The Piper of Arll," the
climactic episode is the death of the piper and of the intruding
ship's crew; in "The Forsaken" an old squaw is left alone by
the tribe to die in the wilds; in "At the Cedars" there is the
double death of a man and his sweetheart in a log-jam. Death
is piled on death in "On the Way to the Mission," where an
Indian trapper, hauling the corpse of his wife to the mission
for burial, is murdered by two rapacious white men. A very
similar poem is "Mission of the Trees," in which an Indian
father collapses and dies on his way to the mission with the
body of his son. A dead son reappears in "A Scene at Lake
Manitou," the emotional centre in this case being the Indian
mother's grief. "Night Burial in the Forest" tells the story of
a fatal love feud, as does the powerful "At Gull Lake: August,
1810."

The vision of a world in conflict finds expression also in
Scott's love poems. Almost all of them deal with frustrated love,
the frustration resulting from enforced absence, unrequited
passion, or death. In "Spring on Mattagami," his conception of
Nature as a violent, frightening but also fascinating power is
used to reinforce a similar conception of love.

But most of Scott's love poems are rather weak. One suspects
that he was inhibited by the puritanism of the Canadian public: it is significant that his frankest poem, "Byron on Wordsworth," which treats of Wordsworth's affair with Annette

Vallon, had to be printed for private circulation only. Perhaps the best lines on love among his published works are these:

> O, what is love but the bee with the clover,
> The passion of plunder,
> The giving, the taking,
> The ecstasy wild and the tearing asunder,—
> And then all is over;
> But somewhere the honey is hid in the hive
> And love to the lover is more than the passion,
> For beauty is stored in some exquisite fashion
> To be eaten in thankfulness, silence and tears
> On the bread of the desolate years.

Scott is undoubtedly at his best as a narrative poet. The directly didactic poems are, like the love poems, relative failures. The philosophy of life which, in "The Forsaken" for example, has resonant suggestiveness and restrained intensity, sounds rather flat and dull when he attempts to express it directly. He is apt to give us uninspired imitations of Victorian poets. Ideas and phrases borrowed from Wordsworth, Browning and above all Tennyson mingle in his most ambitious—and least successful—philosophical poem, "The Height of Land."

Scott does not show a marked preference for any single metrical form. Like the other members of the Group of the Sixties, he is fond of the simple quatrain stanza, but he does not employ it nearly as frequently as Roberts and Carman. He also uses couplets, six-, seven-, and eight-line stanzas, sonnets, blank verse, and free verse. He makes a much greater use of free verse than the other members of the Group, and in general is less given than they are to the more conventional types of verse form. He is fond of strikingly short lines—as in "At the Cedars" and the first part of "The Forsaken"—and of unusually long ones, such as this final line of "Night Burial in the Forest":

> The wings of the Angel who gathers the souls from the
> wastes of the world.

His rhythms are much less emphatic than those of Roberts and Carman, but he is less capable than they of achieving musical effects. "The Piper of Arll" is a striking exception, but generally speaking Scott does not charm us by the beauty of his melodies. He never approaches the haunting cadences of Carman's "Low Tide on Grand Pré" or the sustained music of Roberts' "Tantramar Revisited." His lyrical powers, in other words, are relatively weak, and it is by his narrative poems that he will be remembered.

The diction of Scott's poetry is less ornate than that of his romantic contemporaries. The early poems, it is true, of which "The Piper of Arll" is the conspicuous example, are in the decorative manner of Morris, Rossetti, and the early Yeats, but he resembles the last of these three poets in his transition toward a barer, sparser, more compact mode of utterance. He is less adjectival than Carman, there is less softness, vagueness, and suggestiveness in his verse, but greater precision and strength. At his best, as in the passage quoted above from "The Eagle Speaks," or as in these lines from "Labor and the Angel":

> The wind roars out from the elm,
> Then leaps tiger-sudden; — the leaves
> Shudder up into heaps and are caught
> High as the branch where they hung
> Over the oriole's nest . . .

Scott's verse is swift, vigorous, direct, and plain.

I think we must agree, however, that a gift of striking and suggestive imagery is not one of Scott's strong points. His images are few and far between, and they are not especially memorable. Scott achieves his effects by slower, less spectacular means—chiefly by the accumulation of accurate bits of physical description and of emotional insight—rather than by the sudden illuminating fusion of thought and thing which occurs in the finest metaphors and similes.

The dominant tone of Scott's poetry is quiet, in spite of the violent content of so many of his best poems. Though his poems usually involve a stormy climax, they almost always come to a peaceful close. There is a dialectical pattern to most of his poems: two forces battle one another until their powers are spent or their differences resolved and peace ensues. In "The Piper of Arll," the piper and the crew of the intruding ship exercise their fatal attraction upon each other; a violent climax is reached as the ship suddenly sinks beneath them; but the poem comes to a quiet close as the ship is pictured on the ocean floor:

> And sometimes in the liquid night
> The hull is changed, a solid gem,
> That glows with a soft stony light,
> The lost prince of a diadem.
> And at the keel a vine is quick,
> That spreads its bines and works and weaves
> O'er all the timbers veining thick
> A plenitude of silver leaves.

Throughout most of "Night Burial in the Forest" the birch-bark torches roar, symbols of the violence of the events which have preceded the funeral, but quiet peace is the tone of the final stanza. In "On the Way to the Mission" the white men dog the footsteps of the Indian, kill him, and then, discovering the nature of his load, flee and leave the corpses in the silent moon-light:

> The moon went on to her setting
> And covered them with shade.

The final peacefulness of these poems is achieved not by the transcendental leap, but by the stoical acceptance of suffering as the inevitable lot of man. The dominant mood is heroic endurance. Calm and stability is finally attained through an inner spiritual discipline, not through some magical release. We have the sense of a harsh and lonely world, the vicissitudes of which we can and therefore must endure without disgrace. In Toynbee's language, the challenge of a stern environment has elicited the response of courage. Is it too much to suggest that in these quietly powerful poems, seldom brilliant but always competent in style and solid in substance, we catch an authentic glimpse of the Canadian spirit at its finest?

Literary Criticism in Canada*

L<small>ET</small> me begin by defining the scope of this essay.
It will be concerned not with all literary criticism produced in
this country, but with Canadian criticism of Canadian literature. It is not intended to be a formal analysis and evaluation
of contemporary critics, still less a history of the development
of our criticism; it is an attempt to discover certain basic tendencies of Canadian literary criticism and to suggest possible
explanations for them.

Perhaps the most striking thing about our criticism is that
there is so little of it. The critical bibliography for almost every
Canadian author—Carman is a conspicuous exception—is so
small that it can be covered in a single evening. A series of full-
scale monographs on the best Canadian writers is badly needed.
A start was made, a couple of decades ago, with the "Makers of
Canadian Literature" series, but the project was allowed to
lapse, after a few volumes had appeared, because public support
was lacking. In any case, it is doubtful whether the plan of
this series was adequate, since it conceived of the publication of
a biography, an anthology of selections, and a critical estimate,
all in the space of a very small volume. More comprehensive
studies have appeared sporadically—Chittick's study of Haliburton, for example, and Klinck's study of Wilfred Campbell—but
there are many gaps, gaps which in a more critically conscious
country would be incredible. There is, for example, no satisfactory book-length study of Lampman, nor of Duncan Campbell Scott, nor of Charles Heavysege, nor of John Richardson.

There is an almost equal dearth of general volumes. The

*Published in the *University of Toronto Quarterly*, January, 1950.

only true history of Canadian literature, that by R. P. Baker, stops at Confederation. There are a number of handbooks on the subject, but most of them have defects which seriously impair their value. That by MacMechan is, and was only intended to be, a highly selective sketch, as is Lionel Stevenson's *Appraisals of Canadian Literature*; that by Logan and French is careless in style, over-enthusiastic in tone, and clumsy in construction. The most satisfactory volume of a comprehensive nature, Professor Rhodenizer's *Handbook of Canadian Literature*, is now obviously dated and in need of revision: it includes authors who, from our present perspective, can be seen to be without significance, and it omits authors who deserve a place. There are two good books on Canadian poetry, those by Professors W. E. Collin and E. K. Brown; but Professor Collin's book deals with only a few of our poets, and with none prior to Confederation, and Dr. Brown's is a very brief and necessarily somewhat superficial study for all its acuteness of insight. There is at present no book on the novel in Canada, though, according to the report of the Canadian Humanities Research Council, two are in preparation.

When we turn to periodical criticism, the situation is not much better. There is, to the best of my knowledge, no full-length article in our magazines on the first Canadian novelist, John Richardson; there is only a handful of articles on such an outstanding poet as Duncan Campbell Scott; there are only two articles, and a few review-articles, on Frederick Philip Grove.

Quantity, of course, is less significant than quality; but I think that in this case the two are inseparable, that before the quality of our criticism improves its quantity must increase. No one person can or should determine the stature of a poet or novelist. As Dr. Johnson said, fame is a shuttlecock and must be batted back and forth a good deal before it finds a permanent resting-place. The play of ideas between several critics concerned with the same author is mutually stimulating. Each critic is challenged by his rivals to find new beauties or new flaws, to uncover new layers of meaning or new subleties of technique. In Canada this kind of challenge is almost unknown; for all the response there is to one's appraisals, one's words might never have been read.

The second fact which strikes one about Canadian criticism is its preponderantly academic origin. The best critics of the older generation were professors such as Edgar at Toronto, Cappon at Queen's, Rhodenizer at Acadia, MacMechan at Dalhousie; in this generation they are again professors—Brown, Smith, Collin, Frye, Daniells, MacKay. Non-academic critics such as Lorne Pierce and John Sutherland are conspicuous by their rarity.

This academicism explains many of the peculiar tendencies of our criticism. There is, for example, our addiction to politeness and fence-sitting. It is rare indeed to see a piece of Canadian criticism which either roundly damns or enthusiastically praises a writer; instead, in true pedagogic fashion, we carefully weigh his merits and defects, tentatively relate him to similar English, American, or European writers, and timidly express the hope that the public will see fit to read him. Now this, of course, is a legitimate and praiseworthy part of the critical process; but it is not the only part. In Canada, however, it has tended to be almost the only kind of criticism. It seems to me a very good thing that we have had the un-academic enthusiasm of Lorne Pierce and that we now have the equally un-academic bluntness of John Sutherland to ruffle the placid waters of our critical literature. We need more such critics, not to supersede but to supplement the work of our academic critics.

Another characteristic of academic criticism is its *penchant* for labels and pigeonholes. The most recent example of this tendency was the first edition of A. J. M. Smith's *The Book of Canadian Poetry*. There was considerable controversy about his classification of our more recent poets into the native and the cosmopolitan traditions, and some curious anomalies resulted. It was disturbing to find F. R. Scott, whose verse is very decidedly inspired by and rooted in the Canadian milieu, classed with Finch and Smith rather than with Livesay and Birney. It is significant that in the recently published second edition of the anthology, Smith has dropped these classifications. It was, however, possible to find justification for his rather arbitrary divisions in the fact that recent Canadian poetry was, when his anthology first appeared, a largely unexplored wilderness. His signposts, if occasionally misleading, were on the whole helpful, and they were reasonably few in number.

But if Smith's divisions could be justified, we have only to look at Logan and French's *Highways of Canadian Literature* to see the excesses into which this classifying mania can run. To read that book, one would think that there were more "schools" of Canadian literature than of porpoises in the sea. Even R. P. Baker's *English-Canadian Literature to the Confederation*, a much better book, carries this tendency too far, with its talk of the non-existent "schools" of Goldsmith, Byron, and Burns. We should have been much further ahead if the time wasted in the invention and elaboration of these schools had been employed in the close analysis of individual poems. Close line-by-line analyses, such as that accorded to Birney's "David" by Roy Daniells in the Spring, 1946, number of *Gants du ciel*, have been far too rare in our critical history.

In noting these defects in academic criticism I do not wish to associate myself with those who seek to belittle the contribution of our universities to the development of Canadian literature. On the contrary, I believe that the universities have done more than any other agency to stimulate the production of good writing in this country. As we have seen, almost all our critics have been university professors, and almost all our writers have been university trained. If it had not been for the pioneer critical explorations of men like Baker, MacMechan, Smith, and Brown, Mr. Sutherland's clever sallies would have been meaningless if not impossible. Most important of all, the academicians have, by their influence on their students, done much to create an audience for Canadian writers, and it is in the universities that little magazines such as *Northern Review* and *Here and Now* find their most eager readers.

For if academic criticism has its limitations, it also has its special strengths. The academic critic is a man trained in more than one literature, and is therefore specially fitted to apply one of the tests which any national literature must be prepared to withstand: the test of comparative criticism. He is trained also to sift evidence thoroughly and impartially, and is therefore less prone to fall into the excesses of enthusiastic over-valuation and cynical under-valuation. He has a sense of the past, an awareness of tradition, and can therefore employ the historical method to good advantage. As a teacher, he is experienced in the orderly and clear exposition of ideas, and is thus fitted to present the public with an intelligible picture of our literary development.

There are, however, two respects in which the universities have fallen short of their maximum potential service to our literature: they have been too reluctant to accord it a significant place in the formal undergraduate and postgraduate curriculum, and they have not performed adequately the function which they alone are fitted to perform, namely the scholarly investigation of our literary history.

That the study of Canadian literature should not supplant the study of English literature in our universities is eminently reasonable; but it should supplement it. It should occupy a small part of the freshman English course which, in most of our colleges, is given to students in all faculties; and it should have a place—a small place, possibly one term out of the usual eight—in the curriculum of those students who are specializing in English. This is not the proper context in which fully to argue the case for the undergraduate study of Canadian literature. To confine the argument to the relevant, it is clear that if we are to have more critics of our literature in the future they must first become aware of the existence of this literature, and that one sure place to receive this awareness is in the lecture-room.

Postgraduate study of Canadian literature is, of course, closely related to the task of the scholarly interpretation and investigation of our literary history. It is in the graduate schools that a start should be made on this essential job. And it is essential: to convince oneself of the service which the scholar renders to the critic it is only necessary to attempt to write a critical study of almost any Canadian writer of the ninetenth century. If, for example, one proposes to write a critical study of John Richardson's novels, he finds that he must first do all the scholar's spade-work: biographical details have not been fully explored and verified; the various editions have not been sorted out and compared; there is no complete list of his publications. Surely in performing such tasks Canadian graduate students could get training in research methods as valuable as that which they receive by adding their mite to the store collected on some English or American author?

So much for the academic factor. There are two other factors the influence of which I should like to consider: the relative smallness of our literary community, and the lack of any pre-eminent author.

The number of people who write books and articles in Canada is quite small, and the number of those who write anything which either is or aspires to be "literature" is smaller still. So small is the latter group, that almost all the members are known to each other either directly or indirectly. As Matthew Arnold pointed out, it is always difficult, in judging contemporary or recent productions, to avoid the personal estimate. In Canada it is doubly difficult. To choose an obvious example, almost every literary critic in Canada is familiar with the buoyant and warm personality of Dr. E. J. Pratt. Knowing him, it is well-nigh impossible to be a coldly impartial critic of his poetry. One can never be sure whether it is the verse itself one admires, or the glimpse it reveals of the man. And even if one did detect a weakness in the work of a man so universally admired, the temptation to slur over it would be very great indeed.

The result is that the great bulk of our criticism is characterized by what might be called "tender-heartedness." Very rarely is the work of a living writer attacked, almost never if the quality of his previous work has made him a well-known figure. If the critic is in an aggressive mood, he directs his attack against the dead. This has led, in the recent past, to an under-valuation of the worth of the poetry of Carman, Lampman, Roberts, and Scott, and an over-valuation of the worth of many of our contemporary poets. It is true that the reputations of the members of the Group of the Sixties needed a certain amount of deflation, but when all their defects have been noted it remains true to say of their work that it is nearer to perfection *of its kind* than is that of any more recent poet or group of poets. Where is the modern metaphysical lyric to match the near-perfection of Carman's late romantic lyric, "Low Tide on Grand Pré"?

But if "Low Tide on Grand Pré" is a convenient touchstone of excellence—and many critics would indignantly deny this— it would be rash to maintain that Carman's work as a whole makes him the pre-eminent figure in our literary history. The fact is that there is no single pre-eminent Canadian writer, no one even remotely approaching the stature of Milton or Fielding. This is an obvious statement, but I do not think that its consequences for our criticism have been noted. In the first place, it deprives the critics and literary historians of a centre about which their observations and comparisons may revolve. To see the advantages of possessing such a central point of reference, we have only to look at the criticism of English drama. In that field, Shakespeare is a landmark by which almost all the necessary measurements may be made, and his existence both simplifies and vivifies the critic's task. For standards of measurement, the Canadian critic must invariably look outside the borders of his own country. He must relate the subject of his study to a tradition which is in at least some degree alien.

A second consequence for our criticism of this lack of an outstanding writer is further proof of his potential value: I refer to our constant and rather pathetic search for him. An author of great merit but not of transcendent excellence is chosen by the critic, his strengths are magnified and his weaknesses ignored or excused, until the critic finally persuades himself that he has found the master he seeks. If no writer of established reputation can be found suitable for such a build-up, then some new figure on the literary horizon is selected as the coming genius of the age. Hence the perpetual hopefulness of our criticism, the oft-disappointed but never discarded belief that Canadian literary greatness is just around the corner.

But the most destructive consequence has been the apathy this lack has bred in the young, eager potential critics of our literature. Criticism of Canadian literature is not, on the surface at least, a very challenging or exciting endeavour. The keen young critic, eager to prove his mettle, is much more likely to tackle an English or American writer whose stature is beyond question. When there are the complexities of Donne or Melville to decipher, why waste one's time on the misty transcendentalism of Carman or the rough-hewn pessimism of Frederick Philip Grove?

Well, why? It is a question which cannot be dodged if this article is to have any positive value. In the first place, I should argue that the best critical writing is not always done on the best authors: it is perfectly possible to do first-rate research and first-rate criticism on a second-rate author. Some of the finest of Johnson's *Lives of the Poets* are concerned with second-rate versifiers who are now scarcely remembered. I should say that it is at least as strenuous a critical exercise to detect the precise nature of the flaws in Carman's verse as to reveal the metaphysical brilliance of a song by Donne.

In the second place, there is so much to be done in the field of Canadian literary criticism. The labours of countless doctoral candidates have cultivated the English and American fields to the point where it is difficult to find a fresh area of investigation; but in Canada scarcely the first sod has been turned. Surely this should arouse the instincts of the pioneer which may be assumed to slumber in us all?

Finally, and most important, I feel that as Canadians we have a special right and responsibility to investigate our own literary history. Our social, political, and economic historians have long shown us the way, and they have achieved impressive results. Our American neighbours have come increasingly, in the past two decades, to make their own literary tradition a major subject of study. How long must we wait for our Parringtons and Brookses and Lewisohns to appear? If they do not appear soon, we may find that the Americans know more about our literature than we know ourselves. Already, as I learn from correspondence with the instructors concerned, several American universities are offering undergraduate and graduate courses in Canadian literature, and it is of course well known that some of the best collections of Canadian books and manuscripts are housed in American libraries.

In thus pleading for Canadian study of Canadian literature I am not, let me repeat, arguing that we should ignore or discourage the study of Milton and Shakespeare and all the other great writers of the English-speaking world. They too are part of our tradition, and it is one of our responsibilities as members of a Western civilized community to keep that tradition alive. But we should be willing to devote part of our time to the tracing and fostering of our own special tradition, the tradition of British North America.

I look forward to the day when, from academic and non-academic sources alike, there will flow a steady stream of clear, direct, and vigorous criticism upon our literature of the past and present. It should be criticism which brings to bear upon the work of our writers the finest insights of the best critical minds. It should be criticism which is unafraid and uninhibited, which refuses to make compromises with or concessions to our prudery, our conventions, and our too-tender susceptibilities. The emergence of such criticism will be perhaps the most certain sign that "our day of dependence is over," that our cultural immaturity is on the wane.

in French, Spanish, and English poetry, and he had obviously read intelligently.

Where, then, is the difference between the styles of the poems to be found? Great poetry, I believe, must possess either wit or passion or, preferably, both. Wit and passion are found in *The Deserted Village;* they are almost entirely absent from *The Rising Village.* The lines from *The Deserted Village* which have become a virtual part of the racial memory, which are quoted by people who often have no knowledge of their source, are lines in which one or both of these qualities is present:

> Ill fares the land, to hastening ills a prey
> Where wealth accumulates, and men decay . . .

Here the wit is in the neatly poised antithesis of the second line, in the aptness and epigrammatic brevity of both. At the same time, the passage is an impassioned expression of Goldsmith's deep-seated conviction that the commercial revolution of the seventeenth and eighteenth centuries spelt the doom of the ancestral rural England he admired. Much the same is true of other famous lines in the poem:

> Remote from towns he ran his godly race
> Nor e'er had changed, nor wished to change his place . . .

> More skilled to raise the wretched than to rise . . .

> And fools who came to scoff, remained to pray . . .

In each of these lines, Goldsmith was giving epigrammatic expression to passionately held beliefs.

The Canadian Goldsmith, on the other hand, appears to have felt passionately about nothing: he neither hates nor loves with any of his uncle's vehemence. The latter's diatribes against luxury and the tyranny of wealth have, as we noticed above, no counterpart in *The Rising Village.* The younger Goldsmith obviously admires Britain; but his description of her virtues is so unspecific and so indiscriminate as to become merely a bit of conventional colonial nostalgia. He also admires Nova Scotia; but he does not fully understand her, as we shall see below, nor cling passionately to her.[4] In building his contrast between past

---

[4]This impression, derived from a reading of the poem, may be confirmed by reading his *Autobiography* (ed. Rev. Wilfrid E. Myatt, Toronto, 1943). He was very disappointed when, after crossing to England in 1817, he was posted back to the Halifax commissariat station. He would have preferred to remain in England, or to have been sent to some other British possession. See pp. 6 ff.

and present, the Canadian Goldsmith had no villain comparable to the tyrannical over-rich landlord of *The Deserted Village* on whom to place the blame. The wilderness, the Indians, and the savage beasts one may wish to subdue, but they do not inspire the same vehement hatred as the newly-rich merchant who "takes up a space that many poor supplied" and "indignant spurns the cottage from the green."

If the passion of the English poem is lacking, so to a large extent is the wit. It is the elder Goldsmith's wit which saves his poem from being a mere alternation of sentimentality and invective. The wit remains throughout as the yardstick of sanity, as proof that the poet is in contact with reality. Whenever he is in danger of attributing a fantastically Utopian quality to his memories of village life, his wit steps in to save him. In the midst of his idyllic description of the village inn, he drily comments on it as a place

> Where village statesmen talk'd with looks profound,
> And news much older than their ale went round.

The whole portrait of the schoolmaster is a triumph of this kind of irony, as exemplified in the lines:

> Yet he was kind, or, if severe in aught,
> The love he bore to learning was in fault.
> The village all declar'd how much he knew;
> 'Twas certain he could write, and cipher too . . .

The younger Goldsmith obviously recognized the value of this element in the English poem, and sought to emulate it. Occasionally, as in his portrait of the doctor—

> No rival here disputes his doubtful skill,
> He cures, by chance, or ends each human ill—

or of the schoolmaster—

> Whose greatest source of knowledge or of skill
> Consists in reading, and in writing ill—

he approaches the same deftness; but for the most part his efforts at wit are laborious (see, for example, his long-winded account of the insatiable curiosity of the tavern-keeper).

Another respect in which the Canadian poem falls short of the style of its model is in its relative lack of specific detail. Although both poems are idyllic in their approach to rural life, and therefore may be excused a certain generality in their descriptions, it is notable that the English poet achieves a mixture of the typical and the individual, of the general and the particular, which is beyond the skill of the Canadian. Both schoolmasters are types, but the English schoolmaster is much more of a recognizable person than his Canadian counterpart. Rural festivities in both poems are pretty generalized merrymakings, but there are skilful touches of specific detail (the "swain mistrustless of his smutted face") in the English poem which are almost totally lacking in the Canadian. Occasionally, however, the Canadian poet does use his eyes and describe things in some detail, and then his poem takes on a new authority and strength. One example of such passages is this description of the process then in vogue for clearing the land:

> See! from their heights the lofty pines descend,
> And crackling, down their pond'rous lengths extend.
> Soon from their boughs the curling flames arise,
> Mount into air, and redden all the skies . . .

An even better example, and to my mind the best passage in the entire poem, is this description of the country store:

> Around his store, on spacious shelves arrayed,
> Behold his great and various stock in trade.
> Here, nails and blankets, side by side, are seen,
> There, horses' collars, and a large tureen;
> Buttons and tumblers, fish-hooks, spoons and knives,
> Shawls for young damsels, flannel for old wives;
> Woolcards and stockings, hats for men and boys,
> Mill-saws and fenders, silks, and children's toys. . . .

But such particularity is rare in *The Rising Village*; for the most part the author is content with such vague and general passages as this:

> As thus the village each successive year
> Presents new prospects, and extends its sphere,
> While all around its smiling charms expand,
> And rural beauties decorate the land.

This last passage has the air of being written by rote: it is a bit of padding which adds nothing to our understanding of the village. The tendency towards padding is found throughout the poem and is largely responsible for the diffuse impression which it leaves upon the reader. Here are a few lines which illustrate this tendency:

In search of wealth, of freedom, and of ease.

How great the pain, the danger, and the toil. . .

The danger, trouble, hardship, toil and strife. . . .

His heart seemed generous, noble, kind, and free. . . .

Behold it, wounded, broken, crushed and riven. . . .

The Canadian Goldsmith almost invariably attaches the stock epithet to his noun: woe must be "piercing"; prospects are, of course, "boundless," "charming," or "fair"; passions, it is universally agreed, are "heedless"; a mill is always "busy," a cottage "humble," and a traveller "weary."

Of a writer so given to the use of conventional epithets we should not expect much originality in the use of metaphors and similes. This is another respect in which the Canadian poem is clearly inferior to its English model. The elder Goldsmith was himself no Donne or Shelley to startle us with the brilliance or variety of his figures, but scattered through *The Deserted Village* there are metaphors and similes which impress us by their aptness. Speaking of his desire for a quiet life of retirement, he writes:

. . . I still had hopes, my latest hours to crown,
Amidst these humble bowers to lay me down;
To husband out life's taper at the close,
And keep the flame from wasting by repose. . . .

But one searches in vain in *The Rising Village* for images to equal this and others which might be cited. The younger Goldsmith never gets beyond such stock comparisons as that of a girl to a flower or of a young man to a "captive led by love's endearing chain."

In matters of style and technique, then, the similarity between the two poems is largely an external one. The same structure and metre have been employed, but the Canadian has used them with much less skill. What of the substance of the poems?

There is first of all the question of their documentary value, of their reliability and usefulness as pictures of the contemporary social scene. There has been a great deal of debate on this aspect of *The Deserted Village* ever since its appearance. Was the kind of expulsion of which Goldsmith writes a common thing, justifying his pessimism, or was he drawing extravagant conclusions from a single isolated episode? And in any case, was not his picture of former village life unduly Utopian? On the other hand, there has been, to the best of my knowledge, no debate at all about the documentary truth of *The Rising Village*. Eagerly leaning on this final crutch available to defenders of our early literature, critic has echoed critic in declaring that, whatever its strictly literary merits, *The Rising Village* is a clear and accurate picture of the process of early settlement in Nova Scotia. It is my contention that the documentary aspect of the Canadian poem is at least as debatable as that of its English counterpart.

Recent scholars concerned with the thought of the English Goldsmith seem to have reached essential agreement on the main points raised in the previous paragraph.[5] Goldsmith did exaggerate, both in his assumption that such expulsions as he described were widespread and in his idyllic picture of an English, or Irish, village. On the first point, Howard J. Bell writes:

What little is known about the factual background of the poem is not very helpful in explaining Goldsmith's foreboding. Certainly his friends thought he was conjuring up imaginary dangers. Puzzled by his insistence that the evils described in the poem were real, his early biographers tried to find records of deserted villages, but their searches were not rewarded with prolific evidence. An eviction of the tenants of Lissoy, in Ireland, seemed the only excuse for the outburst. . . . Several of his contemporaries, to be sure, agreed with his presentation of the evils, though how much they really knew about such matters cannot be determined. All that anyone can say on the basis of the very slight evidence is that probably some villagers were wiped out when wealthy men bought land for their estates. (p. 767)

[5]See R. W. Seitz, "The Irish Background of Goldsmith's Social and Political Thought," *Publications of the Modern Language Association*, LII, 1937, pp. 405-11, and Howard J. Bell, Jr., "*The Deserted Village* and Goldsmith's Social Doctrines" *ibid.*, LIX, 1944, pp. 747-72.

On the second point, the same scholar has this to say:

That the poet's description [of the village] is Utopian cannot be doubted. . . . He deliberately magnified the beauty of their simple country life in "the good old days" in order to make more poignant their sorrows and hardships. His purpose was thus to magnify (according to a rhetorical principle as old as Aristotle) the harm done and to arouse popular feeling against the wealthy tyrants and the government's policies that made their depredations possible. (p. 752)

But this exaggeration was, then, deliberate, part of Goldsmith's rhetorical design. And it was exaggeration, not falsehood. In terms of his social and political attitudes—those of an old-style Tory who clung to the traditional virtues of rural England as against the brash arrogance and display of the new oligarchy— what he had to say of conditions in the late eighteenth century was true and deeply considered. Although villagers were not being dispersed in as great numbers as he implies, and although village life had not been quite the pattern of excellence he describes, the basic process which disturbed him was at work. Under successive Whig ministries, English commercial interests had gained much ground at the expense of the landed interests, and the traditional rural way of life was indeed in danger of extinction. In a sense, Goldsmith's picture, drawn when the Industrial Revolution was in its infancy, was prophetic: it was to be drawn again a generation later by Wordsworth and by a variety of writers during the Victorian age. If, then, *The Deserted Village* is inaccurate in some of its details, it neverthe- less expresses a fundamental truth regarding the development of English society in its period.

Much the same, I believe, is true of the documentary aspect of the Canadian poem. It has documentary value, but of a sort at once more general and more limited than has previously been suggested.

It is strange that critics who accept *The Rising Village* at its face value as an accurate picture of social conditions in early Nova Scotia should not have been struck by the contrast be- tween it and Haliburton's *The Clockmaker*, published only a decade later. The contrast is quite as great as that between the English Goldsmith's village and Crabbe's. The Canadian Goldsmith's farmers are all industrious and efficient; Haliburton's are lazy and unenterprising. For Goldsmith, all is for the best in the best of possible worlds; for Haliburton, Nova Scotia is in a slough of apathy and ignorance from which only the lash of satire may arouse her.

If we turn to contemporary histories and journals as a means of arbitrating this dispute, we find that the weight of evidence is on the side of Haliburton.[6] The picture, admittedly, is somewhat confused; but the following general outline emerges fairly clearly. During the Napoleonic and American wars, Nova Scotia had enjoyed a period of great prosperity; but once the wars were over a long period of depression set in. The severity of this depression was aggravated by the restrictions placed by Great Britain upon colonial trade. At the very time when *The Rising Village* was being written, urgent representations were being made to the Imperial authorities to have these restrictions removed; and in the year of its publication some relief was indeed afforded by Huskisson's tariff. But what reflection of all this is there in the poem? None. There we are told that from the shores of Nova Scotia

> with every gentle gale,
> Commerce expands her free and swelling sail. . . .

There is not a hint of the current dissatisfaction with Britain's trade policies; instead Goldsmith declares:

> These are thy blessings, Scotia, and for these
> For wealth, for freedom, happiness, and ease,
> Thy grateful thanks to Britain's care are due,
> Her power protects, her smiles past hopes renew,
> Her valour guards thee, and her councils guide,
> Then, may thy parent ever be thy pride!

If Goldsmith's picture of commerce is unduly optimistic, so is his picture of agriculture. Many of the early settlers of Nova

---

[6]See John M'Gregor, *British America* (London: 1832); Captain W. Moorsom, *Letters from Nova Scotia* (London: 1830); Hugh Murray, *British America* (London: 1839); Abraham Gesner, *Industrial Resources of Nova Scotia* (Halifax: 1849); *A General Description of Nova Scotia* (Halifax: 1823; new ed., 1825), published anonymously but now attributed to T. C. Haliburton.

Scotia were utterly unfitted for agriculture, and despised it as an occupation[7]; during the war many farmers abandoned their farms for trading; agricultural methods were primitive in the extreme; most of the colony's flour had to be imported from the United States. It is true that by 1825 some improvement had been effected, largely through the agitation of "Agricola" (John Young) and the subsequent establishment of agricultural societies. But Haliburton's *General Description of Nova Scotia*, the second edition of which was published in the same year as *The Rising Village*, records:

Although the change produced by these societies is very great, yet it is more visible in the improved breed of cattle, in the variety and quality of the seeds, in the use of coarser grains, and in the attention paid to manure, than in the different branches of work performed upon a farm. The ploughing is still badly executed, land generally undrained, poorly fenced, insufficiently manured, and in many places so neglected as to become very foul with weeds. . . . There is still room for the introduction of further industry and economy. . . . The native farmer is too apt to speculate, to enter into trade, and dabble in small coasting vessels, to the neglect and injury of the farm.[8]

And as late as 1848, Gesner wrote:

That the Agricultural Societies in the different counties of the Province have been in some degree beneficial to the farming interests, and especially to the improvement of the breeds of domestic animals, there can be no doubt; but not more than one farmer in ten has been induced to enrol himself. . . . True it is that the spirit of enquiry slumbers in their bosoms, and they choose to tread the old beaten track of their fathers rather than avail themselves of modern discoveries.[9]

---

[7]See M'Gregor, *British America*, p. 143.
[8]Pp. 102, 109. This book, in its first edition, may well have given Goldsmith the idea for his poem. In chapter XI, "A Brief Sketch of the State of the Province during the Administration of Sir George Prevost, Sir John Sherbrooke, the Earl of Dalhousie, and Sir James Kempt," Haliburton writes: "The origin and growth of a modern Colony affords much matter of curious speculation. To trace the difference between the state of man rising in the progress of years to civilization, and that of an enlightened people operating upon uncultivated nature, is at once an interesting and useful pursuit." He then quotes from *The Deserted Village*, and goes on to write what is in many respects the prose counterpart of *The Rising Village*.
[9]*Industrial Resources*, 208.

But of these unfortunate conditions, there is again no hint in *The Rising Village*. According to Goldsmith, the Nova Scotia farmer watches

> His rising crops, with rich luxuriance crowned,
> In waving softness shed their freshness round. . . .
>
> . . . And boundless prospects stretched on every side,
> Proclaim the country's industry and pride.

In other words, *The Rising Village* is not a documentary poem in the strict sense of that phrase; it does not give us a detailed and accurate picture of social and economic conditions in its age. If this is to some extent true also of *The Deserted Village,* there is this marked difference between the two poems: the English Goldsmith was saying the uncomfortable thing, he was fulfilling one of the functions of the artist in being the conscience of his race; but the Canadian Goldsmith was saying the comfortable thing, saying what he knew everybody wanted to hear about the progress of the colony. There was ample scope in the Nova Scotia of the twenties for a biting satirical poem, for passages of invective similar to those in *The Deserted Village*, but Goldsmith chose to ignore his opportunity and to murmur soothingly that all was well.

But much the same defence can be offered for his departures from strict accuracy as was offered for the English Goldsmith. In the first place, the Canadian poet's rhetorical design demanded a sharp contrast between the wilderness to which the settlers had come and the relatively civilized community which they had managed to build. To have taken account of the shortcomings in the contemporary community would have weakened the force of this contrast. In the second place, for all its inaccuracy of detail, *The Rising Village* does present a truth: Nova Scotia had made tremendous progress in both agriculture and commerce in the half-century preceding the poem. Finally, and most important, the poem testified to a new spirit discernible in the Nova Scotia of the twenties. As various recent writers have pointed out, the colony was at this period evolving a sense of its own identity and destiny.[10] The colony had reached the

---

[10]See, for example, A. G. Bailey, "Creative Moments in the Culture of the Maritime Provinces," Dalhousie Review, Oct., 1949, 231-44, and G. G. Campbell, *History of Nova Scotia* (Toronto: 1948), 199.

stage in its development when it began to have the degree of social cohesion necessary for intellectual and artistic expression. *The Rising Village,* Howe's essays, poems, and speeches, and Haliburton's histories and satires are the literary manifestations of this new spirit. In other words, *The Rising Village* is the document not so much of an economic condition as of a state of mind.

This state of mind, however, is such as to make ridiculous the assertion that the poem is thoroughly eighteenth-century in outlook. Goldsmith may have imitated his English namesake in structure and style, but he did not imitate him in thought. Life in nineteenth-century Canada had given him an attitude which differs sharply from that expressed in *The Deserted Village.* The English Goldsmith was no believer in "progress;" he shared Swift's "negative philosophy of history," and believed that the best hope for Britain lay in a reversion to a simpler society based primarily upon the land. He was consistently opposed to the proliferation of commerce and of the Empire which supported it. Commerce, and the merchants who conducted it, were the villains not only of *The Deserted Village* but of most of his writings. As Mr. Bell puts it: "From beginning to end he despised and feared the commercial spirit. The thirst for gain, as he frequently pointed out in his essays and histories, produced avarice, fraud, debasing subservience to attain an objective, injustice, cruelty, bad faith, venality in public office, and neglect of national welfare. The merchant class would go on as they had begun in 'the rage of gain' until they ruined the nation—or were forcibly stopped."[11] When we turn to the Canadian Goldsmith, how different is the attitude! This Goldsmith is a child of the progressive nineteenth century, and of optimistic North America. To him, the pedlar who "a merchant's higher title gains" is a hero to be singled out for special praise; the wealth and splendour of Britain are her glory, not her shame; the outflung Empire is a token of Britain's progressive spirit:

> . . . Thy flag, on every sea and shore unfurled,
> Has spread thy glory, and thy thunder hurled.

[11]PMLA, LIX, pp. 165-6.

Whereas the English Goldsmith, influenced probably by his reading of classical literature and history, foretold the doom of his over-rich country and ended his poem on a note of sombre warning, the Canadian poet concluded with optimistic prophecy:

> And as the sun, with gentle dawning ray,
> From night's dull bosom wakes, and leads the day,
> His course majestic keeps, till in the height
> He glows one blaze of pure exhaustless light;
> So may thy years increase, thy glories rise,
> To be the wonder of the Western skies;
> And bliss and peace encircle all thy shore,
> Till empires rise and sink, on earth, no more.

This optimism is perhaps not wholly due to the Canadian Goldsmith's time and place: it may be in part due to his youth. It was, however, almost the last as well as almost the first product of his pen. He did turn out a few occasional poems afterwards—they are collected, along with the second edition of *The Rising Village,* in a tiny grey volume published in Saint John in 1834—but none of them are of much significance. There is pathos in the paragraph in his autobiography in which he tells us why he gave up poetry:

I had better have left it alone. My unfortunate Baubling was torn to shreds. My first effort was criticized with undue severity, abused, and condemned, and why? Because I did not produce a poem like the great Oliver. Alas! Who indeed could do so? Whatever merit it possessed in itself was disowned, because the genius that wrote it did not equal that of his great predecessor. I had, however, the approbation of the "judicious few," who thought it an interesting Production. It was very fortunate for me that it was the occupation of leisure hours. My living did not depend on my poetical talent, lucky fellow, and in this respect I had the advantage of the immortal Poet. After this essay I abandoned the Muses, and I have not had the pleasure of any further intercourse with the lovely ladies.[12]

With this in mind, it is difficult to be too severe in criticizing *The Rising Village.* Whatever its shortcomings when compared with its model, it retains its interest for us as the first poem to

---

[12]P. 12.

be published in book form by an English Canadian, and as the first literary testament of an intellectual ferment in colonial Nova Scotia. Moreover, as the *Eclectic Review* put it in its notice of the poem a century and a quarter ago, "who will grudge half a crown for a poem by a descendant of Oliver Goldsmith's?"[13]

---

[13]Sept., 1825, p. 268.

Leacock as a Satirist*

T<small>HE</small> first twenty years of the twentieth century, when Stephen Leacock began to write and produced his best work, saw economic expansion but also cultural barrenness in Canada. The advent to power of Sir Wilfrid Laurier, in 1896, coincided with an economic revival which ended a long depression. The Canadian West began to expand rapidly, gold was found in the Yukon, silver and other mineral deposits were discovered in Ontario, new settlers and new capital poured into the country. Culturally, however, little was accomplished. The leaders of the Group of the Sixties had, with the exception of Duncan Campbell Scott, either died or left the country, and their successors were slow to appear. When they did appear, they were distinguished by their ability to attract large popular audiences rather than by their artistry. Of the best-known writers of this period—Ralph Connor, L. M. Montgomery and Norman Duncan in prose, W. H. Drummond, Tom MacInnes, Robert Service, and Marjorie Pickthall in verse—only Marjorie Pickthall, and she only in a minor way, was a serious artist.

An awareness of these conditions—economic expansion and cultural stagnation—is necessary for an understanding of the one really notable Canadian writer of the period, Stephen Leacock. This new, aggressive, bumptious, and unduly materialistic Canada needed above all a satirist to moderate its pretensions, to question its smugly optimistic assumptions. This rôle was attempted by Leacock, and by him alone. But even Leacock undertook it only half-heartedly and intermittently, and this because the general cultural negligence of the time

---

*Published in *Queen's Quarterly*, Summer, 1951.

made it too difficult, too unpopular, a task. This, in brief, is the thesis of this article.

Stephen Leacock had an ideal background and preparation for the rôle of satirist. He had been born in an English village, had come to Canada as a small boy and had lived on an Ontario farm, had been head boy at Upper Canada College, and after a sound training in ancient and modern languages at Toronto and in economics and political science at Chicago had become head of the Department of Economics and Political Science at McGill. His English birth and background had given him at least a glimpse of external standards by which North American civilization might be judged; his years on a farm had accustomed him to a simple type of life marked by adherence to the traditional processes and decencies. As an ex-head boy of an aristocratic school and as a professor at McGill he had a social prestige which made it impossible to attribute his satires to mere envy and jealousy. His knowledge of languages also helped to give his view perspective, and provided him with models upon which his own satires could be based. A recognized authority on economics and politics, he could not be brushed aside as an ignorant radical whose dislike of unrestricted capitalism arose from a failure to understand it. And the fact that he lived in Montreal and was on intimate terms with many of the leading financiers and industrialists meant that he was placed in an appropriate position from which to survey the crude commercialism of the new century.

That it was this which chiefly attracted his humorous observation is clear from his first book, *Literary Lapses* (1910). It is no accident that the first and most delightful sketch in that book describes the plight of a shy youth entering for the first time that Temple of Commerce, a bank. Beneath all the elaborate clowning we can detect a serious note inspired by the feeling of being out of place in a material civilization. The second sketch, "Lord Oxhead's Secret," is a satire on the type of commercial fiction which thrives on aristocratic titles, clichés, and surprise endings. "Boarding-House Geometry" is perhaps best approached as pure fun, but is not the cheap boarding-house and its petty economies one of the characteristic products of a commercial society? The next two sketches are relatively feeble, but we return to the main theme with

"How to Make a Million Dollars," in which Leacock, whose satire is usually genial, becomes rather unkind:

> So one evening I asked one of the millionaires how old Bloggs had made all his money.
> "How he made it?" he answered with a sneer. "Why, he made it by taking it out of widows and orphans."
> Widows and orphans! I thought, what an excellent idea. But who would have suspected that they had it?
> "And how", I asked pretty cautiously, "did he go at it to get it out of them?"
> "Why", the man answered, "he just ground them under his heels, that was how."

The satire in that cuts more than one way, and it is a good example of the subtlety with which Leacock's seemingly inconsequential fooling is often conducted. There is the obvious satire against exploitation; but the man who is making the accusation is himself one of the exploiters and his words are not so much an expression of honest contempt as of disguised envy. There is satire also at the expense of those who utter the conventional reproaches against great wealth, who over-simplify the complexity of large-scale finance and merely mouth sentimental platitudes about widows and orphans.

I must not here itemize each sketch in *Literary Lapses*. A general summary of the remainder will serve. There is satire on many of the aspects of a commercial civilization—on health faddists, on " lonely hearts" columns, on the "progress" which is merely novelty, on the preoccupation with statistics in particular and numbers in general, on so-called advanced education. The sketch entitled "Self-Made Men" strikes the dominant note most clearly: in it, two successful business men, "men with well-fed faces, heavy signet rings on fingers like sausages," try to outbrag each other about the hard uphill struggle they have had and end characteristically by ordering an elaborate dinner. One of the best sketches in the book—"A, B, and C, the Human Element in Mathematics"—may seem at first glance to lie outside the scope of my thesis; but does not part of its appeal rise from our sense of the anonymity of modern man in the huge metropolis? Is it not, like most of the book, an effort to assert the claims of humanity over the claims of mere number?

However that may be, there is little to my purpose in Leacock's second book, *Nonsense Novels* (1911). These parodies on popular types of fiction might be termed satire on the commercialization of literature, but are more properly conceived as burlesques. This leads me to the admission that in presenting Leacock the satirist I am not presenting the whole Leacock. There are many Leacocks: the writer of literary burlesques, the literary critic and biographer, the student of humour, and the serious economist and historian. But there is also Leacock the satirist, and it is with him that this essay is chiefly concerned.

Leacock's satire is seen most clearly in his three best books: *Literary Lapses, Sunshine Sketches of a Little Town,* and *Arcadian Adventures with the Idle Rich.* The satire is not, however, confined to these books: it occurs intermittently throughout his work; but before we examine other examples, it may be well to consider the basis on which his satire rests.

The satirist is one who makes fun of the follies and foibles of mankind, and who does this by relating men's behaviour to some ideal standard or norm from which they depart. Has Leacock any such satiric norm, or is he, as some suggest, a mere writer of nonsense? I believe that a fundamental unity of outlook underlies all of Leacock's best work. He is, to put it briefly, a country squire of the eighteenth century who revolts against the unbridled acquisitiveness and arrogant commercialism of the early twentieth century. His values are eighteenth-century ones: common sense, benevolence, moderation, good taste. His method of presenting these values, however, is the genial one of Addison rather than the savage one of Swift.

For proof that this is Leacock's attitude we may go to both his life and his books. We see the instinct of the country squire in his dress: he wore good tweeds and serges, but wore them carelessly, chose sizes too large, and deliberately eschewed the elegant and the up-to-date. We see it also in the maintenance of his country home at Orillia, to which he retreated after each academic session. There he was a modern Squire Allworthy. "He liked entertaining in Orillia particularly," his niece tells us in her preface to *Last Leaves,* "to fill the house with week-end guests, friends from everywhere. He liked to look down the broad table and proudly point out that everything was 'off the farm,' except the can of sardines in the hors d'oeuvres."

But we see all this even more clearly in his books. In *The*

Unsolved Riddle of Social Justice (1920), we see it directly, without the mask of irony. This book is the attempt of a benevolent man of the eighteenth century to restore some semblance of decency and order to the chaos of an industrial society. "The tattered outcast dozes on his bench while the chariot of the wealthy is drawn by. The palace is the neighbour of the slum." Here Leacock's effect is less like that which we might expect from a contemporary economist, and more like the probable reaction of Sir Roger de Coverley suddenly confronted with twentieth-century London. It is the sturdy common sense of an eighteenth-century squire dismissing socialism as "a mere beautiful dream, possible only for the angels." It is an eighteenth-century instinct which would patch up the present social order rather than destroy it in favour of a new one. And the patching which Leacock suggests is just that which a benevolent squire of that period would have devised. Let us, says Leacock in effect, look after the children, the workless, the aged and the infirm as those people were looked after in the village by the squire and his lady.

In his greatest book of humour, *Sunshine Sketches of a Little Town* (1912), Leacock uses gentle irony to suggest the same general outlook. Here he creates an idyll of a small community based on the farming life of the surrounding area, and for the closest approach to the picture which emerges we must go again to the eighteenth century—to the "sweet Auburn" whose passing Goldsmith so movingly lamented. In Mariposa, life moves at a snail's pace, and there is time for the courtesies of contemplation which have been crowded out in the industrial world. Dean Drone, sitting in his garden over a book of Theocritus, is more like the parson of Auburn than the modern "go-getting" cleric whom Leacock was later to pillory in *Arcadian Adventures with the Idle Rich*. Josh Smith, with his "chequered waistcoat of dark blue with a flowered pattern," "his shepherd's plaid trousers," "his grey spats and patent leather boots," is an innkeeper whom Fielding would have recognized or Dickens seized upon as a survivor from an earlier and more ample day.

Mariposa, however, is not merely an eighteenth-century English or Irish village transferred to twentieth-century Canada: it is also recognizably a Canadian small town. There were, and happily there still are, such communities in which the noises of the contemporary industrial era are heard only as a faint and distant murmur, and out of them, at this very period, many Canadian regional novelists were shaping their tales. Leacock could write as nostalgically, as sentimentally, as any of them about the beauties of his region. He was not joking when he wrote, in "The Marine Excursion of the Knights of Pythias," that "You may talk as you will about the intoning choirs of your European cathedrals, but the sound of 'O Canada' borne across the waters of a silent lake at evening is good enough for those of us who know Mariposa."

Or was he joking? It is the ambiguity, the subtle irony, of *Sunshine Sketches* which make it so fascinating. Leacock was aware of the sunshine of Mariposa, but also of its littleness—for there is irony even in the title. In contrast with big cities like Montreal and New York, Mariposa is a Utopia, a blessed spot which the tide of industrialism has almost completely passed by. When "The Whirlwind Campaign in Mariposa" fails to produce the results that a similar financial drive had achieved in the city, Leacock drily comments: "It may be that there are differences between Mariposa and the larger cities that one doesn't appreciate at first sight." And the flaws in Mariposa life are chiefly things which, like the whirlwind campaign, arise from a misguided desire to ape the cities. Mariposa isn't content to be a sleepy small town: it wants to become a metropolis. Hence such genial satire as this:

In point of population, if one must come down to figures, the Canadian census puts the numbers every time at something around five thousand. But it is very generally understood in Mariposa that the census is largely the outcome of malicious jealousy. It is usual that after the census the editor of the Mariposa Newspacket makes a careful re-estimate . . . and brings the population up to 6,000. After that the Mariposa Times-Herald makes an estimate that runs the figure up to 6,500. Then Mr. Gingham, the undertaker, who collects the initial statistics for the provincial government, makes an estimate from the number of what he calls the "demissed" as compared with the less interesting persons who are still alive, and brings the population to 7,000. After that somebody else works it out that it's 7,500; then the man behind the bar of the Mariposa House offers to bet the whole room that there are 9,000 in Mariposa. That settles it, and the population is well on the way to 10,000 when down swoops the federal census taker on his next round and the town has to begin all over again.

The best sustained chapter—"The Speculations of Jefferson Thorpe"—is the clearest example of this satire upon the corrupting influence of modern industrialism and the worship of material success. It describes the effect upon Mariposa of one of the great financial booms which were characteristic of this generation of Canadian life—the boom occasioned by the discovery of silver deposits in the Cobalt area. The town goes wild, the young bank-teller commits suicide, and the laconic barber, Jefferson Thorpe himself, loses all his savings. While the dominant tone is farcical, it is the kind of farce which T. S. Eliot detects in *The Jew of Malta*—farce with a bite in it.

The theme is absent from the tedious chapters of nonsense dealing with the love affairs of young Pupkin, but it re-appears in the sketches describing the 1911 election in Mariposa. In election time, Mariposa is inevitably caught up in the stream of the national life. The town exhibits, on a small scale, all the cheap rhetoric which distinguished that most malicious election campaign in Canadian history. How neatly, by the slightest of exaggerations, Leacock suggests the falseness of it all:

I only knew that it was a huge election and that on it turned issues of the most tremendous importance, such as whether or not Mariposa should become part of the United States, and whether the flag that had waved over the school house at Tecumseh Township for ten centuries should be trampled under the hoof of an alien invader, and whether Britons should be slaves . . .

Josh Smith wins the election—Josh Smith, the hotel-keeper, running as a Tory on a temperance ticket—and he wins by a trick, as the result of a premature election report coming, characteristically, from the city!

The satire in *Sunshine Sketches,* is, however, for the most part very mild and gentle. In *Arcadian Adventures with the Idle Rich* (1914) it is sharper and more explicit. The opening pages set the tone:

The Mausoleum Club stands on the quietest corner of the best residential street in the city . . .

The street in the softer hours of the morning has an almost reverential quiet . . . The sunlight flickers through the elm-trees, illuminating expensive nursemaids wheeling valuable children in little perambulators . . . Here you may see a little toddling princess in a rabbit suit who owns fifty distilleries in her own right . . .

Just below Plutoria Avenue, and parallel with it, the trees die out and the brick and stone of the city begins in earnest. Even from the avenue you see the tops of the skyscraping buildings in the big commercial streets, and can hear or almost hear the roar of the elevated railway, earning dividends. And beyond that again the city sinks lower, and is choked and crowded with the tangled streets and little houses of the slums.

As this passage suggests, the book is an indictment of arrogant plutocracy. The first sketch, "A Little Dinner with Mr. Lucullus Fyshe," is an ironical study of the attempts of a typical plutocrat to lure money from an English peer—who is at the same time eager to borrow money to salvage his ancestral estate. The next two sections concern Mr. Tomlinson, who, having made a huge fortune by the chance discovery of gold on his farm, tries vainly to get rid of his wealth only to find that he has acquired a Midas touch. Eventually the mine fails, and Tomlinson is happy to return to his quiet farm. The satire here exposes the myth of the "hard uphill struggle" of which Leacock's plutocrats are fond of talking, and of the supposed "knowhow" which finds itself outmanoeuvred by the simple guilelessness of Mr. Tomlinson. Leacock came as close in these sections to what, in *Humour and Humanity,* he called "sublime humour" as he was ever to come. Tomlinson is at once a tragic and a comic figure, and the laughter of the story is always close to tears.

The next two sections of *Arcadian Adventures* are closer in tone and spirit to the Pupkin sequence in *Sunshine Sketches;* but sections six and seven, dealing with the rivalry between the Anglican Church of St. Asaph and the Presbyterian Church of St. Osoph, resume the main theme. It is characteristic that the ultimate merger of the two churches is achieved in the manner of a big business deal—and for the same purpose!

In this book, indeed, Leacock ridicules practically every aspect of the plutocratic society of his time. Entertainment has become a mere adjunct of business: a dinner with Mr. Fyshe is a business conference in disguise. "Culture" has become a mere outlet for the idle wives of financial barons or a means of display for the barons themselves. Education, especially university education, has also been corrupted by the influence of Big Business. The university is symbolized by Dr. Boomer, whose whole aim as an administrator is to pry money out of business men by offering them honorary degrees and similar privileges. With such a president guiding its destinies, it is no wonder that the university has come to resemble a factory rather than a seat of learning:

The university, as everyone knows, stands out with its great gates on Plutoria Avenue, and with its largest buildings, those of the faculty of industrial and mechanical science, fronting full upon the street.

These buildings are exceptionally fine, standing fifteen stories high and comparing favourably with the best departmental stores or factories in the city.

Leacock, however, was no social revolutionary who would, in Yeats's phrase, "hurl the little streets upon the great." He was, in outlook and in actual political affiliation, a Tory; but he was a Tory of the old school. His Toryism had nothing of the cynical callousness of Big Business; it was the Toryism of Goldsmith and Burke, which saw in the traditional decencies and duties of of an agricultural society the proper basis for community. His literary purpose was similar to that of Chaucer, seeking to preserve amid the growing commercialism and corruption of the fourteenth century the values of feudal solidarity, chivalric courtesy, and the ancestral faith; similar also to that of Addison, attempting to persuade the new middle class to take on something of the culture and humanity of the landed gentry; similar to that of Dickens, calling amid a squalid industrialism for the colour and kindness of a slower age; similar, finally, to that of Mark Twain, yearning amid the tinsel of the Gilded Age for the simple virtues of pioneer America.

It was from such men that Leacock learned, and with whom he had his closest affiliations. Like him, they were all laughing philosophers, but in them all, as in him, there was a serious underlying purpose. Was Leacock of their tribe? The late Dr. G. G. Sedgwick came close to an answer when he declared: "He is not one of the Great Ones, but he may sit at the same table."

If he was not "one of the Great Ones"—and it is true that most of his work is ephemeral and that even his best books leave one with the feeling that the man who wrote them could have written better—it was partly because of the nature of Canadian society in his time. The prevailing materialism was too strong even for him to resist. In most of his books he went along with the crowd and wrote the kind of nonsense for which they were willing to pay. Canadian culture was still too shallow to support such an artist. But Leacock came closer to greatness than any other Canadian writer of his generation, and in *Sunshine Sketches of a Little Town* the period found its highest literary level.

Areas of Research in
Canadian Literature*

Iт is symptomatic of our growing self-confidence that Canadian literature, the very existence of which was seriously debated in academic circles a generation ago, should now be recognized as a legitimate subject of research. Already valuable pioneer work has been done by faculty members and graduate students in several Canadian, and in a few American, universities. Canadian literature remains, however, a very rich and virtually unexploited field. So far, our operations in it may be compared to those of a harvesting machine which merely removes the heads from the grain: we have still to examine the soil in which the seed grew, and to investigate the processes of growth.

To state that Canadian literature offers a rich field for academic literary research is not necessarily to imply that Canadian literature is itself a luxuriant growth. We need have no illusions about the quality of Canadian writing in order to believe that the conditions under which it has been produced and the characteristics which it has manifested are worthy of serious study. A stunted plant may offer more excitement to the investigator than its more prolific neighbour.

There seem to me to be seven major areas in which research in Canadian literature might profitably be conducted: bibliography, biography, literary sociology, cultural analysis, philosophy, comparative literature, and the study of reputations. This list does not pretend to be exhaustive, but it at least should provide a broad basis for discussion and a sufficiently challenging programme of action.

---

*This article formed the substance of an address delivered to the National Conference of University Teachers of English, Toronto, May, 1952. It was published in the *University of Toronto Quarterly*, October, 1953.

It is a grim commentary on our cultural apathy that there is as yet no satisfactory and comprehensive bibliography of Canadian literature. The only two bibliographies—one of poetry, the other of fiction—which aim at comprehensiveness were published over fifty years ago. Recently, Professor R. E. Watters of the University of British Columbia has been preparing an up-to-date bibliography with the aid of grants from the Canadian Humanities Research Council. His work will be immensely valuable, but, if I understand its scope correctly, it will leave considerable room for the researches of the expert bibliographer. The Watters bibliography will be in the nature of a check-list, compiled largely on the basis of existing partial bibliographies rather than upon a volume by volume examination of the books themselves. It will leave unsolved such bibliographical puzzles as the existence or non-existence of Major John Richardson's *Westbrook,* a novel which is listed in several bibliographies of that author but about which no precise information is given. I have made inquiries about *Westbrook* from all the leading libraries of this continent and from several abroad, but have not succeeded in tracing a single copy. My guess is that the novel was advertised for sale, but that it was either never written or never published. It will also be left for subsequent researchers to sort out all the special and limited editions in which Bliss Carman's poetry appeared in the first two decades of this century: a task, I suspect, which will challenge the energy and ingenuity of even the most devoted student. Similar bibliographical puzzles will readily occur to most of my readers. Think, for example, of Stephen Leacock, whose books were so multifarious, were translated into so many languages, and excerpts from which appeared in so many anthologies. There will also be the task of tracing the periodical contributions of Canadian authors. Who can guess what new light might be shed upon the development of Lampman or Roberts or Duncan Campbell Scott if we had an accurate chronological record of their poems as they appeared in the magazines of the last two decades of the nineteenth century?

If bibliography seems too specialized a field for the potential scholar, perhaps the work waiting to be done in biography will arouse his excitement. It would not be too rash to assert that there is not yet a single definitive biography of a Canadian author. Perhaps Professor Carl Klinck's study of William Wilfred Campbell may remain the standard work on that rather minor figure, but if so it is a solitary exception. V. L. O. Chittick's study of Haliburton is a scholarly one, but it is now thirty years old and, for all its erudition, it does not really penetrate the personality of that delightful old Tory satirist. We must pay our tribute to other pioneer studies such as those of Lorne Pierce on William Kirby, Elsie Pomeroy on Roberts, and Carl Connor on Lampman, but each of these books has serious flaws. We badly need a series of biographies of our major authors, a series which should include books on Thomas Chandler Haliburton, John Richardson, Charles Sangster, William Kirby, Gilbert Parker, Bliss Carman, Archibald Lampman, Charles Roberts, Duncan Campbell Scott, Marjorie Pickthall, Frederick Philip Grove and Stephen Leacock.

To fill this need will be no easy task. To give some idea of the kind of difficulties that may be encountered, perhaps I may illustrate from my own experience in trying to put together a biography of Canada's first native novelist, Major John Richardson. Not only are the existing biographies of the man brief and sketchy in the extreme, they are not even accurate regarding the major events of his life. Facts disclosed in the papers of Richardson's maternal grandfather, John Askin, make it reasonably certain that the novelist's mother was half-Indian. This, if true, is of great help in understanding Richardson's personality—he seems always to have suffered from a sense of insecurity—and his books, for in the latter he frequently introduces Indian characters and endows them almost always with great nobility. Yet none of the existing biographies even allude to the possibility of such ancestry! There is another mystery about Richardson's marriage. I have secured a copy of a return made by Richardson himself to the British War Office which not only gives a date for his marriage quite different from that given in the biographies, but also gives the name of a quite different lady! Whether the biographies are quite wrong, or whether Richardson married twice, is a question yet to be unravelled. At any rate, with these two instances of inaccuracy before us, we are apt to look sceptically at the highly coloured accounts given us of Richardson's death. He is said to have died of starvation in New York City, after having sold his Newfoundland dog to buy a last meal; but all this may well be sheer fantasy.

Adequate biographical treatments of Richardson and other

authors will of course demand a study of the social backgrounds from which they emerged; and indeed, this whole subject of what may be called literary sociology will form a fascinating area for research. On the one hand, we must investigate the manner in which our literature reflects our society. There has been much loose talk of the documentary accuracy of our authors, and it is time that we decided what exactly we mean by this phrase and to what extent its use is justified by the facts. I have recently sought to show that Goldsmith's *Rising Village* is far from being a true picture of colonial life in early Nova Scotia, and yet its claim to be such has been attested by critic after critic. It is strange that often the same critic declares for the documentary accuracy of both Goldsmith and Haliburton, when they were inhabitants of the same colonial society and yet gave such divergent accounts of it! Isabella Valancy Crawford, again, is said to give us an accurate account of pioneer life in Ontario; but it is difficult to believe that the singing, ranting, murdering lumbermen of her *Malcolm's Katie* are typical early inhabitants of staid Ontario. How accurate is the image she gives us? How accurate are the images of their societies provided by Lampman, Grove, and Leacock?

On the other hand, we must attempt to establish what social forces precipitated the various literary movements in Canada. Dr. A. G. Bailey made a brilliant beginning on this subject some years ago in his article "Creative Moments in the Culture of the Maritime Provinces," but what he did for the Maritimes needs to be done for the other parts of the country. A host of urgent questions spring to mind. Was there any real connection between the excitement generated by Confederation and the sudden upsurge of literary activity in the eighties and nineties of the last century? To what extent was the nationalism of the nineteen-twenties responsible for the literary revival of that decade? Why was World War II such a productive period in Canadian literary history, whereas World War I was so barren?

Anyone who thinks at all seriously about such questions will be struck by the fact that not only has our literature tended to occur in clusters but that the other arts have tended to flourish at the same moments and to take similar forms. Thus the decades following the achievement of Confederation saw not merely the work of Carman, Roberts, Lampman, Scott, Kirby, Parker, and others in literature, but the beginnings of significant work in painting and music. In the twenties, when Pratt, Grove, de la Roche, and the Montreal Group were producing their poems and stories, the Group of Seven were doing experimental and creative work in painting. World War II saw an upsurge not merely of Canadian writing but also of Canadian music, ballet, sculpture, and of other allied arts. Here is another fruitful subject for investigation—especially fruitful if undertaken by someone sufficiently skilled in several of these art forms to be able to make significant comparisons between them. As a casual observer, I think I see interesting parallels between the rugged northern landscapes of Thomson, Harris, Jackson and company and the landscape poems of E. J. Pratt, F. R. Scott, A. J. M. Smith, and others. Again, it takes no great discernment to see similarities between the tendency of Canadian poetry in the forties towards social analysis and protest, and the gradual decline in the dominance of landscapes among our paintings. It would indeed be most interesting to see what there is in common between the images of Canada presented to us by workers in the various forms of art.

If the foregoing subject of research would commend itself particularly to those trained in the fine arts, the one next to be considered would be most appropriately undertaken by those trained in philosophy. We need to investigate the relation of literature to the various currents of ideas which have circulated through Canada. In speaking of the poetry of Carman and Roberts, critics frequently refer to their transcendentalism. What is the exact nature of transcendentalism, as they express it? Is it an accurate copy of the transcendentalism of Thoreau and Emerson, or is it significantly modified to suit the Canadian environment? Whence was their transcendentalism derived? Did they receive it directly from its New England exponents, or was transcendentalism diffused throughout the eastern seaboard, without regard to international boundaries? Again, where did Lampman derive the ideas, particularly the social ideas, which animate his later poetry? Was a vague sort of Utopian socialism common in intellectual circles in Canada in the late nineteenth century, or did Lampman borrow it directly from William Morris? When did the Darwinian hypothesis begin to make an impact on Canadian habits of thought? These are just a few of the questions which any student interested in the history and diffusion of ideas might profitably undertake to answer.

As ideas are diffused, so are other literary influences. The student skilled in detecting such influences and similarities would find much to challenge him in the comparative study of Canadian literature. Our writers are commonly said to be imitative, but it is only rarely that the nature and extent of their imitation is considered in serious detail. We have not yet, I think, sufficient evidence to say categorically whether our writers have tended to look across the Atlantic Ocean or across the American border in their search for models. Was Thomas Chandler Haliburton, for example, an American humourist, or a transplanted English satirist? Was the early literature of colonial Nova Scotia an offshoot, as R. P. Baker argues, of New England literature, or were its writers more closely allied to English literature of the late eighteenth century? Are our poets of today more aware of Spender, Dylan Thomas, George Barker, and John Betjeman, or of Stevens, Williams, Jarrell, and Lowell? Particular writers will offer particular forms of difficulty. Carman is a case in point. Shelley, Swinburne, Poe, Whitman, Stevenson, Browning, Mallarmé, to mention but a few, have been cited by critics as influences on his work. Is it possible to sort out these influences? Is Carman merely a maker of pastiches, or is there some distinctive and personal quality in his vision and form of expression?

A subdivision of this comparative inquiry might well be the relations between literature emanating from English-speaking Canada and that emanating from French-speaking Canada. It is my conviction that these two literatures have developed in virtual isolation one from the other, and yet there are some remarkable parallels between them. The novels of each group, until recently, were predominantly historical romances or regional idylls. The poems of each group were predominantly, again until recently, romantic lyrics of love and landscape. In the last two decades, the writers of both groups have become increasingly realistic and social in their emphases. Have these similarities been accidental, the result of a similar physical and social environment, or the product of international forces?

A very specific form of this last inquiry might be the investigation of the amount of translation from the two major languages in Canada. In the nineteenth century, it was quite common for English-Canadian novels to be translated into French for the benefit of readers in Quebec. Today a casual observation would indicate that this practice has largely ceased and that the translations are made rather from French into English. Is such a casual impression borne out by the facts? If so, is it because the residents of Quebec are no longer interested in reading English-Canadian novels, or because a much higher proportion of the literary-minded people of that province are capable of reading the novels in English?

I come to the last possible area of research which I listed at the beginning of this article: the study of reputations. It may seem a little premature to suggest this type of study for authors whose claim to lasting interest has scarcely been established. In my view, however, this kind of inquiry can be very helpful in deciding what is permanent and what is transient in an author's work. A careful study of the curve of Bliss Carman's literary reputation at home and abroad, for example, should bring us much nearer the desirable goal of deciding what his ultimate rank as a poet will be. Interesting studies might also be made of the critical reception of Canadian writers in England and the United States. All such studies would tend to put our literary output in some kind of perspective, would enable us to look at our authors with less prejudice.

These, then, are a few of the areas of research in Canadian literature. Other areas will doubtless occur to other persons. My hope is merely that I have indicated something of the scope of the subject, of its potential excitement, and that I have given some glimpse of the immense task that awaits our minds and pens.

A Reading of Lampman's "Heat"*

ALL critics of Archibald Lampman, and notably Duncan Campbell Scott, Carl Y. Connor, Raymond Knister, Norman G. Guthrie, and E. K. Brown, have agreed that he was one of the most conscientious craftsmen in the history of Canadian poetry. They have confined themselves, however, either to general appreciations of his skill, or to the analysis of a few selected lines. So far as I am aware, no one has undertaken the full dress analysis of a Lampman poem as an organic whole, and that is the purpose of this article. I propose to examine the famous "Heat," because it is the poem which I know and like best and because it is easily accessible. Since it is in almost every Canadian anthology, I shall quote from it sparingly, assuming that the interested reader will provide himself with the text.

Many readers must have felt that "Heat" has a fascination out of proportion to its surface meaning. It is, of course, remarkable enough for its descriptive accuracy, perfection of tone, and unwavering concreteness. Here, beyond doubt, is a typical Ontario summer day, caught as cleanly as words could ever catch it. The plains "reel" in the strong sunlight both in the sense that they unwind from the eye to the horizon like a fisherman's line and that they seem, in the currents of hot air, to waver back and forth like a drunken man. This latter effect of the atmosphere also explains the poet's choice of the word "swim" to describe the progress of the road as it nears the top of the hill. The poem throughout is filled with examples of such verbal exactitude: the wheels of the haycart, slightly loose on their axles, are said to be "clacking," which is the precise onomatopeic word to describe that odd but familiar sound; the slow

*Published in *Culture*, 1953.

song of the thrush is exactly expressed in the description of him "sliding" his "thin revolving tune," as is the more shrill and rapid chirrup of the grasshopper by the contrasting "spin."

But this accuracy, this exact translation of sensation into word, does not of itself seem sufficient to explain the spell which the poem weaves. Nor is the secret, I think, in the metre and melody of the verse, apt and haunting as they are. Lampman has used stanzas of eight lines, rhyming ababcdcd, and of these lines the first seven are in iambic tetrameter and the eighth in iambic trimeter. This final shorter line has the opposite effect to that of Spenser's final alexandrine: instead of bringing each stanza to a majestic close and suggesting a pause, it implies inconclusiveness and urges us on to the next stanza. Lampman, in other words, is less interested here in painting a series of tableaux than in projecting a linked sequence of emotional impressions.

As in his choice of stanza form, Lampman has shown great tact in varying the metrical pattern to suit his special purposes. In the first stanza, for example, a trochee replaces the iamb in the first foot of each of the third and fifth lines for the obvious purpose of suggesting the difficulty of the upward climb of the road and the wagon. In the third stanza, the first foot of the second line is inverted to suggest the extraordinary power of the sun as it "soaks in the grass," and the third line has an extrametrical syllable to provide the retarded pace necessary for the act of counting the marguerites one by one. Similar metrical modifications, all clearly justified, can be found in each of the stanzas.

Similar skill is evident in Lampman's use of alliteration and assonance. As we might expect in a poem whose subject is slow, silent, summer heat, the most heavily alliterated consonant is "s." In the first stanza we get "southward," "steep," "seems," "swim," "summit, slowly steals;" in the second, "side," "slouching slowly," "sky to sky," and "sole;" in the third, "the sun soaks," "still," "spider;" in the fifth, "spin," "small," "sound," "sometimes," "skyline," "sight;" and in the sixth stanza, "sharp," "sweet," and "sloped shadow." For all this, the alliteration is seldom if ever overdone: the repeated sibilants and labials have their effect but they do not, with the possible exception of the line "Is slouching slowly at his ease," obtrude themselves.

Lampman's cunning and functional use of assonance can perhaps best be illustrated by examining the four middle lines of the second stanza:

> Half-hidden in the windless blur
> Of white dust puffing to his knees.
> This wagon on the height above,
> From sky to sky on either hand . . .

The short "i" and short "u" vowels of the former two lines suggest the close-up effect of the picture: here the eyes, as also the vocal organs in pronouncing the vowels, are being held within narrow limits. In the latter two lines, as the scope of the picture broadens and our eyes are invited to view the scene panoramically, the long "i" vowels allow our mouths to expand also.

But not even yet, it seems to me, have we reached the essence of the poem's appeal. To do that, we must consider the imagery, and see how cunningly Lampman has woven and interwoven certain motifs.

The poem is constructed on the principle of balanced opposites: dry is set over against wet, hot against cold, light against dark, near against far. Let us look at each of these pairs in turn.

The clay road being "white" is dry, but it seems to "swim;" cart and wagoner are dusty, but the sun "soaks" in the grass; the water-bugs are close to the water of the brook, elm-tree shadows are like a "flood," but the burnt grass is dry and the ground is "droughty."

Heat is suggested almost continuously throughout the poem—by words such as "melt," "heat-held land," "burning," and "full furnace"—but cold is there too, in "the cool gloom" beneath the bridge and in the shade of the trees.

Now for the light-dark antithesis. The distant plains of the opening line are "dim," but the road is "white and bare;" the wagoner is half-hidden in dust but the wagon is bright against the skyline; the marguerites are so clear in the sunlight that they can be individually counted, but the water-bugs are in the shadow of the bridge; the elm trees cast shadows but the thrush is singing into "the pale depth of the noon," the woods are "blue with haze" but the hills are "drenched in light;" the poet is in "the sloped shadow" of his hat, but he is also in "the full furnace" of the hour.

The deliberate opposition of near and far is equally apparent. The first stanza is panoramic until the last two lines, when the eyes, having swept the horizon, come to rest on the wheels of the haycart. The first half of the second stanza continues the close-up effect; then the gaze widens to take in the whole panorama again. In the third stanza we begin with panorama and then narrow down to the flowers and tiny insects near at hand. The fourth stanza gradually leads the eye from the nearby trees and cows to the limitless distance suggested by "the pale depth of the noon," and much the same is true of the fifth stanza, where we are carried from the grasshoppers and crickets to the distant woods and hills. And in the final stanza the ultimate in narrowing is effected as we are brought completely away from the external world into the poet's mind.

There are several other types of physical contrast in the poem: the slow song of the thrush against the rapid chirp of the grasshopper, the tiny midges and water-bugs against the great hills and woods, for example. But the principle of balanced opposites does not merely apply here to physical things: it applies also on the personal and the cosmic planes. There are two persons in the poem, and they are as unlike as two men could well be. One is the wagoner, the manual labourer, the other the poet, the sensitive intellectual. And in the lines

> Beyond me in the fields the sun
> Soaks in the grass and hath his will . . .

we have at least an implicit suggestion of the ancient cosmogony, widely diffused in myth and legend, whereby all creation is the result of the intercourse of the male Sun with the female Earth.

But if the poem merely set forth, and did not reconcile or unify, these sets of opposites, it would be interesting but not as significant as it really is. Readers of this poem are often puzzled by the final stanza; some critics have even gone so far as to consider it superfluous; I think it provides the essential clue to the poem's meaning. Lampman asserts that "in the full furnace of this hour" his thoughts have grown "clean and clear." He also says (in an obvious reference to the pairs of opposites of which we have seen the poem to be composed) that to him "not this nor that/Is always sharp or always sweet." What he is claiming, and claiming justly as I hope to demonstrate in a moment, is that somehow this experience has brought him a special insight, a moment of vision, and epiphany. He has become aware of both the full sharpness and the full sweetness of life, and of them both at once and as necessary complements of each other. The same applies to all the pairs of opposites in the poem; wetness and dryness, heat and cold, light and dark, near and far, fast and slow, are not merely opposites but complements of one another. Similarly, the wagoner is the complement of the poet, and the Sun of the Earth.

That it is Lampman's real theme to reveal and reconcile these opposites can be demonstrated from the way in which he deliberately links them, and weaves them in the pattern of a larger unity. The wagoner is linked with the poet by the phrases used to describe them: the wagoner "is slouching slowly at his ease," the poet "leans at rest." The grasshopper is linked with the thrush in that the song of each is said to revolve in the air. But it is this notion of revolution, of cyclical movement, the dominant image of the whole poem, which is the chief means by which these seemingly incompatible opposites are reconciled.

We see this image most clearly in the "idly clacking wheels" of the haycart, the "thin revolving tune" of the thrush, and the spinning song of the grasshopper, but once we have become aware of it we can see it almost everywhere. Cyclical movement is suggested by the "reel" of the plains (whether it be the weaving circles of the drunkard or the unwinding fisherman's reel that we envisage), by the "puffing" of the dust around the wagoner's feet, by the sun (its circular shape and its diurnal revolution), by the marguerites with their spokelike petals, by the ruminant cows with their slowly turning cuds. It is also suggested by the rhythm of the lines: throughout there is a gentle rise and fall as of a slowly moving wheel. Look, for example, at the first two lines: the voice rises to "reel," slowly sinks to "dim," rises again to "by," and falls to "bare." Circular motion is also conveyed by the structure of each stanza: in each the eye is invited to make the circuit of the horizon and then to settle on a specific point of rest.

This dominant image of the turning wheel is symbolic of the unity of the poet's experience, and of the vision of a unified world which this moment of insight has vouchsafed to him. The turning wheel is Lampman's version of that glimpse of eternity which Vaughan described as a ring of pure and endless light. The wheel slowly turns, and as it turns light succeeds dark, heat cold, dry wet, and so on. These opposites are the spokes of the wheel: they have their place in an endless cycle which gives them each meaning and a final unity.

This may be, of course, to read too much into an apparently simple nature lyric, though I have sought throughout to follow the poem's own suggestions and to discover its pattern rather than to impose a pattern upon it. Whether the poet consciously put all these suggestions there seems to me irrelevant: any poet must work at least in part intuitively, and especially when he is seeking to project a mystical moment of vision.

I trust that I have at least demonstrated that there is a little more to Lampman's poetry than meets the casual eye. For my own part, I fully subscribe to the assertion of Norman Gregor Guthrie[1] that Lampman's verse "looks at its best through the microscope." "His verse," Guthrie writes, "is of a texture and character that commends itself to the most intimate study and re-reading . . ." If this article has provoked some careful re-reading, I shall be satisfied.

---

[1] In *The Poetry of Archibald Lampman* (Toronto, 1927) p. 16.

The Innocent Eye —
The Art of Ethel Wilson*

"The day that Mrs. Dorval's furniture arrived in Lytton, Ernestine and I had gone to the station to see the train come in. It was a hot day. The heat of the sun burned down from above, it beat up from the ground and was reflected from the hot hills. Mr. Miles, the station agent, was in his shirt sleeves; the station dog lay and panted, got up, moved away, lay down and panted again; and the usual Indians stood leaning against the corners of the wooden station (we called it "the deepo") in their usual curious incurious fashion, not looking as though they felt the heat or anything else. The Indians always looked as though they had nothing to do, and perhaps they had nothing to do. Ernestine and I had nothing much to do, but school was out and supper wasn't ready and so we had drifted over to the station. Neither of our mothers liked us to do this every day; but we were not absolutely forbidden."

THIS, the first paragraph of *Hetty Dorval* (1947), was for most Canadians their first introduction to the art of Ethel Wilson. They might have been excused for not seeing anything especially remarkable in the paragraph—Mrs. Wilson is a writer who wins one gradually and gently rather than with a sudden shock of delight—but in fact the paragraph contains in embryo nearly all the qualities which have distinguished her subsequent work and made her the most interesting Canadian writer of fiction to appear since World War II.

There is, first of all, Mrs. Wilson's casualness of tone and manner. Nothing pretentious here, nor portentous. Simply, matter of factly, with quiet restraint and dry humour, she conveys the essence of a scene and a situation. The details seem

*Published in *Queen's Quarterly*, Spring, 1954.

chosen merely at random—the heat, the shirt sleeved agent, the panting dog, the stolid Indians, the gaping girls—but insensibly we find ourselves placing the scene and the characters by means of them.

There is also apparent Mrs. Wilson's feeling for nature, and especially for animate nature. That panting dog might have been overlooked—but Mrs. Wilson is always very aware of dogs, and cats, and seagulls, indeed of all living creatures. There is her ear for colloquial language—apparent here in the parenthetical reference to "the deepo"—and her use of the "double take" for humorous effect: the Indians who looked as if they had nothing to do and who perhaps *had* nothing to do.

Above all, there is apparent the quality which more than anything else gives Ethel Wilson's work unity and distinctiveness: the vision of the innocent eye.

Although *Hetty Dorval* was the means by which most Canadians became aware of Ethel Wilson, it was not her first published work. Her first story, entitled "I Just Love Dogs", appeared in *The New Statesman and Nation* on December 4, 1937, and was reprinted in E. J. O'Brien's *Best British Short Stories*, 1938. Two more stories appeared in *The New Statesman* in 1939 ("Hurry, Hurry," Mrs. Wilson's own favourite, reprinted in the second edition of my *Book of Canadian Stories*, and "I Have a Father in the Promised Land," which eventually appeared as a chapter in *The Innocent Traveller*.) During the war she devoted most of her writing time to editing a Red Cross magazine, but one of her stories appeared in *Orion IV* and another in *The Canadian Forum*.

Since the end of the war Mrs. Wilson has continued to contribute to the literary magazines, especially to *Here and Now* and *Northern Review*, but she has reached a wider audience by her three books of fiction: *Hetty Dorval* (1947), *The Innocent Traveller* (1949), and *The Equations of Love* (1952.)

All three of these books, and a fourth which Mrs. Wilson now has ready for publication, are relatively short. *Hetty Dorval*, which the author modestly describes as "a hasty squib," runs to a mere one hundred and fourteen pages; *The Innocent Traveller*, a series of sketches given continuity by their concentration upon the members of a single family, contains two hundred and seventy-seven pages; and *The Equations of Love* contains two novelettes — "Tuesday and Wednesday" and "Lilly's Story"—in its two hundred and eighty-one pages. Mrs. Wilson attributes this brevity to the fact that "these people's lives are not epic," and says that even if they were she has not the ability to write of them at greater length. A more charitable view would attribute the brevity rather to the severe economy and restraint which she imposes upon herself.

Each of her books has been an improvement upon its predecessor; she has steadily progressed towards a more subtle and profound study of the vagaries of human nature. In *Hetty Dorval* she was obviously feeling her way, for the characters are relatively thin and conventional and the plot is frequently contrived. *The Innocent Traveller* is much more suave and accomplished, and its characters are more finely delineated, but it is somewhat superficial and episodic. *The Equations of Love,* however, is perfect of its kind, and explores the human predicament much more thoroughly and sincerely. It has all the earmarks of a minor classic, and is already being translated into Italian, Danish, and German.

This very rapid development in Mrs. Wilson's writing skill is perhaps to be attributed to the fact that she began to write relatively late in life and had perforce to crowd her apprenticeship into the shortest possible period.

She was born in Port Elizabeth, South Africa, in 1888, the daughter of Robert William Bryant and Lila (Malkin) Bryant. Her early childhood was spent in England, but when she was orphaned at the age of eight she came to Vancouver to live with the grandmother and aunts so charmingly re-created in *The Innocent Traveller*. After four years at school in Vancouver, she went back to England for a four-year stint at boarding school, receiving an education which she describes as "rigorous, almost Spartan, sound, and often very amusing." Her London Matriculation achieved, she returned to Vancouver, attended the Provincial Normal School, and was a schoolteacher until her marriage to Dr. Wallace Wilson in 1921. She has travelled widely with her husband, a distinguished doctor who was president of the Canadian Medical Association in 1946, but has continued to make her home in Vancouver.*

One naturally wonders what led this busy doctor's wife, in

*For this, and the other biographical information, I am indebted to Mrs. Wilson herself, who generously and fully answered my letters of enquiry.

middle age, to turn to the craft of writing, and how she was able to attain such quick success. We have some clues, but no final answer. There was, she tells us, "a tendency in my father's family towards writing—never very much, never very good, but certainly never very bad, because they were a critical lot." Her mother's family, with whom she grew up in Vancouver, were great readers, and had, as we learn from *The Innocent Traveller,* been on good terms in Staffordshire with Matthew Arnold and the father of Rudyard Kipling.

Mrs. Wilson herself has been a great reader, and from her admirations we can learn much of her own aims as a writer. Among the novels she most admires are Fielding's *Tom Jones,* Defoe's *Moll Flanders* and *Roxana,* E. M. Forster's *Howard's End* and *A Room with a View,* the first two or three volumes of Proust, all of Trollope, and Arnold Bennett's *Old Wives' Tale.* Surprisingly enough, there is not a woman novelist on the list. When questioned about this, Mrs. Wilson replied, in effect, that although she knew and admired the work of Jane Austen, Virginia Woolf, and Willa Cather she did not find them as congenial as the male writers listed.

What are the qualities in her favoured novels and novelists which make them congenial to her and which are embodied also, to some extent, in her own work? In Defoe, obviously, it is the matter-of-factness and the patient accumulation of detail. "Lilly's Story" especially, the second novelette in *The Equations of Love,* has Defoe's fidelity to fact, his awareness of the harsh pressure of circumstance, his admiration of the woman who lives by sheer dogged nerve, his capacity to accept and even to delight in human nature in its less flattering aspects. Neither Defoe nor Mrs. Wilson, it is clear, would be easily shocked—it is part, paradoxically, of their "innocence."

What attracts Mrs. Wilson to Forster, I suppose, is his irony, his suavity, his deep moral seriousness which never becomes pomposity, his caustic yet kindly humour, and, as with Defoe, his deep-seated tolerance and humanism.

Proust and Mrs. Wilson (who is a very modest woman and would be the first to dispute this casual juxtaposition of their names) have in common their interest in the recovery of lost time and in the ramifications of family. In *The Innocent Traveller* especially, although admittedly on a much smaller scale, Mrs. Wilson has recreated the past in all its sensuous immediacy with a loving fidelity similar to that of Marcel Proust.

The easy normality of Trollope may seem very distant from the strained neuroticism of Proust, but in their patient accumulation of domestic and social detail they find a meeting-place where Ethel Wilson too can join them. There is, also, a faintly old-fashioned Victorian saintliness about Mrs. Wilson's novels, especially about *The Innocent Traveller*, which reminds one of Trollope. Aunt Topaz would have been thoroughly at home in *Barchester Towers*.

With Arnold Bennett, of course, it is detail again, as well as the common interest in Staffordshire and in style. But what of Fielding? What possible connection is there between the robust, masculine world of *Tom Jones* and the femininity of *Hetty Dorval, The Innocent Traveller*, and *The Equations of Love*? Social realism, humour—these are links, but tenuous ones. More basic, perhaps, is the common delight in people, the fundamental conviction that human beings, for all their vices and failings, are enormously interesting and amusing.

Summing up her reasons for liking the novelists we have just discussed, Mrs. Wilson writes "The fact that these people have something to say, with skill, with good heart, often with deep feeling yet with some scepticism, their detachment as well as their involvement, gives me inexpressible pleasure. They have style, each his own, and without style . . . how dull." This statement applies with equal force to her own work.

Like those novelists she most admires, Ethel Wilson has something to say. It is not a message that can be expressed in a neat moral aphorism; rather it is an attitude which pervades her fiction. Stated negatively, it is a mild ridicule of everything which pretends to be what it is not; stated positively it is an eager delight in forms of human life which are sincere, honest, and integral. She is ever ready to give her characters the benefit of the doubt; even a villain such as the Chinese cook, Yow (who appears both in *The Innocent Traveller* and *The Equations of Love*) is shown to have his good side, evident in his devotion to the grandmother. Mrs. Wilson's satire at the expense of those who do not meet her standard of integrity is always of the gentlest sort, so that Mort and Myrtle, for example, in the first section of *The Equations of Love*, are people with whom we

are in fundamental sympathy in spite of their self-deceptions
and self-evasions.

Mrs. Wilson's tolerance makes her aware of the paradoxical
nature of many moral questions. A moral paradox is at the
heart of both sections of *The Equations of Love*. In "Tuesday
and Wednesday," it is the fact that Vicky's lie about the
manner of Mort's death is nearer the truth than the more
accurate accounts of witnesses, and that from the lie flow
consequences which can only be considered good; in *Lilly's
Story* it is the fact that Lilly earns our moral admiration not
merely in spite of but in part because of the series of lies and
deceptions by which she continues to exist.

But this inclination to look on the bright side, to seek out
good in evil rather than evil in good, does not mislead Mrs.
Wilson into ignoring the heart of darkness. There are glimpses
of the abyss in her novels which restore moral perspective and
make it clear that her basic serenity is an achieved attitude
rather than a temperamental optimism. We see the abyss of
despair many times in the chapters in "Tuesday and Wednesday" dealing with Vicky, and again in "Lilly's Story" in the
episode on the beach when the robin hunts the snake, the kitten
the robin, and the eagle the kitten—"She felt uneasy . . . seems
like everything's cruel, hunting something."

There is nothing particularly original in all this of course,
and Mrs. Wilson would not claim any profundity of thought.
But her gentle, unprejudiced, open-eyed humanism is timely in
this age of dogmatism, and very refreshing.

It is the skill with which she projects and objectifies this
attitude, however, rather than the attitude itself, which is her
surest claim to distinction. She is skilful with words, with
technique, with description, and with characters. With plots
she is less successful.

Her skill with words is perhaps most evident in the fact that
until one deliberately looks one is likely not to notice it. She
is, in other words, the master of an unobtrusive prose style
which does not draw attention to itself because it is so unerring.
Consciously clever phrases, such as that "curious incurious
fashion" in the first paragraph of *Hetty Dorval*, are very rare
in her work. She has a quick hand for similes and metaphors,
but they too are unobtrusively woven into the fabric of her

prose. That fabric is far from colourless, but its colours are delicate, and its texture is firm, even, and fine.

Mrs. Wilson's prose style is most impressive in her descriptive passages, especially in decriptions of personal appearance and of natural scenery. Though there is no self-conscious Canadianism in her work—she is convinced that such literary nationalism is misguided—no prose writer has given us more striking descriptions of the Canadian landscape. A long quotation could alone do justice to this feature of her art, but here are a few sentences from a description of a train journey westward which will give some idea of it:

And the next day they still ran along the prairie, but now the land broke into rolling country . . . and the world became lightly wooded again. Then, beyond increasingly high hills they looked westwards and saw, coldly blue and white against the sky, a tumult of mountains.

In the gullies of the little hills through which they now passed there were aspens and birches the early frost had turned from green to gold. The birches with their white maidenly stems and honey-yellow leaves shone against the dark conifers. . . . As the train hurried towards the mountains, Rachel looked up at the railway cutting and saw, for one moment, poised alone against the blue sky, a single slender white-stemmed aspen tree whose golden leaves trembled and shone and sang in the sunshine. It was there. It was gone. It was hers.

How perfectly right this is, in diction, tone, and rhythm, and yet how effortless it seems!

There is a similar effortlessness in Mrs. Wilson's narrative technique. She writes her stories as simply and casually as if she were actually talking to us beside the fireplace, making her own personal comments on the action with an unabashed frankness. It is only when we observe closely that we notice how cunningly her effects are achieved. One very effective device of hers is the sudden shift in perspective, so that after examining a scene at close range we abruptly move backwards and see it from a distance. And what a novel way she has of introducing the main characters in *The Innocent Traveller*: by a child's inspection of their feet under the dining table! She can lead up to and display very dramatic scenes—as, for example, the

unexpected shipboard meeting in *Hetty Dorval* or the reappear-
ance of Yow in "Lilly's Story"—but we never have the cheated
feeling that a surprise has been deliberately "arranged." And
usually, too, she is ready to prick the bubble of her own drama
with the needle of irony, as in this delightful passage from *The
Innocent Traveller*:

The river was immense, a prince among rivers. When at last the
ship moving with stately slowness approached the city of
Quebec, Mr. Otis Skinner stretched out his hand. "See," he said
pointing, "over there are the Heights of Abraham." In Aunt
Topaz, as in Mr. Otis Skinner, the spirit of History began to
swell.
    Mr. Otis Skinner spoke again. His voice was lower, and he
spoke as it were unaware, to his own breast. *"There,"* he said
"Wolfe fell." And he added, still more low, "And Montcalm."
There was a moment of silence. Everybody looked respectfully
and with deep interest at the steep Heights of Abraham.

Another conspicuous example of Mrs. Wilson's skilful technique is her adroit handling of time. In almost all her novels
she has set herself the difficult task of covering long stretches of
time in a relatively short book. Seven years transpire in the
course of Hetty Dorval, nearly ninety years in *The Innocent
Traveller*, and approximately fifty in "Lilly's Story". (On the
other hand, she has demonstrated her versatility in "Tuesday
and Wednesday" by confining the action to thirty-six hours.)
In each case she has cleverly avoided mere expository summary
by isolating scenes for detailed treatment, and has created the
illusion of time passing by unobtrusively noting the changes in
the physical and mental capacities of her characters. We do
indeed feel at the end of both *The Innocent Traveller* and
"Lilly's Story" that we have lived through a lifetime with the
central characters.
    Mrs. Wilson's characters are extremely skilful creations, and
they seem to grow more vivid with each book she writes. Hetty
Dorval is a convincingly spoiled and selfish minx, but Aunt
Topaz is more real to us than any aunt of our blood, and Lilly
than any waitress who has served us. They seem real, perhaps,
in part because they are "characters" in the slang sense of that
word: they are eccentrics, people with marked peculiarities of

appearance, dress, speech, gesture, and behaviour. But they are
not mere caricatures, and as we proceed with their stories we
become increasingly aware of complexities and subtleties which
identify them as living beings.

So abundantly are her characters endowed with life that we
almost overlook Mrs. Wilson's occasional lapses in plot.
Whether from conviction or a desire to satisfy her audience, she
accepts the old convention that a plot must involve coincidence
and surprise. The fact is that this convention seems out of place
in stories as real and authentic as hers. Thus it offends us to be
asked to believe, in *Hetty Dorval,* that Hetty's housekeeper was
actually her mother, or in "Lilly's Story" that the Chinaman
Yow turned up years later as cook in the very hospital where
Lilly was the housekeeper.

There are other flaws in Mrs. Wilson's work. She becomes, on
occasion, almost embarrassingly coy—as, for example, in the
references to Mort's "angel" in "Tuesday and Wednesday."
Sometimes her personal intrusions into the plot annoy us and
break the continuity of the narrative.

But these flaws are not serious, and are more than compensated for by the fact that Mrs. Wilson, like her models, writes
always "with good heart, often with deep feeling yet with some
scepticism," and that she maintains a fine counterpoint of
involvement and detachment. It is refreshing, in this cynical
age, to read an author who obviously delights in the spectacle
of human existence, to whom life, for all its pathos, is something rich and rare and joyful. Mrs. Wilson has gusto, a hearty
appetite for experience. She feels deeply for her characters—
delights in Aunt Topaz, pities Victoria May Tritt, looks at
Lilly with a mixture of admiration and compassion—and yet is
capable of seeing them objectively. She does not romanticize
these people, and is constantly aware of the superficiality of
Aunt Topaz, the mousiness of Victoria May, and the coarseness
of Lilly.

But has Mrs. Wilson like Defoe, Fielding, Proust, Trollope,
Bennett and Forster, a style of her own? By style here she clearly
meant style in the widest sense, that sense in which the style
becomes synonymous with the man. Has Mrs. Wilson a style in
this sense, a distinctive character as a writer, a personal vision?
I believe that she has, and that its nature can best be expressed
by the phrase "the innocent eye."

The innocence of Ethel Wilson's vision has nothing to do with ignorance or lack of sophistication. It is rather innocence in the sense Blake used it in his *Songs of Innocence*, the antonym of jadedness, ennui, conventionality, and prejudice. Mrs. Wilson looks at the world freshly, openly, as if she like Blake believed that "all that lives is holy."

Frequently she embodies this innocence in her characters. What gives piquancy and poignancy to the story of Hetty Dorval is the fact that this evil woman is observed through the innocent eyes of an adolescent girl. Aunt Topaz, in *The Innocent Traveller*, is described as a child to be "as innocent as a poached egg," and she retains this innocence to the end of her days. As an old woman having an audience with the Queen, Topaz is as wide-eyed, eager, curious, and excited as she would have been at the age of eight. Victoria May Tritt, in "Tuesday and Wednesday," is another innocent: to her Mort and Myrtle are an ideal couple, and Mort an indubitable hero; and Lilly Walter, in "Lilly's Story," retains her fundamental innocence in spite of the seductions, thefts, lies, and deceptions to which she is a party.

But the innocence of Ethel Wilson's work does not merely consist in the fact that in most of her stories there is an important character who is an innocent of this sort. It is the basic quality of Mrs. Wilson's own vision. To her the sight of a kitten relieving itself, for example, is not a vulgar fact to be avoided, or a trite episode to be ignored, but an intensely interesting experience to be recorded:

When Morty came back having put down the spoon and left it in Baxter's garden he set the box on the floor. "Mioo, mioo," said the kitten, and with croons of delight ran to the box, scrambled up the side, scratched the dirt, and sat down. The kitten's face took on a look of blissful angelic abstraction. The kitten wore the same distant ineffable look as does a young child occupied in the same business.

Time and again Mrs. Wilson discovers interest and delight in things which the ordinary jaded human being ignores.

Another facet of her innocence is her ability to treat conventionally solemn subjects lightly. Of a funeral she writes: "The day of Mother's funeral was long remembered in Ware. It was so sad that people almost enjoyed it." Of a husband leaving his wife she writes: "Never having heard of a Mr. and Mrs. Porter before, she pictured Mr. Porter in a peaked cap taking Mrs. Porter for a railway journey (a novelty) and leaving her in a strange Ladies' Waiting Room all alone, as Mother had left her and the alarmed Hannah, only a week ago, with instructions not to budge." Even repulsive things such as tapeworms are transformed into objects of innocent merriment in the novels of Mrs. Wilson:

I s'pose you didn't know I'd had the tapeworm? Well, I did. You can't tell *me*. Went to prett' near every doctor in Canada and U.S.A. Couldn't do nothing for me till I went to a feller here and he delivered me of two tapeworms head and all. A yard long apiece them two reptiles was if they was an inch. I regret I never kep' them two reptiles but they sure were a spectacle for any museum.

Examples of this sort of thing could be multiplied. The basic fact is that Mrs. Wilson sees the world freshly and clearly, that she innocently refuses to wear the spectacles of convention and prejudice. She gives us, as a result, the refreshing sensation that the world is young and exciting and that it awaits our delighted discovery. With a writer of her sort we are certainly never moved to say ". . . how dull."

English-Canadian Poetry, 1944-1954*

THE past decade has been a period of considerable but often confusing activity in English-Canadian poetry. It is probably impossible, at this close range, to perceive the really significant directions and achievements, but the attempt is worth making: at best, one may succeed in marshalling the facts in some sort of provisional order; and at least one may provoke discussion and debate.

1944 was a good year, perhaps the most productive single year in our poetic history. It saw the publication of E. J. Pratt's long-awaited *Collected Poems,* two books of verse by A. M. Klein, Dorothy Livesay's *Day and Night,* Ralph Gustafson's *Flight into Darkness,* Arthur S. Bourinot's *Nine Poems,* Dick Diespecker's *Between Two Furious Oceans,* and Joseph Schull's *I, Jones, Soldier.* In addition, there appeared a small anthology, *Unit of Five,* which gave the public its first substantial sampling of the work of five most promising new poets: P. K. Page, Louis Dudek, Raymond Souster, James Wreford, and Ronald Hambleton.

The four years that followed were each almost equally productive. One became accustomed to expecting, instead of the one or two annual volumes of good verse of the twenties and thirties, five or six books worthy of serious attention.

1949, however, brought a sudden ominous pause in this triumphant progress. Only one really striking book of verse was published that year—James Reaney's weird but fascinating *The Red Heart.* Much the same was true of 1950, which produced only James Wreford's *Of Time and the Lover,* Norman

*Published in *Culture,* 1954.

Levine's tiny *The Tight-Rope Walker*, and a couple of slim chapbooks by Livesay and Bourinot.

How are we to explain the surge of activity from 1944 to 1948, and the sudden slackening of 1949 and 1950? The last years of the war and the first years of the peace were the high-water marks of economic prosperity and of the sense of national well-being in Canada. The country was prosperous, prices were still controlled, and more people had money for relative luxuries such as books of verse; and at the same time the sense of national excitement and pride created by the war made more people interested in Canadian books. Even those who opposed the war, or had doubts about the nature of the peace to follow it, were stirred up by it, and were anxious to learn of other people's reactions to it. This interest was heightened by the appearance of several anthologies and critical studies of Canadian poetry: Ralph Gustafson's *Canadian Poetry* (1942), A. J. M. Smith's *Book of Canadian Poetry* (1943), E. K. Brown's *On Canadian Poetry* (1943), Ronald Hambleton's *Unit of Five* (1944), and John Sutherland's *Other Canadians* (c. 1947).

Underlying all these developments, and affecting both the poets and their audience, was a community of values such as Canada had not known for many years. In foreign relations, there was general agreement that victory and a stable peace were the most urgent objectives, that the Nazis must be stopped and the Russians supported. Domestically, the Canadian mood was almost unanimously leftist. Price controls, family allowances, subsidized housing, all the elements of the planned economy and the Welfare State, were fundamental shared convictions.

And then, in a period extending from 1947 to the present, all this brave atmosphere began to evaporate. The Russian spy scare, inflation, the Cold War, the Truman Doctrine, the Korean War, the war in Indo-China—these developments, in their various but connected ways, smashed the unity of Canadian thinking. We were left relatively embittered, bewildered, cynical, or frustrated. In this new atmosphere of indecision and confusion, both the writing and publishing of poetry became much more difficult. Poets, not quite sure of the direction of their thinking, wrote less, or wrote with less conviction; publishers, uncertain of the future and aware that their potential customers were distracted, cut back their lists. *Here and Now,* which had offered Canadian poets the most handsome magazine outlet they had ever had, expired in 1949 after a lifespan of only eighteen months.

The profound nature of the crisis can perhaps best be realized by reference to the other leading literary magazine of the period, John Sutherland's *Northern Review*. Sutherland has been an important figure in Canadian poetry for a dozen years, ever since in 1942 he began to edit *First Statement*. At that time Mr. Sutherland was quite clearly, to paraphrase Mr. T. S. Eliot's famous pronouncement, a socialist in politics, a nationalist in literature, and a sceptic in religion. He remained such for the next five years. In 1945 he began to publish *Northern Review*, with the avowed purpose of creating "a national magazine." Not content with that contribution, he began to issue from his press books of verse by other young writers with socialist and/or nationalist convictions—books such as Irving Layton's angry *Here and Now* (1945) (this should not be confused with the magazine of the same name), Patrick Anderson's impassioned *A Tent for April* (1945), and Miriam Waddington's pity-filled *Green World* (1945). In 1946 or 1947 (the book is not dated) Sutherland followed these with his lively and radical anthology, *Other Canadians*.

In the introduction to this anthology, with a bravado which can now be seen to have resulted from his own uncertainty, he nailed his rather lurid colours to the mast. A. J. M. Smith was condemned as a conservative, pious, spiritual old fuddy-duddy, and the Canadian poetic future was charted according to Karl Marx: "If God still talks to these poets in private, he carries less weight than Karl Marx or Sigmund Freud . . . Mr. Smith's oxygen tent with its tap to the spirit will keep a few remnants breathing for a while, but can hardly impede the growth of socialism in Canada, or prevent the radical consequences which must follow for the Canadian writer."

Shortly after the appearance of these words, Mr. Sutherland began to undergo a great mental transformation. His series of books of verse ceased for several years, and when it was resumed in 1951 it brought us non-political volumes such as Kay Smith's liturgical *Footnote to the Lord's Prayer* and Anne Wilkinson's neo-pastoral *Counterpoint to Sleep*. The verse of left-wing poets such as Dudek, Layton, and Souster ceased to appear in *Northern Review*, and instead the contents of that magazine, including Mr. Sutherland's own contributions, took on a preponderantly religious tone. Lately he has sponsored lecture tours, and published work by, politically conservative and religiously orthodox writers such as Roy Campbell and Peter Viereck.

All this is not to be construed as an attack upon Mr. Sutherland. He is entitled to his own beliefs and in outspokenly expressing them he has proved that he has the courage of his convictions. But his fundamental change of direction is indicative of the spiritual crisis which overtook Canadian intellectuals at the end of the nineteen-forties.

The period when this crisis was in its most acute phase—roughly 1948 to 1950—was a kind of interregnum in the history of Canadian poetry. By 1951 the left-wing school had given Sutherland up and had established its own press and magazine—*Contact*. Augmented by their contributions, but fed largely by writers who had made their reputations before or during the War, the stream of verse began to flow again. Two or three new poets of promise have joined the stream—Philip Child, Elizabeth Brewster, Alfred G. Bailey, Eli Mandel — but no startling change of speed or direction has occurred.

For all its interruptions and uncertainties, the stream of Canadian poetry in the past ten years has brought us many good things.

E. J. Pratt's *Collected Poems* is probably the most important single volume to appear in the decade, if not in the half century. In range, in power, in diversity he easily outstrips all Canadian rivals. His work has originality of texture and bears the imprint of a distinctive personality. Although his name is chiefly associated with vigorous narrative poems like "The Cachalot" and *Brébeuf and His Brethren*, he is almost equally at home with the lyric, satire, and the verse-portrait. For a few years after the publication of his *Collected Poems* he seemed to be in a decline—*They Are Returning* (1945) and *Behind the Log* (1947) are only superior verse journalism—but his *Towards the Last Spike* (1952) has done much to restore his reputation. Here, in the story of the building of the C.P.R., Pratt found a theme in which his talents could display themselves at or near their best. The poem is rich in humour, in characters of legendary proportions, in suggestive symbols, and in that sense of struggle between vast forces which is Pratt's special note.

The combination of strength and tenderness, of force and subtlety, which we find in E. J. Pratt may be found also in his chief rival for the position of English-Canada's greatest living poet, A. M. Klein. Klein's poetry, however, because of his Hebrew religious origin and his Montreal residence, has a very different substance. His Jewishness was a very prominent quality in *Poems* (1944) and the source of the intense bitterness of the satire in *The Hitleriad* (1944). In his most recent volume, *The Rocking Chair* (1948), his knowledge of Montreal has enabled him to treat, with a piquant mixture of sympathy and satire, the life of French Canada. He has been keenly conscious of social injustice and personal malice, and has deliberately made his verse a weapon against them. At the same time he has been aware of the love, pity and splendour lurking in ordinary people and places. This combination of anger and delight, together with the audacity of his images, the strength and richness of his diction, and the variety of his rhythms, has made his poetry fresh and distinctive. Occasionally he goes too far—his pathos at times degenerates into bathos, his satire into invective—but he never becomes dull by lack of daring.

Another poet whose energy occasionally betrays her into shrillness is Dorothy Livesay. The poems in *Day and Night* are bold and passionate in their denunciation of capitalism, but they sometimes sound forced, as if their author were trying to convince herself. In *Poems for People* (1947), however, her aggressive radicalism has been replaced by a more tolerant humanism, and in the process her technique has become firmer. The subjects of her later poems are more specifically feminine—love, children, the family—and in treating these traditional subjects in a modern vocabulary, contemporary metaphors, and experimental forms, she has often seemed excitingly creative.

Earle Birney, whose *David* was the sensation of Canadian poetry in 1942, has been a more consistent poet than either Klein or Livesay: he has produced poetry more steadily, and he has changed remarkably little in either subject-matter or style. Although he has written movingly of war, love, and mountain climbing, his chief concern has always been with the interpretation and evaluation of the Canadian social scene. This concern is uppermost in all the best poems in the three volumes he has published in the past decade: *Now Is Time* (1945), *The Strait of Anian* (1948), and *Trial of a City* (1952). No other poet is more successful than he in capturing the feel of contemporary Canada: he sees the ugliness of its slums, the shallowness of its values, the adolescence of its culture; but he also sees and appreciates its attempts at self-understanding, its naive optimism, its basic goodwill, and its real promise. These themes he treats in our own idiom, and in a style which owes singularly little to outside influences. His long, loose, loping lines, his casualness of tone and diction, his indigenous images—all seem genuinely of our own stuff.

These four—Pratt, Klein, Livesay, and Birney—have been the major figures of the decade; the remaining poets must be considered more briefly and arranged, for convenience's sake, in groups.

The main tradition of Canadian poetry until at least 1925 was that of romantic nature verse, associated chiefly with the names of Carman, Roberts, Lampman, and D. C. Scott. This tradition was largely displaced in the thirties and forties by two others: the metaphysical tradition stemming directly from T. S. Eliot, Ezra Pound, and the later Yeats, and indirectly from English poets of the seventeenth century; and the tradition of social protest stemming from Auden, Spender and Day Lewis. In the forties two new but closely related influences made themselves felt—Gerard Manley Hopkins and Dylan Thomas—but the effect of these poets was to enrich and modify existing traditions rather than initiate a new one. American influences, strangely enough, have had little effect, although in recent years there have been some indications that Robert Frost is making a belated impact.

The old and honourable tradition of romantic nature verse has not been altogether abandoned. It has survived in the work of Arthur S. Bourinot, Audrey Alexandra Brown, and a host of minor versifiers. Mr. Bourinot and Miss Brown have both produced some fine poems. Bourinot is at his best in the simple, precise description of the flora and fauna of the Gatineau country, while Miss Brown achieves her best effects in the expression of deep personal feeling and in the creation of glowing effects of colour.

The metaphysical tradition in Canada was first espoused by the so-called Montreal Group of the twenties—A. J. M. Smith,

F. R. Scott, A. M. Klein, and Leo Kennedy. These poets, with the exception of Klein, have been relatively quiet in the last decade, though I understand that Scott, Smith and Kennedy have volumes ready for early publication. Generally speaking, they have not yet fulfilled the high hopes that were expressed for them by E. K. Brown in his *On Canadian Poetry*. Smith has been increasingly engrossed in his pursuits as an anthologist and critic, Scott in politics and constitutional law, and Kennedy in advertising and public relations work in the United States.

But the type of poetry which the Montreal Group introduced into Canada—erudite, intellectual, complex, impassioned, ironic, and anxiously contemporary—has been widely practised in the last decade. Ronald Hambleton (*Object and Event*, 1953), Ralph Gustafson (*Flight into Darkness*, 1944), Roy Daniells (*Deeper into the Forest*, 1948), Robert Finch (*Poems*, 1946; *The Strength of the Hills*, 1948), James Wreford (*Of Time and the Lover*, 1950), Alfred G. Bailey (*Border River*, 1952) and Douglas LePan (*The Wounded Prince*, 1948; *The Net and the Sword*, 1953)—all these men have produced poetry to which the above adjectives apply. They are not indistinguishable, but they have a great deal in common. Most of them are professors, all of them are highly educated, and they draw upon their special knowledge to set the present time in perspective. Daniells, for example, achieves distinctive effects by drawing upon his knowledge of myth and symbol, Bailey by introducing material and images from his knowledge of anthropology and history, Wreford by employing images from his geological and geographical learning. All of them are conscious and conscientious poetic craftsmen, aware of the English tradition and of contemporary masters such as Eliot and Thomas. All of them are repelled by the vulgarity, cruelty, and violence of the modern world, and all seek to redress the balance by appealing to the traditional values of Christian humanism. Their collective influence in the country, both as poets and teachers, is far greater than in their moments of despondency they believe; in the young they keep alive all that is best in the Western heritage.

Many of these poets protest against various conditions in our society, but a more direct and blunt type of social protest is associated with the left-wing school of Louis Dudek, Irving Layton, and Raymond Souster. In the early forties these three were colleagues of John Sutherland in the production of *First Statement*; more recently they have collaborated in the publication of the magazine *Contact*, the collection *Cerberus* (1952), and the anthology *Canadian Poems, 1850-1950* (1953). They have, then, been extremely active, and deserve our thanks for helping to keep poetry alive in a difficult age.

The energy they have exhibited in their publishing enterprises they have also displayed in their poetry. With an unsparing hand they have flayed our complacency, our conservatism, our prudery, and all the other sins to which we bourgeois Canadians are prone. The picture they paint is not a pretty one, nor altogether fair, but it is always lively if sometimes too lurid. They have at least had shock value, and they have dared to say many things that needed saying.

The most blunt and powerful of the trio has been Irving Layton: he has often scattered his ammunition, but he has scored some fine hits. His poems are sometimes rough and ready in technique, but his frequent revision of them is proof that he has an artistic conscience. Dudek is a more deliberate craftsman, more ready to perceive fragments of beauty amid the rubble of actuality, more diverse in subject and style. Souster is a quieter, simpler poet than either of them. His special and often very appealing quality is a kind of naive wistfulness and sincere pity which only rarely bursts into anger or grief.

Because they have been impatient of criticism and quick to scent condescension, these three young poets have not received their full due from our preponderantly academic critics. Theirs are fresh and genuine voices without which the present Canadian choir would be much less interesting.

Standing midway between what we have loosely labelled the metaphysical and social protest schools is a group of poets who combine many of the features of both. P. K. Page, Patrick Anderson, Miriam Waddington, and Anne Marriott are more complex and sophisticated than the Dudek-Layton-Souster group, but they have been usually more directly concerned with immediate social and political objectives and problems than the metaphysical school.

Patrick Anderson arrived in Canada in 1940 with his head full of the social philosophy of Karl Marx and the verse rhythms of Dylan Thomas. He proceeded to establish the magazine *Preview* and to urge Canadian poets to dedicate themselves wholeheartedly to the world struggle against Fascism. His own books—*A Tent for April* (1945), *The White Centre* (1946), and *The Colour as Naked* (1953)—are full of light and fire. His words leap and tumble, his images proliferate with exciting rapidity and range. There is an irresistible swing to his verse and a power to move us now to anger, now to love. It is only after the initial excitement has worn off that we begin to wonder where we were being led, and for what precise purpose. Sober second thought reveals much rhetoric and not a little sentimentality, but still plenty that is genuine and powerful. In his latest volume especially there is more discipline and artistic cunning, and a greater maturity of outlook.

P. K. Page seemed likely, about 1945, to become the leading poetess of Canada. The poems she contributed to *Unit of Five*, and her own volume *As Ten, As Twenty* (1946), were obviously influenced by Auden and Anderson, and yet they were sufficiently personal in both technique and substance. They expressed, in unusual but effective imagery, a sensitive woman's response to the world of war, want, and fascism. Such poems as "The Stenographers" seemed to hold out the promise, if not quite the reality, of greatness. Unfortunately, Miss Page has published very little during the last five years: it will be a great pity if her very subtle talent is lost to our poetry.

Anne Marriott is another woman poet who has not yet lived up to the expectations her early work aroused. Her first book—*The Wind Our Enemy* (1939)—is already established as a minor Canadian classic. It records, in colloquial language and consistently domestic imagery, the plight of the Western farmer during the dust storms of the thirties. Since that time she has published a number of reputable poems in the magazines, and one book of poetry (*Sandstone*, 1945) but nothing to rival her first success.

The emotion of pity, dominant in *The Wind Our Enemy*, is also dominant in Miriam Waddington's *Green World* (1945). A social worker by profession, Mrs. Waddington has seen much of the seamy side of Canadian city life, and has become aware of "The slow surge of cold hatred/Flowing through secret passages/Under our tunneled cities." Against this hatred, she sets the positive values of love and tenderness. Her technique is less complex than that of Page and Anderson, and reminds us rather of Souster. Her diction is simple and colloquial, her images are drawn from familiar sources, and there is almost no obscurity in her verse. She is one of the most immediately attractive of our poets.

These, then, have been the major trends, but some new directions have lately been apparent. For one thing, there has been a revival of the regionalism which was a strong element in the poetry of Roberts and Lampman in the late nineteenth century. Charles Bruce, especially in *The Flowing Summer* (1947) and *The Mulgrave Road* (1951), has dealt sincerely, lovingly, and unpretentiously with his memories of youth amid the fishermen and farmers of Nova Scotia; Philip Child, in *The Victorian House* (1951), has recorded his own early years in Hamilton, Ontario, in a poem that is grave, straightforward, and patently honest; Thomas Saunders in *Scrub Oak* (1949) and *Horizontal World* (1951), has recreated in simple but often convincing fashion the places and people of Manitoba; and Elizabeth Brewster, in *East Coast* (1951) and *Lillooet* (1954), has etched clear if slightly satirical pictures of her native New Brunswick landscape and society. These poets are exceptional too in that they have been influenced as much by American as by English examples. Thomas Saunders, for instance, is an obvious disciple of Robert Frost, and Elizabeth Brewster more subtly blends the influences of Emily Dickinson, E. A. Robinson, and Edgar Lee Masters. The regionalist vein these four poets have struck has still much poetic ore to yield, and it is to be hoped that they will attract other workers.

But perhaps the most distinctive poet to emerge in the past decade has been James Reaney. He has as yet published only one volume—*The Red Heart*—but his poems have continued to appear in the magazines and we may expect a second volume in the near future. His originality consists not so much in technique as in the revelation of a unique sensibility. He makes his poems of seemingly familiar subjects—plum trees, farm kitchens, car-crowded highways—but he makes these things new by describing them from an unexpected and exciting angle. He has Wordsworth's gift of investing the familiar with strangeness, of making that which we had seen many times seem suddenly exciting and exotic. He is almost certainly the most promising of the younger poets.

In the last year or two there have been signs of a revival of interest and energy in Canadian poetry. New anthologies have been edited by Earle Birney and (jointly) by Louis Dudek and Irving Layton; new magazines (*Contact, Civ/n*) have been established and older ones (notably *The Fiddlehead*) expanded in scope. Best of all, new poets such as Fred Cogswell, Phyllis Webb, Robert Gibbs, Eli Mandel, Gael Turnbull, and Colleen Thibaudeau have begun to publish regularly in the magazines, and their work may soon be expected to appear in book form.

Progress in the arts is slow, and we need not feel discouraged that no single poet or school of poetry of world significance has yet appeared in English-speaking Canada. There has been an advance, more than we often recognize. We have left behind us many obstacles that once deterred us. We no longer debate the futile question of the distinctiveness of our poetry: the Canadian poet worthy of the title cannot avoid introducing his environment into his poetry—it is simply there, in the idioms, the images, the rhythms if not in more obvious form. We no longer argue the merits of cosmopolitanism as against nationalism: we recognize that the poet must be aware of both his place and his time. We no longer feud over the respective claims of free verse and regular metres: the poet is free to choose the medium which suits him best. We need no longer defend the poet's right to treat any subject that pleases him, for this right is now almost universally conceded. And if our poets at the moment are somewhat confused and uncertain, if they write chiefly, as Patrick Anderson has lately put it, poems "Where anxiety trembles upon the rim of faith," they are only accurately recording the temper of our time. After all, it is not the function of the poet to remake the world, but to make us more intensely aware of it.

A Group of Seven Poets*

SEVEN new books of verse[1]—and one of them entitled *Friday's Child!* Since playing with nursery rhymes seems to be the latest fad among the poets, perhaps a mere critic may be pardoned if he takes the hint and assigns each of these volumes to its most appropriate day of the week.

Monday's child is fair of face—this is certainly Miss Phyllis Webb, who in both person and poetry is very beautiful. Her poems have almost always a lovely liquid flow, they are full of bright colours and especially of green, and they are packed with images which reveal the fertility of her fancy. I should say that her greatest gift is her capacity to find the apt concrete symbol for idea or feeling—the smooth pebble of prayer, the muffled velvet of patience, the sharp razors of pain. Miss Webb, then, has the *donnée* of the poet; but to say that her work is fair of face implies a certain lack of substance, and I do feel that she has not yet decided just what it is that she must say. Much of her work gives me the feeling that it is the product of the desire, rather than of the necessity, to write poetry. It is significant that three of the best poems in the book—"Marvell's

*Published in *Queen's Quarterly*, Autumn, 1956.
[1]*Even Your Right Eye.* By Phyllis Webb. (Toronto: McClelland and Stewart, 1956), p. 64.
The Hangman Ties the Holly. By Anne Wilkinson. (Toronto: Macmillan, 1955), p. 57.
The Selected Poems of Raymond Souster. (Toronto: Contact Press, 1956), p. 135.
Let Us Compare Mythologies. By Leonard Cohen. (McGill Poetry Series). (Toronto: Contact Press, 1956), p. 79.
Friday's Child. By Wilfred Watson. (Toronto: British Book Service (Faber), 1955), p. 56.
The Haloed Tree. By Fred Cogswell. (Toronto: The Ryerson Press, 1956), p. 16.
The Bull Calf and Other Poems. By Irving Layton. (Toronto Contact Press, 1956), p. 49.

Garden," "Poetry," and "In Dublin"—are about poets and poetry rather than about first-hand experience. Another indication of this same tendency is her proneness to lapse occasionally (see, for example, "Lament") into conventional complaints about the state of the world in the whining manner of Stephen Spender. Indeed there is rather too much wistful pathos in this book, and I long for more of the exuberance of which she has shown herself capable in the poem on Marion Scott and in the gaily cynical "Earth Descending." For example, why in her love poems does she restrict herself to bemoaning "the end of the affair," when she might as well have told us something of the delight of the beginning? It is true, as C. S. Lewis says in the quotation from which Miss Webb takes her title, that there are some journeys on which we must leave behind even our right eye; but these are rare journeys, and I hope that Miss Webb will keep both eyes open as she prepares her next book. Knowing her gifts for melody and imagery, we shall await that next book with pleasant anticipation.

If Miss Webb is fair of face, Miss Wilkinson is certainly full of grace. I cannot remember another Canadian book of verse, unless it be A. J. M. Smith's classic *News of the Phoenix*, which has so impressed me with its absolute perfection of finish. Every word, every phrase, every stanza and every poem in this book gives one the impression of having been weighed, measured, trimmed, cleaned and polished until it has the flawless opacity of the lens which is one of Miss Wilkinson's favourite images. For all this, the poems do not seem laboured but spontaneous, full of a kind of ironic playfulness which modifies a basically serious view of life. This is the sort of thing she does, as though without effort:

> And I was born a boy for I bore a boy
> And walked with him in the proud
> And nervous satrapy of man—
> Though who can hide the accent of a mother tongue?

> And I was a maiden all forlorn
> A long long time ago.
> But the time for maidens is said to be brief
> And I do not remember it otherwise. . . .

That is a representative passage of Anne Wilkinson's verse, and it illustrates most of her qualities. There is the playfulness—in

the pun on "mother tongue," in the snatch from the nursery
rhyme in the first line of the second stanza—but there is also
the tragic sense of the tensions of boyhood and the transitoriness
of youth and innocence. There is also evident Miss Wilkinson's
sense of empathy—the capacity which she here reveals to feel
her way into the life of a boy extends elsewhere to many other
persons and things—and her ability to transmute the material
of her own personal, feminine experience into the stuff of
poetry. Another quality present is that of economy: Miss
Wilkinson's poems are short, distilled, quintessential statements
of deep feeling. The form is disciplined, quite devoid of the
longueurs and languors of mediocre free verse. Most of the
diction is simple, colloquial, even commonplace, but when she
does use an unusual word, as the "satrapy" above, it is always
the word with just the right connotations. A few lines, however,
canot represent the variety of this Tuesday's child, whose work
runs the gamut of feeling from the despair of "I Am So Tired"
and "Dirge" to the exaltation of "In June and Gentle Oven"
and "Once Upon a Great Holiday." Indeed this book is so rich
in meaning and suggestion that if I had to choose one of the
seven to take with me on a journey, my choice would inevitably
fall on *The Hangman Ties the Holly*.

Wednesday's child is full of woe—and so, it would seem, is
Mr. Raymond Souster. The little poem "Search," which Louis
Dudek has here selected from 1944's *Unit of Five*, illustrates
the sad manner and matter which Souster has consistently made
his own:

> Not another bite, not another cigarette,
> Nor a final coffee from the shining coffee-urn before
>   you leave
> The warmth steaming at the windows of the hamburger-
>   joint where the Wurlitzer
> Booms all night without a stop, where the onions
>   are thick between the buns.
> Wrap yourself well in that cheap coat that holds
>   back the wind like a sieve,
> You have a long way to go, and the streets are dark,
>   you may have to walk all night before you find
> Another heart as lonely, so nearly mad with boredom, so
>   filled with such strength, such tenderness
>   of love.

The manner is casual, almost careless—Souster rambles on, piling up apparently insignificant details more or less at random, until, just when you have relaxed and lowered your guard, he lets you have a swift punch in the solar plexus. You get so used to his technique that you think he will never manage to bring it off with you again—but he does. There is obviously much more art here than meets the eye. The matter is the life of the more squalid areas of our large cities, especially of Toronto, with an occasional journey to a crowded nearby beach or park. Love, treated realistically as something at least primarily physical, is the chief anodyne, and the beauty of nature is a poor second. The poems in this book have been selected from ten separate books published over the last twelve years, and give us an opportunity to trace Souster's development. It can be analyzed briefly: there is no development, unless it be a development to have grown a little more tired, a little more disillusioned, and a little more jaded with the passing of the years. One would expect, then, that this would be a very monotonous and disappointing book; the reverse is true. If Souster has not improved or changed, he has at least not declined: the last poem in the book, a gay fantasy about the roller-coaster at Sunnyside, is as fresh and surprising as the first. Indeed as these poems are read again and again one begins to see that there is more variety than one expected—that Souster can be gay as well as sad, clipped and epigrammatic as well as rambling and casual, angry and rebellious as well as wistful and resigned. There is something very appealing about his work— something genuine, honest, nakedly direct. I think he misses a lot of good things in life—he is quite blind, for example, to the virtues of Fredericton and of universities—but he sees things that the rest of us miss all the time.

Leonard Cohen, whose first volume is published in the newly-launched McGill Poetry Series at the age of twenty-one, is my Thursday's child, for he certainly has far to go. Anyone who can write this poem before his majority has a great future as a poet:

> Do not look for him
> In brittle mountain streams:
> They are too cold for any god;
> And do not examine the angry rivers
> For shreds of his soft body

Or turn the shore stones for his blood;
But in the warm salt ocean
He is descending through cliffs
Of slow green water
And the hovering coloured fish
Kiss his snow-bruised body
And build their secret nests
In his fluttering winding-sheet.

Cohen has a fine ear for the music of words, as we can see from the almost constant use in this poem of assonance, alliteration, and onomatopoeia. He also has a keen sensuous response to the natural environment. He is not merely a sensuous lyric poet, however—he is preoccupied with violence, particularly the sacrificial deaths of gods, and more particularly with the crucifixion of Christ, an event which occurs and recurs throughout his book as a thematic motif. Cohen's vision of the world is of a place of violent contrasts, where gentleness is in constant collision with brutality. This contrast figures in almost all his poems, but never more movingly than in "Lovers," in which a love story is played out against the background of the concentration camps of Nazi Germany. But the poems which I like best of all are "Summer Night," in which the fact of man's essential loneliness emerges from the forced gaiety of a teenagers' rustic orgy, and "Warning," with its urbane, genial threat of doom. This latter poem has some overtones of Auden's earlier phase, but in this respect it is unique in his work—Cohen's is a fresh and exciting talent which owes little to previous poets. All in all, *Let Us Compare Mythologies* is a brilliant beginning of what we hope may be a long and distinguished poetic career.

Friday's Child is not only a striking but also an apt title for Wilfred Watson's first book of poems, for most of his poems are about loving or giving or a combination of the two. This too is an exciting volume and resembles Cohen's in its interest in the juxtaposition of cruelty and tenderness, ugliness and beauty. But whereas Cohen strikes us as an original poet, Watson, for all his brilliance, is a maker of pastiches. As we read through his book we find ourselves writing in the margin "cf. Donne," "cf. Yeats," "cf. Auden," "cf. Eliot," "cf. Dylan Thomas," "cf. Coleridge," "cf. Herrick," "cf. Keats," or "cf. Hopkins." This, in other words, is "literary" poetry, the product rather of reading than of living, and I cannot disguise my feeling that I therefore find it less compelling than that of all the other poets in this group. It is not my cup of tea: it is pretentious, self-consciously clever, pedantically erudite. And yet there are poems in the book that overpower even me with their scintillating virtuosity. "The Windy Bishop," for example, is a terrific poem about guilt and fear, in which the searing cold and driving blizzards of the Canadian prairies provide ideal objective correlatives for the theme. Here are a few sample lines:

> Flakes of cold
> Curdled my blood
> Into sleet, my limbs
> Stiffened, and I stood dumb
> In the sick of fear.
> Even the fox shuddered
> In his pelt and the hills
> Huddled like cattle
> When the windy bishop lashed me with his word,
> When the windy bishop preached my heart home.

At first the poems seem obscure, but we soon learn our way through Watson's symbolic landscape, especially if we have read our Eliot. But what bothers me most about this poetry is that it is a denial of life, that it keeps reiterating that earthly love inevitably corrupts into lust or declines into grief, that man's proper home is not earth but heaven. We have heard a lot about facile optimism in poetry, but not much as yet about the now prominent facile pessimism. I for one am not ready to write off life on the earth as a hopeless failure, and I suspect that most members of the human race agree with me. It may be a poor place, but it is our own. But it is presumptuous for a critic to argue with a poet about his ideas, and I should like to sum up my impression of *Friday's Child* by expressing the hope that these poems are the difficult finger exercises of a young writer who will soon employ his acquired technical virtuosity to project his own rich and peculiar version of the world about him.

The tag of Saturday's child who works hard for a living must serve, somewhat unfairly, for Fred Cogswell, whose second booklet of verse, *The Haloed Tree*, is number 164 in the Ryerson Chapbook series. This slim, sixteen-page booklet falls far short of doing justice to Cogswell, whose output of verse is astonishingly large. The poems selected for inclusion here are not, taken as a whole, the equal of those in his first publication, *The Stunted Strong*. In the latter, one felt that Cogswell was writing honestly and sincerely of the life and people he knew best; in *The Haloed Tree* one has the feeling that he is trying on a series of masks to see how they suit him. The standard of craftsmanship is high, and the tight discipline of the form reminds us somewhat of the terse economy of Anne Wilkinson. But whereas Miss Wilkinson retains spontaneity and variety, Cogswell, in these particular poems at any rate, seems to get rutbound in recurrent rhymes and rhythms. After reading sixteen similar lines of the first poem, "Death Watch," for example, I find myself intoning these last eight as a meaningless and monotonous sing-song:

> But though I feel death's arms enfold
> To rob me of my living gold,
> The wench has gifts to recompense
> The last surrender of my sense;
> Unlike those wrung from human love
> Her charms I cannot weary of:
> Long worms destroy alike remorse
> And longing for a second course.

Moreover, just as the single lines fail to add up to a whole greater than the parts, so do the poems fail to cohere into an overall pattern of meaning. Individually the poems are clever, true, perceptive; but collectively they reveal no single shaping personality. In *The Stunted Strong*, on the other hand, there was such a collective impression: a personality emerged in which tenderness and irony, compassion and anger, touched and modified each other. In short, as so often happens, Cogswell's second book is something of a disappointment to admirers of his first. Knowing the rich energy and persistence of the man, I have no real fear for the survival of the poet.

And the child that is born on the Sabbath day—Is bonny and blithe, and good and gay. There may be a certain irony in reserving this description for Irving Layton, who until lately was the *enfant terrible* of Canadian letters. Certainly it would have been a misleading description of the Layton of a dozen years ago, when an awkward but terribly honest anger was his chief expression. But it is a tribute to Layton's perseverence and un-failing energy that by constant practice he has won for himself the stature and reputation from which he can permit himself to be blithe and gay. Poems such as "Sacrament by the Water," "Earth Goddess," "The Way of the World," "Astarte," "Song for a Late Hour," "The Fertile Muck," "Letter from a Straw Man," and "Intersections" are essentially happy poems, in which Layton affirms his values, especially the value of physical love. The old bitterness is there, even occasionally in these poems, and more prominently in "Abel Cain," "Spikes," and "On Seeing the Statuettes of Ezekiel and Jeremiah in the Church of Notre Dame," but it is now a ripe bitterness. In that respect, the tone of these poems is akin to that of the later Yeats, and indeed it is of Yeats now that Layton most frequently re-minds me. It is not the kind of literal reminiscence that one finds in Watson, but more of a spiritual affinity, of a mellow mixture of illusion and disillusion which refuses to deny the fact that man is of the earth earthy and there must abide. In contrast with Watson, Layton is a life-affirming poet, who de-lights in people, even in those he dislikes. He says of Ezekiel and Jeremiah (whom he describes, incidentally, much as others have described Layton—as rugged, troublesome, angry, sultry, and coarse) that they should not be in the church but in "the sunlit square opposite/alive at noon with arrogant men," and one knows that for him the word arrogant is not, as it would be in Watson, derogatory, but appreciative.

I find Layton a refreshing poet to read. He has honesty and energy and an infectious vitality. Even his poorer poems—in this volume, for instance, "The Mosquito," which seems to me merely trivial—are provocative; and his best, such as the wonder-fully tender "Bull Calf" which gives its name to this volume, are tremendously evocative and moving.

Deserting our nursery rhyme, I should like now to say a few words about the format and means of publication of these seven volumes. It is interesting to observe that only three of the seven books are brought out by the regular commercial publishing houses of Canada. Poetry, it seems, is going to have to depend more and more upon the private presses for circulation. Writers' co-operatives, such as Contact Press, are a fine idea and should be given every assistance; also it is good to see the universities beginning to play their part: the University of New Brunswick initiated such projects in Canada with Cogswell's *The Stunted Strong*, and now McGill has followed suit with Cohen's book. But could not the private or co-operative or university presses seek at least to match the commercial houses in making their books attractive to look at and read? Even our commercial houses have much to learn in this respect: much the best bound and printed of these volumes is the Watson book, the product of Faber and Faber. McClelland and Stewart's Indian File books, of which Phyllis Webb's is number 8, look attractive, but they are not well bound: after a few readings the pages begin to fall out. Macmillans, who were turning out some execrable printing and binding jobs a few years ago, have done an excellent piece of work for Anne Wilkinson: let us hope the trend continues. But why should Contact Press turn out Cohen's book on sickly yellow paper with great fat type faces? And would not hard covers for Souster's *Selected Poems* and Layton's *Bull Calf* have been worth the small extra investment? A final point about format. Mr. Cohen's book is illustrated with line drawings by Freda Guttman, and although I do not think her drawings are especially skilful or apt I think this is a practice which should be encouraged. Anything which tends to draw the arts in this country into a mutual relationship is a good thing.

Format aside, the present state of poetry in Canada is a healthy one. Probably only twice before in our history—in the mid-'nineties of the last century and in the mid-'forties of this— have so many good books of verse appeared within so brief a period. Two tendencies seem to me especially important. One is that for the first time a poetic flowering in this country has not begun to fade after a decade or so of life: the renaissance that began during World War II seems to be gaining momentum rather than the reverse, as poets such as Souster, Layton and Wilkinson maintain or improve their standards and new poets such as Webb, Cohen and Watson continue to appear. Secondly, there are growing indications of a fusion between the two main recent schools of Canadian poetry, the proletarian school of Layton, Dudek, Souster on the one hand and the academic school of Smith, Daniells, Wreford and company on the other. Apart from Layton himself, whose poetry as we saw is gaining in urbanity and wit and erudite allusiveness anyway, only two of the poets in the above list fit neatly into either camp. Raymond Souster, of course, belongs to the former group, and Wilfred Watson is clearly the latest recruit to the latter. But Miss Webb, Miss Wilkinson, Mr. Cohen and Mr. Cogswell combine some of the best elements of both schools: all have learning, grace, wit, and a gift for metaphysical conceits; at the same time they have much of that close contact with contemporary reality, that compassion, and that naked honesty which made the first productions of Souster, Layton and Dudek so fresh and exciting a departure.

All in all, I feel a glow of paternal pride as I contemplate my week of children.

The Canadian Writer and His Public 1882-1952*

Iₙ his inaugural address as the first president of
the Royal Society of Canada, delivered on May 25, 1882, Dr.
J. W. Dawson announced: "We meet today to inaugurate a new
era in the progress of Canadian literature and science." It therefore seemed fitting, when I was asked to take part in this Royal
Society Symposium, that I should concern myself with the questions whether the foundation of the Society did inaugurate a
new era, and, if so, what form the progress has taken.

At a later point in his address, Dr. Dawson said, "In Canada
at present, whether in science, in literature, in art, or in education, we look around in vain for anything that is fully ripe. We
see only the rudiments and the beginnings of things." This was
undoubtedly a fair and accurate statement of conditions obtain-
ing in Canadian literature in 1882. There had been in Nova
Scotia in the 1820's and 1830's a colonial flowering which produced the poetry of Oliver Goldsmith, the essays and orations
of Joseph Howe, and the satirical sketches of Thomas Chandler
Haliburton. In the two colonial Canada's during the 1830's and
1840's, there had appeared the highly coloured romantic novels
of Major John Richardson and Mrs. Rosanna Leprohon, the
documentary prose of Mrs. Moodie and Mrs. Traill, and the
earnest but amateurish poetry of Charles Heavysege, Charles
Sangster, and Alexander McLachlan. All this constituted a far
from shameful beginning, but none of it, with the possible
exception of Haliburton's satire, was, in Dawson's phrase, "fully
ripe."

*An address delivered to a symposium conducted by Section II of the Royal
Society of Canada, Montreal, June, 1956.

In the years immediately preceding the foundation of the Royal Society there had been signs of greater things to come. In the novel form, William Kirby's *Golden Dog* (1877) had attained a standard beyond the reach of Richardson and Leprohon; and in poetry, Charles G. D. Roberts' *Orion* (1880) had betokened a literary flowering in New Brunswick that might well surpass that of its sister province, Nova Scotia. But he would have been a rash prophet indeed who would have postulated the development of a great literature on such isolated phenomena as these.

But move forward a decade, to the year 1893, and what a revolutionary development had occurred! If the Royal Society had held this symposium in 1894 what unbounded optimism over the prospects of Canadian literature, and especially of Canadian poetry, it would have been justified in expressing! For in 1893 had appeared Bliss Carman's first and finest volume, *Low Tide on Grand Pré,* Charles G. D. Roberts' greatest single book *Songs of the Common Day,* Duncan Campbell Scott's *The Magic House,* William Wilfred Campbell's *The Dread Voyage,* and the anthology which displayed the work of all these young poets and of others such as Archibald Lampman, Frederick George Scott, Pauline Johnson, Ethelwyn Wetherald, Isabella Valancy Crawford, Frances Harrison, and Sara Jeannette Duncan—*Later Canadian Poems,* by J. R. Wetherell. Wetherell could say in his introduction, without fear of contradiction, that his book demonstrated "that we have writers who are justly claiming recognition in English literature."

There was plenty of other evidence of this rapid development. The leading American magazines of the day—*The Atlantic Monthly, Scribner's, Harper's, The Century, The Independent* —frequently printed the work of these young Canadian poets. References to the remarkable efflorescence of poetry in Canada were frequent both in these American periodicals and in such English magazines as *The Athenaeum* and *The Saturday Review.* At home several magazines with a marked interest in literature has been established—*The Week* in 1883, and both *Queen's Quarterly* and *The Canadian Magazine* in 1893. Here the poems were published, the books of poetry intelligently reviewed, and the strengths and weaknesses of Canada's literary position carefully assayed by writers such as G. Mercer Adam, Goldwin Smith, L. E. Horning, and J. G. Bourinot.

But it would be inaccurate not to indicate the more unfavourable features of this period. Symptomatic of one such feature is the fact that a sixth book of fine poetry, which should also have appeared on the 1893 list, did not—Archibald Lampman's *Lyrics of Earth*. Lampman tried to find a publisher for it all that year, but did not succeed until 1895. The fact is that Canadian publishing houses were deplorably weak at this time —of the five books of poetry which appeared in 1893 only two (Campbell's *Dread Voyage* and Wetherell's anthology) were published in Canada. Throughout this period, and indeed until after the first World War, it was the exception rather than the rule for Canadian books to be published in Canada. There were many reasons for this, but the most tangible was the fact that Canada had no proper copyright act until 1921. The columns of *The Week* often contained pleas for the passage of such an act, but as usual in cultural matters the Canadian government continued to delay.

Another negative factor to be noted in the 1893 situation is that Canadian fiction had not matched the rapid development in Canadian poetry. The only fiction of any moment published in 1893 was Sara Jeannette Duncan's novel *Simple Adventures of a Memsahib* and Robert Barr's book of short stories, *The Face and the Mask,* and these were both the products of expatriates. Even if we examine the whole output of the decade since the foundation of the Royal Society we can only add another pair of books to this short list—Gilbert Parker's *Pierre and His People* (1892) and W. D. Lighthall's *The Young Seigneur* (1888) —and these two novels merely continued, on a slightly more professional plane, the tradition of historical romance which had been established by Richardson, Leprohon, and Kirby.

However, taking the achievement of the first decade all in all, there was real ground for optimism. Especially in poetry, it appeared that Canada was on the way to becoming one of the great literary nations of the world.

The next thirty years, however, failed miserably to fulfil these hopes. This first wave of literary activity in the newly federated nation, instead of continuing to gain momentum during the early years of the twentieth century, reached its highest point in 1893 and thereafter ebbed away. A second wave did not begin to gather force until about 1923.

The losses, between 1893 and 1923, far outweighed the gains.

Even within ten years, by 1903, Lampman had died without ever quite fulfilling his early promise, Carman had settled permanently in the United States and had provided evidence that he was never likely to equal the success of his first volume, and Roberts had also emigrated and published a series of books of verse each of which marked a decline from its predecessor. Of the "big five" of Canadian poetry, only D. C. Scott and W. W. Campbell were still writing verse in Canada, and they had not shown any significant improvement since 1893. Only one new poet had appeared in the interval—W. H. Drummond—and he was but a superior versifier. In fiction, Gilbert Parker, T. G. Marquis, and Agnes Laut had all become famous historical romancers, Sara Jeannette Duncan had established herself as a witty if superficial painter of Anglo-Indian customs, Robert Barr and Norman Duncan had won fame as popular novelists of the journalistic variety, and Ralph Connor had begun to attract world-wide attention for his piquant mixture of violent action and high moral sentiment. Famous as these novelists were, none of them could be taken seriously by a literary critic with strict standards, and none of them set themselves to analyze profoundly the nature of Canadian individual or social life. Such nascent realism as there was, was to be found intermittently in E. W. Thomson's volume of short stories, *Old Man Savarin* (1895) and Joanna Wood's novel *The Untempered Wind* (1894), and even here it was mixed with a good deal of folksy humour and coy sentimentality.

Conditions of publication had also worsened in the decade. The great loss had been the demise of *The Week* in 1896, and it was far from being compensated for by the establishment of *Maclean's* in 1896 or of *The University Magazine* in 1902. *Maclean's* was too "popular," and *The University Magazine* too academic, to fulfil the needs of Canadian creative writing as adequately as *The Week* had done, although each was to make some contribution to the cause as the years passed. There was still no adequate copyright protection for Canadian authors, and very few books were published in Canada.

The next decade, to 1913, saw little improvement in the situation. The only new poets to emerge were the rough popular rhymesters, Robert Service and Tom MacInnes, and the wistfully romantic lyricist Marjorie Pickthall. *Rhymes of a Rounder* and *The Drift of Pinions,* both published in 1913, typify the divided state of Canadian poetry in the period—the former book full of gusto but lacking in polish, the latter full of delicate nuances but lacking in substance. In fiction the historical romance was still pursuing its swaggering march to wealth and fame, its only rival for popular attention the domestic or regional idyll as practised by L. M. Montgomery, Marian Keith, R. E. Knowles, and a host of others. In humour alone was a genuinely new and promising talent in evidence—that of Stephen Leacock, whose *Literary Lapses* had appeared in 1910 and *Sunshine Sketches of a Little Town* in 1912. In Leacock, though in small and rather innocuous doses, was found the tonic the period demanded: the tonic of satire.

For substantial evidence of the beginning of a second creative movement in Canadian literature we have to look to the year 1923. By that time several new poets had made their appearance —Katherine Hale, Arthur S. Bourinot, Florence Randal Livesay, Louise Morey Bowman, Wilson Macdonald, and, most distinctive of all, E. J. Pratt—and at least there were signs of a renaissance of Canadian prose. In 1922 and 1923 the first two novels by Mazo de la Roche were published, and the first two books by Frederick Philip Grove. There was even some evidence of the beginnings of a genuinely Canadian drama, in the publication in 1923 of Merrill Denison's *The Unheroic North*. Moreover, there was a marked improvement in conditions of publication. The passage of the Canadian Copyright Act in 1921 made possible a marked increase in publishing activity in Canada, and the formation of the Canadian Authors Association in that year created for the first time a body which would devote organized efforts to the improvement of the Canadian writer's financial position. New magazines had been founded to provide additional outlets for Canadian writing—*The Canadian Bookman* in 1919, *The Canadian Forum* in 1920, and *The Dalhousie Review* in 1921.

The achievements of the next decade did to a very large extent fulfil these promises. By 1933 Pratt had established himself in poetry by the publication of *The Witches' Brew* (1925), *Titans* (1926), *The Iron Door* (1927), and *The Roosevelt and the Antinoe* (1930). A new school of poets had arisen in Montreal, including A. J. M. Smith, F. R. Scott, Leo Kennedy, and A. M. Klein, and their work had appeared regularly in *The*

Canadian Forum along with poems by other promising young poets such as Robert Finch and Dorothy Livesay. In fiction, Grove and de la Roche had each published four relatively distinguished novels in the decade, including the former's poignantly tragic *Our Daily Bread* (1928) and the latter's brilliant prize-winning *Jalna* (1927). These two had been joined by several other promising new novelists—Morley Callaghan, who by 1933 had published three novels and two volumes of short stories, Martha Ostenso, Robert Stead, and Raymond Knister. Canadian drama had not made the progress hoped for it, but the existence throughout the decade of a vigorous Little Theatre movement in Canada had kept hope alive, and had led to the composition of several plays by Mazo de la Roche, L. A. MacKay, D. C. Scott, and Fred Jacob. *The Canadian Forum* had survived and had provided a vehicle for the publication of both creative and critical writing, and it had been joined in the course of the decade by *The McGill Fortnightly Review*, *The Canadian Mercury*, and the *University of Toronto Quarterly*. Another sign of the new impetus in Canadian literature was the publication during this decade of several anthologies of Canadian writing, of the first histories and handbooks of Canadian literature, and of reprints of Canadian classics such as Susanna Moodie's *Roughing It in the Bush*, Major John Richardson's *Wacousta*, and Haliburton's *Sam Slick*.

The impetus of this movement was, however, distinctly slowed down in the decade from 1933 to 1943. Pratt, Grove, de la Roche, and Callaghan had continued to publish, but their rate of production had decreased. Grove, for instance, published six books between 1922 and 1933, but only one between 1933 and 1943; Callaghan had published five books in the five years 1928-1932, but published only four in the course of the next fourteen years. The most conspicuous evidence of the slowing down was the failure of the young poets who had been appearing in the magazines in the twenties to publish the books that would ordinarily have been expected of them in the thirties. Only Dorothy Livesay and Leo Kennedy managed to publish individual books of poetry during the decade; the remainder had to be satisfied with a section in the anthology *New Provinces* (1936). Other signs of the slowing down in literary activity in the thirties were the paucity of anthologies and of books of literary criticism. *New Provinces* was the only important anthology in the decade, and W. E. Collin's brilliant and provocative *White Savannahs* (1936) the only book of criticism. *The Canadian Forum* continued throughout this decade to provide a magazine outlet, but *The McGill Fortnightly Review* and *The Canadian Mercury* did not survive the twenties. It was not until 1941 that new literary magazines made their appearance—*Contemporary Verse* in Vancouver and *Preview* in Montreal.

The ebb in the second wave of literary activity can, I think, be directly attributed to the Great Depression. Canada was still a marginal market for books—the tradition of publishing and reading books was not yet sufficiently established—and the nascent publishing trade was thus very hard hit by the economic stringency of the period. That the publishers were justified in their caution is demonstrated by the almost total failure of the one outstanding book of poetry published in the period, *New Provinces*. Almost the whole edition was remaindered; many of the remainder copies were kept in the possession of its editor, F. R. Scott, and were not sold until last summer at the Canadian Writers' Conference in Kingston.

By 1943, however, there were some more favourable developments which indicated that a third wave of Canadian literary activity was gathering force. In poetry, one of the members of the Montreal Group, A. M. Klein, had his first book of verse published in 1940, and two new poets, Anne Marriott and Earle Birney, made their *débuts* in 1939 and 1942 respectively. In the novel, Hugh MacLennan's *Barometer Rising* and Sinclair Ross's *As for Me and My House* both appeared in 1941, and led critics to anticipate that the established trio of Grove, Callaghan, and de la Roche was at last to be significantly augmented. But perhaps the most effective developments of all occurred in the year 1943 itself, in the appearance of an excellent book of verse (A. J. M. Smith's *News of the Phoenix*), an excellent anthology (A. J. M. Smith's *Book of Canadian Poetry*), and an excellent book of criticism (E. K. Brown's *On Canadian Poetry*).

These three books were indeed the signal for an accelerated development in Canadian literature, and especially in Canadian poetry, during the next ten years, a development without parallel except for that of the 1880's and 1890's. The poets who had had their poems published in the magazines during the twenties and thirties—poets such as F. R. Scott, A. M. Klein,

Dorothy Livesay, Robert Finch—began to practise their art with new enthusiasm and skill and to issue their work in book form. They were soon joined by a veritable host of younger poets, who made the vigorous little magazines of the period, such as *Contemporary Verse, First Statement, Preview, Northern Review, Fiddlehead,* and *Here and Now,* their steppingstones to book publication. P. K. Page, Irving Layton, Louis Dudek, Patrick Anderson, Miriam Waddington, Raymond Souster, James Wreford, James Reaney, Roy Daniells, Alfred Bailey, George Whalley, Douglas LePan, Anne Wilkinson, Elizabeth Brewster—the list is almost incredibly long, and yet could easily be extended without significantly lowering the standard of inclusion. None of these poets was or is perhaps "great," but such widespread literary activity creates the atmosphere in which great work is likely to spring up.

It would be pleasant to paint an equally bright picture of recent Canadian activity in fiction. Some of the magazines which printed the poems of the writers we have mentioned did print some almost equally interesting short stories, and other short stories found a place on the national network of the C.B.C., but generally speaking the short story in Canada is a neglected art. The novel finds more practitioners, but I do not think that we have yet any solid evidence to suggest that we have a group of young novelists to equal or surpass Callaghan, Grove, and Mazo de la Roche. Hugh MacLennan, Philip Child, Ethel Wilson, Thomas Raddall, Robertson Davies, among the seniors, and W. O. Mitchell, Ernest Buckler, Henry Kreisel, and Joyce Marshall among the juniors, have all done competent and sometimes more than competent work—but they have not filled us with the exciting feeling that a really creative epoch in the history of the Canadian novel is in progress. It is in French Canada, in the work of Gabrielle Roy, Roger Lemelin, Robert Elie, and others, that there has been a real renaissance in Canadian fiction.

Looking back, then, we may say that there have been, so far, three creative periods, three waves of progress, in Canadian literature since the foundation of the Royal Society in 1882. The first, confined almost wholly to poetry, took place in the 1880's and early 1890's; the second, extending to both poetry and fiction, occurred in the 1920's; the third, again concentrated in poetry though not excluding fiction, came in the 1940's. What were the factors which precipitated these movements?

If we examine these three periods we find that they had three elements in common. First, they were periods when Canada's sense of her own destiny was undergoing a process of transformation, and when there was a resultant sense of national excitement. During the seventies and eighties, as the columns of *The Week* abundantly illustrate, the great debate concerned the form of Canada's future: should it be that of an independent national state, that of a constituent part of an imperial federation, or that of an appendage to the United States? During the twenties, the national excitement was generated by the series of steps taken to implement the first of these alternatives, national independence, which by now, and largely as a result of World War I, was the almost unanimous choice. During the forties, the debate took an economic rather than constitutional form, and the question was the degree of socialization which should occur in the Canadian economy. This is, of course, to oversimplify, but a more detailed analysis would, I believe, only confirm my conclusion that these periods of intense literary activity were also periods of intense ideological activity. When ideas and convictions are passionately held and debated, literature will flourish. It will not necessarily directly reflect or express the social and political debate, but the very existence of that debate creates an atmosphere in which literature can live.

I recently came across a passage in F. Scott Fitzgerald's notebooks that seems to be relevant here:

Art invariably grows out of a period when, in general, the artist admires his own nation and wants to win its approval. This fact is not altered by the circumstance that his work may take the form of satire, for satire is the subtle flattery of a certain minority in a nation. The greatest grow out of these periods as the tall head of the crop. They may seem not to be affected but they are.

In the three periods of creative activity I have mentioned, Canada was in a state of excitement which commanded the writer's admiration and which made him anxious to win its approval.

Secondly, these were periods when exciting new literary developments were occurring abroad, and especially in Great

Britain and the United States. In the seventies and eighties, Roberts, Carman, Lampman, and Duncan Campbell Scott were deeply influenced by the work of the English Pre-Raphaelite school and of Swinburne, and of such Americans as Emerson, Whitman, and Poe; in the twenties, the Canadian poets of the Montreal Group were stimulated by the experiments of T. S. Eliot, the later Yeats, and the American Imagists; in the forties the influences were those of Auden, Day Lewis, and Dylan Thomas, and to a lesser extent those of American proletarian poets such as Fearing and Rexroth.

Thirdly, these were periods when new magazines had been founded to provide an outlet for experimental work. The influence of *The Week* in the eighties, of *The Canadian Forum* in the twenties, and of *Contemporary Verse* and *Northern Review* in the forties, can scarcely be overestimated. The importance of these periodicals was not confined to their part in publishing the creative work of the young writers. The fact that all of them carried on controversies about the role and nature and merits of Canadian literature was equally important, for it gave the writers the feeling that they were a significant part of an important national activity.

Finally, what part has the Royal Society had in these developments? Reading over the addresses of the first patron of the Society, the Marquis of Lorne, and its first president, Dr. Dawson, it is difficult to determine in precisely what way they believed the Society should fulfil its aim of promoting our literature. The Marquis of Lorne was the more specific, and his proposals might be summarized as the awarding of prizes for literary excellence, the strengthening of emulation among us by discussing the progress of literature abroad, the encouragement of libraries and archives, and the inspiration to be derived from the presence in the nation of such a body of eminent men. I think we may without complacency say that the Society has actually promoted the growth of Canadian literature in at least three of these ways. The Lorne Pierce Gold Medal has been judiciously awarded to writers who have, over a period of time, made a worthy contribution to our store of literature; by their many excellent papers on writers of other countries the members of the Society have reminded Canadian writers of the high standards they must ever seek to meet; the Society has taken a prominent part in encouraging the establishment of the

National Archives and the National Library. Whether we have
been an inspiration to the nation as a whole and to Canadian
writers in particular is a question modesty forbids us to answer!

But it seems to me that in a symposium such as this the Royal
Society is making a new and valuable contribution to the promotion of Canadian literature. Since this is, to the best of my
knowledge, the first such symposium, we might be held to have
been negligent in the past. Certainly, it is my hope that other
symposia will be held in the future, and that at intervals of a
decade or so the members of the Society will attempt to assess
the progress of Canadian letters.

In conclusion, it behoves me to attempt to assess the progress
of the past seventy years. I am reminded of Dr. Dawson's 1882
statement that "at present we look around in vain for anything
that is fully ripe. We see only the rudiments and the beginnings
of things." I hope I shall not be accused of cynicism if I say
that that is almost as true today as it was then. The progress, I
think we must admit, has been slight.

It has been slight, but it has been real. Perhaps it has been
most obvious in the improvement in conditions of publication
and in the degree of public response. Whereas it was extremely
difficult to have a book published in Canada in 1882, it is now
relatively easy. Mr. John Gray of the Macmillan Company of
Canada stated at the Canadian Writers' Conference in Kingston last summer that he believes that any reasonably good novel
by a Canadian will find a publisher today, and I think he is
right. That in turn implies, since publishers do not publish
regularly at a loss, that such a novel will find an audience of
roughly three thousand readers in Canada. I believe that this
achievement of a domestic audience large enough to warrant
the publication of books primarily designed for it is the single
most important literary development in Canada in the last
seventy years. The audience for Canadian biography, anthologies of short stories, books of travel, and works of criticism is
also large enough now to make publication possible. For poetry
the audience is smaller, but it is more consistent, and Dr.
A. J. M. Smith and Miss Phyllis Webb, at the Writers' Conference last summer, were both emphatic that we have a poetry-
reading public comparable with that in Great Britain and the
United States.

As far as book publication is concerned, then, there has been a real improvement. The situation may not be perfect, but it is encouraging. We cannot be so complacent about the conditions of periodical publication. The magazines which will print creative work of high quality—*Queen's Quarterly, Fiddlehead, Northern Review, Dalhousie Review, Canadian Forum*—are all, except the last-named, quarterlies, and thus the volume of writing they can publish in the course of a year is small. We are badly in need of a literary magazine which could be published on a weekly or at least monthly basis. The foundation of the modern counterpart of *The Literary Garland* or *The Week* would be the single most important contribution we could make to the course of Canadian letters. Let us hope that the heralded *Tamarack Review* will fulfil this function.

The foundation of such a magazine would not only stimulate creative writing, but also the criticism thereof. There has been some improvement in the quantity and quality of Canadian criticism, especially since about 1925 when the first handbooks began to appear, but much remains to be done. Really informed and intelligent criticism, such as that of the late E. K. Brown in his *On Canadian Poetry*, of W. E. Collin in *The White Savannahs*, or of the *University of Toronto Quarterly's* annual survey, "Letters in Canada," is precisely what a nascent literature such as ours most requires. And if anyone doubts that such criticism is stimulated by the appearance of a new literary magazine, let him examine the pages of *The Week* in the eighties, of the *Canadian Forum* in the twenties, or of *Northern Review* in the forties.

But criticism cannot exist unless there is a literature worthy of criticism, and though our literature has made some progress in the past seventy years it has still a long way to go. We have behind us now the romantic lyrics of the group of the sixties, the humour of Leacock, the grim but powerful novels of Grove and Callaghan, and a score of good modern poems, but we have not yet a literature that can compare with the great literatures of the world. Even if we restrict the comparison to our own domestic scene, it seems to me that the second and third waves have not reached significantly higher than the first, that there has been little measurable advance. The only real improvement has been quantitative rather than qualitative; the first wave was restricted to a few poets, whereas the second and third have included considerably larger groups of poets and prose-writers as well; but I at any rate should be very hesitant to say that any single volume published in the 1940's is demonstrably superior to the best of the volumes published in 1893. Yet this should not discourage us. A great literature is not created in a day or even in seventy years. We should recall the remainder of Dr. Dawson's statement on May 25, 1882: "If these [beginnings] are healthy and growing, we should regard them with hope, should cherish and nurture them as germs of greater things in the future."

The Poetry of Dorothy Livesay*

Dorothy Livesay is one of the most important poets of her Canadian generation—of that generation which came to maturity between the two World Wars. She has certainly combined more successfully than any other poet, with the possible exceptions of E. J. Pratt and Earle Birney, what have come to be known as the cosmopolitan and native traditions in Canadian poetry. On the one hand she has been constantly alive to the poetic experiments being carried on in her lifetime in France, England and America, and to the main movements of world affairs and international thought; on the other hand she has never lost sight of the distinctive features of the literature, landscape and life of her own country. Moreover, this time with the single exception of Pratt, she has a longer record of continuous and even composition than any other Canadian poet. She has been writing poems of high merit for over thirty years, and gives every indication of being ready and able to do so for another thirty.

Dorothy Livesay was fortunate in the date and circumstances of her birth. Born in Winnipeg on October 12, 1909, she came to maturity in the nineteen-twenties when poetic excitement was at its height in England, the United States, and Canada. In England, the Georgian poets and the Imagists had won their battle for simplicity and directness against the ornateness and involved rhetoric of late Victorian verse, and Ezra Pound, T. S. Eliot and Edith Sitwell were leading poetry beyond imagism into the exciting new complexities of symbolism. In the United States, Frost, Sandburg, Masters, Jeffers and Lindsay had won a similar struggle against late Victorian artificiality and were

---

*Published as the Introduction to *The Selected Poems of Dorothy Livesay* (1957).

demonstrating the possibility of making poetry out of the lives and speech of ordinary American people, while women poets like Amy Lowell, Elinor Wylie, Hilda Doolittle and Edna St. Vincent Millay were experimenting with new technical effects. In Canada, A. J. M. Smith and F. R. Scott had been stirred by these developments abroad to launch *The McGill Fortnightly Review* and to publish in it their tributes to Eliot and Sitwell and their own experiments in the new poetic modes.

It was almost inevitable that Dorothy Livesay should become aware of these poetic movements, because she had the good fortune to be the child of literary parents. Her mother, Florence Randal Livesay, was herself a not inconsiderable poet and author of short stories; and her father, J. F. B. Livesay, was a distinguished Canadian journalist who was largely responsible for the foundation of the Canadian Press. The Livesay home had a well-stocked library, and Dorothy's early education, obtained at home because of her delicate health, consisted largely of reading not only the best of English and American literature, but also the great French and Russian writers of the late nineteenth and early twentieth centuries.

Her literary proclivities were given further encouragement after 1920, when the family moved to Ontario. Here the summers were spent at Clarkson, on the estate which figures as the setting for the Jalna novels of Mazo de la Roche. Mazo de la Roche herself lived in a nearby cottage, and was writing *Jalna* when Dorothy was in her middle teens. The phenomenal success of that novel in 1927 must have been a great stimulus to the budding poet. The winters were spent in Toronto, where Dorothy attended the Glen Mawr School for Girls and received excellent instruction in English, French and Latin. In 1927 she entered Trinity College, which half a century earlier had welcomed Archibald Lampman, and registered as an honours student in Modern Languages, majoring in French and Italian.

The University of Toronto was at this time a very congenial environment for a young writer. E. J. Pratt was lecturing at Victoria College and had recently published *The Titans* and *The Witches' Brew*, Robert Finch was lecturing in French at University College and publishing his imagist poems in *The Canadian Forum*, and L. A. MacKay was lecturing in classics and writing his brilliant verse satires. Penetrating literary critics such as Pelham Edgar, Herbert Davis, Felix Walter, J. S. Will and the young E. K. Brown were also on the faculty. Charles G. D. Roberts had recently returned from England and had settled in Toronto as the acknowledged dean of Canadian letters. The result was the existence of several lively literary clubs on the campus, and of a general air of literary excitement. Hart House Theatre was then the centre of the Canadian dramatic movement, and for the first time it seemed possible that a native Canadian theatre would become a reality. Toronto was also the publishing centre of Canada. It was the home of *The Canadian Forum,* the leading literary monthly which had been founded in 1920, and of the three chief Canadian publishing houses—Ryerson, Macmillan, and McClelland and Stewart—whose editors, Lorne Pierce, Hugh Eayrs and John McClelland respectively, were vying with one another to publish promising young writers.

Thus it was that when Dorothy Livesay won the Jardine Memorial Prize for poetry in her first year at Trinity, Hugh Eayrs of The Macmillan Company was immediately interested and undertook to publish a brochure of her poems. This was *Green Pitcher,* a tastefully printed chapbook of sixteen pages which appeared in 1928 when its author was only nineteen. The poems in it show remarkable skill and maturity for one so young. They are brief lyrics, describing nature or states of personal feeling, and they have the simple, direct, concrete quality which both the Georgians and the Imagists had been seeking. But their simple directness serves only to intensify the strong feeling which these poems express: they are all stretched tight as the skin of a drum. Dorothy Livesay has never surpassed the restrained intensity of such of these early poems as "Reality," "Such Silence" and "Fire and Reason."

For her third undergraduate year, with the permission of the university and on the advice of L. A. MacKay and his wife, Constance Charlesworth, Dorothy went to France, to the University of Aix-Marseilles. During this year, 1929-1930, she became very interested in the work of Katherine Mansfield and D. H. Lawrence and wrote several short stories and part of a novel. She had no success in publishing the short stories at that time, but two of them—"The Last Climb" and "The Glass House"—were published in *Northern Review* in 1950 and 1951, and "The Glass House" was chosen by Martha Foley for her *Best American Short Stories,* 1951.

Miss Livesay returned in the fall of 1930 to a Canada whose atmosphere had greatly changed during her absence. The Great Depression had set in, and left-wing politics were replacing literature and nationalism as the chief interests of the more alert undergraduates. Dorothy plunged into the popular front movement, and poetry began to take second place in her mind. This process was accelerated during the year 1931-1932 when she returned to France to do postgraduate work at the Sorbonne in Paris. Although she faithfully attended the lectures of Cazamian and completed a thesis on the influence of French symbolism on modern English poetry, it was the bohemian life of the Left Bank, the mass demonstrations against unemployment and war, and the social revolutionary ferment of such movements as Henry Barbusse's League of Revolutionary Writers that most impressed her.

While she was in Paris, her second book of verse, *Signpost,* was published by Macmillan in Canada in 1932. This event was not as significant as it might have been because the book contained mainly poems which she had written before her political interests became dominant. The poems differ little from those which had appeared in *Green Pitcher:* they are mainly lyrics of personal emotion or nature description, short, simple, direct and restrained. The nervous intensity which had been the most distinctive quality of the best poems in *Green Pitcher* remains the most attractive quality here, in poems such as "Climax," "In the Street," and "Song for Solomon." Two of the poems in *Signpost,* however, are truly signposts leading to the poet's future: "Old Man" and "City Wife" show a sympathetic understanding of the plight of other people which prepares us for the later social poetry.

But for the time being Dorothy Livesay was more interested in social work than in social poetry. Instead of remaining at the Sorbonne or returning to a North American university for the doctorate, she entered the School of Social Work in Toronto in the fall of 1933 and became more and more involved in radical political groups. She had temporarily almost given up her interest in writing, and had decided to do what she could as a social worker to alleviate the sufferings of the unemployed. In Montreal in 1933-1934 she worked as an apprentice in the Family Welfare Agency and saw the dreadful misery of mass unemployment at first hand. In her spare time she assisted in youth conferences called to protest the drift toward war and fascism. What writing she did took the form of ephemeral propaganda plays and sketches.

The revelation that the writer could most effectively play his part in the revolutionary social process *as* a writer came to her during the winter of 1934-1935, when she was working with Negro and white families in a relief agency in Englewood, New Jersey. In the bookshops of New York City she encountered for the first time the dynamic left-wing poetry of Cecil Day Lewis, Stephen Spender, W. H. Auden and Louis MacNeice, and was immediately seized with the desire to emulate their work. When her health broke down because of the strenuous work she was doing, she took a month's rest-cure in rural Ontario where she wrote her two famous social-revolutionary poems, "The Outrider" and "Day and Night." When "Day and Night" was chosen by E. J. Pratt as the featured poem for the first number of *The Canadian Poetry Magazine* (January, 1936) its appearance caused a sensation. Other poets—A. J. M. Smith and F. R. Scott especially—had written social satire in Canada, but this was the first poem by a Canadian unashamedly to preach social revolution.

By the time "Day and Night" was published, Dorothy Livesay had moved to Vancouver to continue her career as a social worker. For a few years she continued her interest in politics and wrote more documentary verse, but in the nineteen-forties a distinct reorientation in her political position became evident. Although she has remained a woman of strong humanitarian sympathies and of independent opinions, she has dropped her revolutionary dogmatism and regained her interest in personal emotions and in natural description. She has also discovered an interest in religion, and has found a spiritual home in the liberal Unitarian Church.

Two factors have been chiefly responsible for this development. The first was her marriage to Duncan Macnair, a Scottish accountant, which occurred on August 14, 1937, and the subsequent births of her son Peter in April, 1940, and of her daughter Marcia in July, 1942. Not only did her marriage create domestic responsibilities which made political activity more difficult, it also provided her with a new focus of personal interest, a renewed sense of the importance of the human individual. Many of the best of her later poems have dealt with child-bearing and child-rearing, the splendid "Serenade for Strings" (now re-titled "Nativity") and the glowing "Carnival," for example. The second factor was the approach, outbreak, and course of World War II, which produced such bewildering shifts of Communist policy and disillusioned so many of the idealists who in the thirties had seen in a popular front the chief hope for peace and freedom. Although Dorothy Livesay is no fashionable anti-communist, she was too honest and forthright a person to attempt to follow the sinuous twistings of the party line during the forties.

It is ironical that, just as *Signpost* had appeared when its author had lost confidence in its mode of private lyricism, so *Day and Night,* Dorothy Livesay's chief volume of social revolutionary poetry, appeared only in 1944, when she had lost faith in the Communist experiment. Its delayed publication is, of course, to be explained by the fact that the depression had almost eliminated the publishing of poetry in Canada, and that it was not until World War II had brought a new wave of prosperity and national consciousness that the process was resumed on a large scale. The appearance in 1943 of E. K. Brown's *On Canadian Poetry* and of A. J. M. Smith's *Book of Canadian Poetry* had created an interest in Canadian poetry such as had not existed since the nineteen-twenties. After the long drought of the thirties, a veritable spate of books of verse began to pour from the presses and *Day and Night* was one of the first of the series. As a result, the publication of the book created as much enthusiasm as had that of the title poem in the *Canadian Poetry Magazine,* and won for its author the Governor-General's Award. This was no mean honour, since other books in competition included A. M. Klein's *Poems* and Ralph Gustafson's *Flight into Darkness.*

The same award was accorded to Dorothy Livesay for her next book of verse, *Poems for People* (1947). Here for the first time was evident the temperate humanism of her maturity, especially in the first two sections, "Poems of Childhood" and "Poems for People." In her early poetry, Dorothy Livesay had shown a capacity to project her own personal feelings; in her poetry of the thirties she had revealed her power to project the hopes and fears of the inarticulate masses; but in these later poems she reveals her gift of empathy, her power to project the feelings of other individuals. Poems such as "Page One," "Inheritance," and "The Mother" point the way to the perfectly expressed compassion of the still more recent "Lament," perhaps the finest elegy in Canadian poetry.

The year 1947 brought to Dorothy Livesay the award of the Lorne Pierce Medal by The Royal Society of Canada. This medal, the highest native honour which can come to a Canadian writer, is awarded in recognition of a sustained and distinguished contribution to Canadian letters.

Having achieved such recognition, some writers might have been content to rest on their laurels. Not so Dorothy Livesay, whose energy and enthusiasm are indefatigable. Since 1949 she has published many poems in the magazines and two chapbooks of verse (*Call My People Home,* 1950, and *New Poems,* 1955), has prepared an anthology of her poems to be read on the Trans-Canada Network of the C.B.C., and has compiled this book of her selected poems.

It is impossible to predict just what turn Dorothy Livesay's poetry will take in the future, but we can be confident that it will continue to develop. Since her earliest youth she has been constantly experimenting and growing in skill and power. From her early imagism she has moved through the social revolutionary phase of the thirties and early forties, and has now reached a temporary plateau from which she looks down at life with fresh but sophisticated vision. The result is a fascinating combination of innocence and experience, of hope and fear, of faith and doubt. She now proclaims her faith in man, but recognizes human fallibility and the need for some supernatural guidance; she still believes in the need for social regeneration but admits its difficulty and necessary gradualness; she believes that the world of nature is essentially good and beautiful but recognizes its latent power to destroy. In a world which often seems in imminent danger of disintegration she lyrically proclaims the values of love, joy and art which are at once the justification and the salvation of the world.

And she proclaims these things in a voice that is and always has been rich in music. At its best, her poetry sings and soars in ecstasy. Whether it be in these words of the nineteen-twenties:

> Some silence that is with beauty swept
> With beauty swept all clean

or in these of the nineteen-fifties:

> O landscape lovely, looped
> With loping hills, wind-woven,
> Galloping through cloud—
> Landfall of love . . .

the voice is the same, and it is a voice we delight to hear.

As an addendum to this 1956 article, I append this review, from the Canadian Forum, *of Dorothy Livesay's 1967 book,* The Unquiet Bed:

The conventional image of the poet as a delicate person who dies young has little foundation in Canada. We had our Lampman and our Knister, true, but Charles Sangster lived to be 71, Charles Roberts to be 83, Bliss Carman to be 68, Duncan Campbell Scott to be 85, and E. J. Pratt to be 82. Today, F. R. Scott is still going strong at 68, A. J. M. Smith at 65, Earle Birney at 63—and Dorothy Livesay at 58. Nor does age wither them: Scott is as lively a satirist as he ever was, Smith as exigent a craftsman, Birney as witty and perceptive a chronicler of times and places, and Livesay as impassioned an amorist and as frank an emotional autobiographer.

The Unquiet Bed is an apt title for Dorothy Livesay's latest collection—as *Green Pitcher* (1928) and *Signpost* (1932) were apt titles for her earliest. This woman refuses to lie down—or at least to lie down for any but amatory purposes. If one did not know better, one would take this to be a book by a woman in her early twenties—a woman who sees the best poetry not as words on a page but as living speech ("Without Benefit of Tape"), who rejoices in the fact that in Canada now poetry is "bursting out/all over the place" ("The Incendiary"), who goes to soccer games ("Soccer Game") and has the fashionable abortion ("Ballad of Me"), who is hoydenishly "one/with rolling animal life" ("Sunfast"), who rejoices in the fact that she is alive and "can stand/up still/hoarding this apple/in my hand" ("Eve"), who wants love to "move over" and "make room for me" ("The Unquiet Bed"), and who quite frankly hungers for sex:

> the body blunt
> needing the knife
> the forked light-
> **ning of tongues**

> your blow
> eased me so
> I lay quiet
> longer . . .
>
> ("Four Songs")

But if this almost frightening vitality, this emotional intensity which at times embarrasses someone like me who has grown tired at fifty—if this were all, the book would be monotonous. Alongside the persistent, defiant assertion of earth and sense and sex there sounds a quieter, wiser, sadder note. Mortality and modesty are there—or the book would not be the moving human document it is. Dorothy Livesay can mock herself, as

> Misbegotten
> born clumsy
> bursting feet first
> then topsy turvy
> falling downstairs . . .

More cruelly self-revealing, she admits

> I go incognito
> in sandals, slacks
> old sweater
> and my dyed
> hair . . . ,

or describes herself as

> a shrunken, bowed and heavy-bellied form
> skirt hugging the knees.

Even in the most erotic poems she is frank to admit the ravages of mortality:

> Crow's feet your finger follows
> circling my eyes
> and on the forehead's field
> a skeleton of leaves. . . .

But there is still more to the book than intense vitality and honest self-revelation. Dorothy Livesay is aware not only of herself but of others. A rich vein of compassion, or more properly of empathy, has always streaked her work—and in this latest book the vein still yields its ore. No soccer player herself (she makes a mistake about officials, to prove *that*) she can make us feel what it is like to shoot and score—

> the toe's a needle
>   quivering
> towards the net—
> ball circles, soars
> and lunging
> it is plunged
> straight to the win—

just as she can suggest what it was like to be Malcolm Lowry, frustrated in his compassion:

> He wanted to take us all
>   all
> and fold us in the comfort
> of his huge bed
> but he stood by the window
> unable to move . . .

She can make us feel the situation of children in the prison of school in springtime ("Spring"), and the agonizing loneliness of the only child ("Isolate"). Her empathy extends even to the Emperor Franz Josef, whose feelings on seeing his drawings reproduced she re-creates most credibly ("The Emperor's Circus"). More predictably, she can write with almost unbearable poignancy about the tragic silence of A. M. Klein ("For Abe Klein: Poet"). The final proof of the empathetic reach of her imagination is the last section of the book, in which she records with amazing sensitivity her reactions to the people and places of Africa, where for several years she taught English under the auspices of UNESCO.

The Unquiet Bed, is, in short, a rich and vital book which proves beyond a shadow of a doubt that poetry is not a peculiar secretion of adolescence but pre-eminently an expression of mature humanity.

The Poems of Marjorie Pickthall*

T̲H̲E̲ process of publishing selected editions of the poetry of the best-known Canadian poets of the past must now be nearing completion. The books of Bliss Carman, Charles Roberts, Archibald Lampman, and Duncan Campbell Scott have all been winnowed during the past decade, their chaff discarded and their grain preserved in a more or less permanent form. It is doubtful whether there are any other poets worthy of such treatment, although Charles Sangster, William Wilfred Campbell, Frederick George Scott, Isabella Valancy Crawford, and Tom MacInnes might be considered. At any rate the effort involved so far has been well worthwhile, as it has kept alive poetry which was in danger of being forgotten in its original format, and has provided the occasion for a revaluation of each poet's contribution.

The latest volume in the series is this selection of the poems of Marjorie Pickthall[1], made by Dr. Lorne Pierce, editor of the Ryerson Press. Dr. Pierce is well qualified for such a task, since he has long been an admirer of Marjorie Pickthall and produced a book-length study of her life and work in 1925.

Dr. Pierce's introduction indicates that even he is now much less sure of the lasting value of Miss Pickthall's poetry than he was then. In the earlier essay he praised her unreservedly for her colour, cadence, contour, and craftsmanship, and said:

She possessed a genius for taking pains. Never rugged, and incapable of standing long and concentrated study, she nevertheless acquired the finest fruits of culture—a sound appreciation

---

*Published in *The Canadian Forum*, December, 1957.
[1]*The Selected Poems of Marjorie Pickthall*: edited and with an introduction by Lorne Pierce (Toronto: McClelland and Stewart), 1957.

of the best, and a vital experience of the true, the beautiful and the good. But to this she added a high-souled purposiveness, which was never satisfied with anything less than perfection. Her work, therefore, reveals that quality frequently lacking in the work of others with more native brilliance, namely, a high ethical purpose which saw things clearly and saw them whole, and held straight on to the high object of her adoration . . . Whatever may have been lacking in profound scholarship was atoned for in reverence to her ideals of beauty and in her lofty, restless passion for perfection.

It is symptomatic of the general drift away from a purely emotional to a more rationally disciplined view of poetry that Dr. Pierce begins the introduction to his new book by summing up the strength and weakness of Marjorie Pickthall as follows: "On the one hand, there are grace and charm, restrained Christian mysticism, and unfailing cadence; on the other, preoccupation with the unearthly, with death and regret, with loneliness and grief, where the tendency is toward emotional interpretations of life, and rapture and intuition are substituted for the discipline of reason." He admits that after the *Drift of Pinions*, her first book, published in 1913, Miss Pickthall only repeated herself, and that her work marked the end of the old romantic tradition of Canadian poetry rather than a new departure. He deplores her failure to face her own age, and her tendency to take refuge in the past. In other words, the present introduction is for the most part a just and clear-sighted estimate of Miss Pickthall's verse. It is Lorne Pierce at his best—allusive, suggestive, mercurial. The criticism may be impressionistic rather than systematically scholarly, but the impressions are those of a very sensitive, sensible, and widely-read human being. Only occasionally, as when he speaks of the poems as "private acts of devotion—reticent, wistful, and personal, a kind of oblation jewelled with symbolism, bright with imagery, and always softly cadenced as if joining in the age-old litany of the Mass," does Dr. Pierce fall into the rhapsodic tone which is the chief fault of his criticism.

The brief introduction, then, is excellent. What of the selected poems themselves? If one approached the book seeking a new revelation of Miss Pickthall's genius one would be disappointed. The best poems in it are those which have been kept in print in the anthologies and which every Canadian reads in his schooldays—poems such as "Père Lalemant," "Duna," "The Bridegroom of Cana," "The Little Sister of the Prophet," and "A Mother in Egypt." These undeniably do have charm, a kind of adolescent wistfulness which, I rather shamefacedly confess, still has the capacity to bring tears to my eyes and a choking sensation to my throat—until I sternly remind myself that I should be past that sort of thing. It is only when one subjects these poems to a deliberately sceptical analysis that their charm evaporates. One realizes, first of all, that they are designed to trigger stock responses, that what makes "The Bridegroom of Cana," for example, so superficially moving, is not so much the language of the poem itself as the fact that the appeal of Christ has centuries of ritual and tradition and preaching to back it up. Undertake the admittedly difficult task of disentangling the actual technique of the poem from the heavily loaded subject-matter, and immediately weaknesses become apparent. There is redundancy, pathetic fallacy ("Slenderly hang the olive leaves/Sighing apart"), and a general overripeness of expression ("rose-and-silver doves," "Honey and wine in thy words are stored," "the golden lure of thy love"). And yet the verdict of a detailed analysis is not wholly negative: "The shaft of the dawn strikes clear and sharp" is a good metaphor, and lines such as

> And the lifting, shimmering flight of the swallow
> Breaks in a curve on the brink of morn . . .

are at once musical, emotive and accurate.

Perhaps the clearest proof of the essential hollowness of Marjorie Pickthall's poetry is that the more it is read and pondered the less impressive and the more cloying it seems. Her faults, which on a quick first reading are apt to be obscured by her talent for weaving a pleasant pattern of sounds around a traditionally emotive subject, become more and more apparent as the book is re-read.

The first of these faults, though not the most serious, is her heavily imitative tendency. Chameleon-like, she seems to have taken on the characteristics of any literary movement with which she came in close contact. She learned most from the Pre-Raphaelites, and leaned very heavily upon Dante Gabriel

Rossetti's sensuousness, colourfulness, and rather hectic emotional intensity, and upon his sister Christina's mysticism and
preoccupation with loneliness and death. She also owed a good
deal to the Celtic Revival, and especially to the early Yeats—so
that her work is full of twilight, tears, sleep, sighs, mists and all
the other late Romantic paraphernalia. Such a stanza as this,
for example, might have come straight out of *The Wanderings
of Oisin:*

> When the rooks fly homeward and the gulls are
>   following high,
> And the grey feet of the silence with a silver
>   dream are shod,
> I mind me of the little wings abroad in every sky
> Who seek their sleep of God.

Imitativeness, however, is not always fatal to good poetry.
The monotony of Marjorie Pickthall is a more serious matter.
Bliss Carman too has been charged with monotony, but he did
develop through several phases and he did have at least two
distinct tones—one wistful, tender and sad, the other buoyant,
vigorous, and optimistic. Marjorie Pickthall uses the same
words, the same images, and the same rhythms in poem after
poem to cast the same spell. Words such as silver, gold, dream,
little, shadows, hushed and sweet echo and re-echo; the images
are drawn almost exclusively from jewellery and metalcraft
("Rain has jewelled all my fingers," "The moon's my golden
ring," "Every pool a sapphire is," "And cleft with emerald
spears of sedge," "The sunlight falls in amber bars," "The slow
sun sinks to the sand like a shield," "St. Ignace and St. Louis,
little beads on the rosary of God"); and the rhythms are slow,
hesitant, and undulant like a chant or litany heard from a great
distance.

Together with this monotony of style there goes, rather paradoxically, an apparent variety of subject-matter. Her poetry
has no local centre—it shifts from primitive Canada to medieval
Britain, from modern Wiltshire to ancient Brittany, from the
Virgin Islands to Turkey, from Palestine to Egypt. Although
she manages, by dint of her wide reading, to give a kind of
factitious authenticity to these places, they all tend to blur into
one romantic landscape.

Now we are approaching, I think, the essential weakness of Miss Pickthall's poetry. It is a poetry of escape, dealing with the remote in time and place. She seems to have shared Yeats' early conviction that "only beautiful things should be painted, and that only ancient things and the stuff of dreams were beautiful." In poem after poem Miss Pickthall makes clear her preference for the dream rather than the reality, for dawn and twilight rather than the clear light of day, for sleep and death rather than wakefulness and life. "The Princess in the Tower," in which she expresses a preference for the solitariness of the tower to the realities of human intercourse, is a key poem in this connection: Miss Pickthall was afraid of life, and though we may have compassion for her as a person we must coldly state that this fear was fatal to her as a poet.

The poet, surely, must be fully alive in his own age; but there is almost nothing in Marjorie Pickthall's poetry to indicate when or where she lived. It is not, of course, that a poet must always or even usually write directly about his own time and place—such an absurd attitude would rule out Milton's *Paradise Lost* and most of Shakespeare. But Milton and Shakespeare, whatever their nominal subjects might be, always had one eye on the readers of their own time. Milton was justifying God's ways to men, and that meant that through the Biblical narrative he was addressing his contemporaries. Miss Pickthall seems to have had no awareness of her contemporaries whatsoever, so that Dr. Pierce can say with some truth that her poems seem like *private* acts of devotion. But true poetry is not a private but a public act, an act of communication. The poet is, as Wordsworth said, a man speaking to men. Because she did not really speak to her own generation, Miss Pickthall cannot speak to ours. Already her faint litanies are barely overheard from her private chapel.

It has often been pointed out in reference to English literature that a literary movement which begins as a protest against the artificiality of the dominant school in its turn becomes artificial and must be replaced. The same process has operated in Canadian literature. The romantic tradition which Charles Roberts inaugurated in our poetry was a protest against the artificiality of poets such as Sangster and Mair—Roberts was actually looking at the landscape of the Maritime provinces, and this was his strength. But by the time Marjorie Pickthall came on the scene that tradition had forgotten its realistic origin, and her work was even more artificial in its way than had been that of Sangster and Mair. It was Pratt and the Montreal Group, in their different ways, who made the necessary protest and brought poetry back to earth. Sometimes I wonder whether, in the very clever and mythologically sophisticated young poets of today, we are not witnessing another retreat into artificiality. For poetry, wherever it ends, must always begin in the close observation of the here and now. And this, I believe, is the lesson that Miss Pickthall has to teach us.

A Colonial Romantic:

MAJOR JOHN RICHARDSON, Soldier and Novelist*

MAJOR JOHN RICHARDSON was the first Canadian novelist to achieve an international reputation; his best novel, *Wacousta*, has appeared in some twelve editions and was in print for over a century; he was the first Upper Canadian poet to have a volume of verse published in Great Britain; as a soldier he distinguished himself for gallantry before he was seventeen years old; as a journalist he played a significant role in the 1837 Rebellions. He was undoubtedly the most colourful figure in our colonial literature, and as certainly the most obnoxious. Excitable, belligerent, haughty, and quick to take offence, his life was a succession of quarrels, controversies, and duels. Yet no full-length biography of this colonial romantic has ever been written,[1] and the facts of his birth, marriage, literary and military career and death are still in doubt. The purpose of this essay is to shed some new light on these obscure facts.

Various dates have been suggested for Richardson's birth, but there seems to be no doubt that the correct date is October 4, 1796. His birthplace was the village of Queenston, near Niagara Falls. His father, Dr. Robert Richardson, was a Scottish surgeon attached to Simcoe's Queen's Rangers, and the scion of a Jacobite family. His mother was Madelaine Askin, second daughter of the prominent Detroit merchant, Colonel John Askin. The biographies of Richardson all state that his maternal grandmother, the first wife of John Askin, was a French lady. *The John Askin Papers*,[2] however, which fully document

*Published in *Canadian Literature*, Autumn, 1959 and Winter, 1960.
[1]The nearest approaches to a full biography of Richardson are to be found in A. C. Casselman's introduction to his edition of *The War of 1812* (Toronto: 1902) and W. R. Riddell's *John Richardson* (Toronto: 1923).
[2]The *John Askin Papers*, Vol. I: 1747-1795, edited by Milo M. Quaife, Secretary-Editor, The Burton Historical Collection. Published by the Detroit Library Commission, 1928.

that merchant's career, make it clear that the novelist's grand-mother was an Indian: "Askin was the father of a numerous family of children. The three elder children, John Jr., Cath-erine, and Madelaine, were by an Indian mother, concerning whom we have no certain knowledge." This Indian blood in Richardson helps to explain the great interest in and admira-tion for the Indian which is revealed in all his work: his long narrative poem, *Tecumseh*, is a tribute to the bravery of that famous Indian warrior; *Wacousta* is a tale of Indian warfare; and Indian characters appear, usually in a very favourable light, in almost all his novels.

The *John Askin Papers* shed other new light on the parent-age and early life of John Richardson. There are a number of letters from Richardson's mother to his grandmother both before and after her marriage to Dr. Richardson, and there are also letters from Richardson's father. Some of these letters include direct references to the future novelist. For example, on February 18, 1798, Madelaine wrote in part as follows: "The children are well. John walks everywhere and is as fat as ever. He is very fond of sleigh riding for he loves a horse." Already, before he was two years old, Richardson was revealing the love of fast horses that was to be one of the constant passions of his life! On August 6, 1801, Dr. Richardson wrote to Colonel Askin from St. Joseph's as follows:

I hope John is a good boy and attentive to his Grandpapa. Madelaine frets a little sometimes about him, but I am per-fectly easy myself as I am certain he is with his best friends, next to ourselves.

This letter reflects the fact that, since Dr. Richardson's duties compelled him to move about a good deal from station to sta-tion, John spent a large part of his boyhood with his grand-parents in Detroit. His grandfather filled the boy's mind with stories of colonial warfare and of trading expeditions into the wilderness, and his grandmother told him of her own experi-ences during the siege of Detroit in Pontiac's Rebellion. Many of these reminiscences he was later to incorporate into his novels.

Thus fired with dreams of heroic combat, young John Rich-ardson did not hesitate when the United States declared war on

Great Britain in June, 1812. Although he was only fifteen, he immediately enlisted as a gentleman volunteer, and during the next sixteen months fought in every engagement in which his regiment—the 41st—was involved. On August 3, 1813, Richardson was commissioned as an ensign, and it is interesting to note that in his *Eight Years in Canada* Richardson declares that it was his friend Sir Isaac Brock who secured his commission for him: thus early was born another of Richardson's lifelong habits, that of relying upon personal influence for advancement. However, Richardson was taken prisoner in October of 1813 at the disastrous battle of Moraviantown, and spent the following year as a prisoner-of-war in Kentucky. His harrowing experiences as a prisoner are vividly described in his first novel, *Ecarté*.

His sufferings in captivity in no wise cooled Richardson's martial ardour. Once released on exchange, he joined the 2nd Battalion of the 8th King's Regiment as a lieutenant, and sailed for Europe in June, 1815, to take part in the war against Napoleon. He reached Europe to find that the Battle of Waterloo had been fought during his ocean passage and, along with many other junior officers, was almost immediately placed on half-pay. By pulling strings, he managed to win a return to active status on May 25, 1816, and sailed with his regiment for the West Indies. During this voyage, made in November, 1816, Richardson's haughty temper had an opportunity to display itself; he was disgusted by the pranks played when the ship crossed the Equator, and refused to submit himself to shaving and other indignities.[3] His spirits were, however, restored by his first glimpse of the beauty of Barbados—his description of which provides a sample of his romantic enthusiasm:

Nothing could exceed the beauty of this island which, as we approached sufficiently near to distinguish trees and plantations, appeared to rise like a bed of emerald from the deep bosom of the waters. Much of that beauty moreover arose from the association of ideas, for having left England at a moment when the bleak winds of autumn had robbed the fields of their green and the trees of their foliage, to be thus, as it were, transported suddenly into a new and luxurious season, excited a sentiment

[3]For this and other information relating to Richardson's experiences in the West Indies, see his *Recollections of the West Indies, New Era*, March 2, 1842 *et seq.*

of delight . . . Alas! how few reflected that in that island, so fair
to the eye, lurked the seeds of death, and that in the light atmosphere which crowned its ever-green summits played those exha-
lations which are fraught with subtlest poison to the health of
the European.

Richardson is referring in that last sentence, of course, to the
yellow fever which at this period of history made the West
Indies a graveyard for British soldiers. Within ten days of his
arrival, Richardson himself fell victim to the disease, and although he temporarily recovered sufficiently to undertake military duties, he was eventually invalided home. He remained
long enough in Barbados, however, to form strong feelings
of disgust for the moral laxity, the caste-snobbery, and the
slave-system of the island. Richardson's impassioned but well-
reasoned attack on slavery, in his *Recollections of the West
Indies*, is one of his most attractive passages.

By October, 1818, Richardson was again back in England,
and on the half-pay list. Almost nothing is known of his activities during the next ten or twelve years. It is assumed, largely
from the interval evidence of his first novel, *Ecarté*, that he
alternated between London and Paris, leading the life of a
young man-about-town and of a minor journalist. He is supposed to have contributed articles to English newspapers and
magazines describing life in Canada and the West Indies, but
no one has ever documented this statement, and I have been
unable to trace any of his periodical writings. We do know
that in 1828 he published his narrative poem *Tecumseh*, in
1829 his novel *Ecarté*, and in 1832 *Wacousta*. Another certain
glimpse of Richardson during this period is provided by a
War Office Return of Services for 1828.[4] Under the heading
"The officer is here required to state, whether he is desirous
of service." Richardson has written in his flowing, impatient
script: "Desirous, and anxious for Service—Repeated applica-
tions having been made and replied to on the subject by his
late Royal Highness the Duke of York." It is a characteristic
glimpse: Richardson eager and impatient, and furiously pulling
strings.

But the chief significance of this Return of Services is that

[4]Public Record Office. War Office Return of Services etc. (wo 25), Vol. 772,
p. 130.

it allows us to clear up, at least to some degree, the mystery of Richardson's marriage. Previous biographies have agreed that "about 1830" Richardson married "an Essex lady," whose first names are always given as Maria Caroline and her last name either not at all or as Wrayson. The Return of Service, however, gives the date of his marriage as August 9, 1825, and the place the British Embassy in Paris. This lead made it possible to trace Richardson's marriage certificate among the Miscellaneous Foreign Records in the General Register Office, Somerset House, London.[5] The certificate reads as follows:

Marriages solemnized in the House of H. B. M.'s Ambassador in Paris in the Year 1825 John Richardson, of the Parish of St. George in the County of Middlesex, Bachelor, and Jane Marsh of Leamington in the County of Warwick, Spinster, were married in this House this Twelfth Day of August in the Year One Thousand eight hundred and Twenty five by me George Lefevre for Ed. Forster, Chaplain.

This marriage was solemnized between us   John Richardson
                                            Jane Marsh
In the presence of E. Bloque
           J. F. Lemaire

Thus is established beyond all doubt the date of Richardson's marriage and the name of his bride. But, as so often happens, to solve one problem is only to create others. Previous biographers have felt confident in giving Maria Caroline as the first names of Richardson's wife because there is a tombstone in the Butler Burial Ground at Niagara-on-the-Lake, Ontario, reading as follows:

Here reposes Maria Caroline, the generous-hearted, high-souled, talented and deeply lamented wife of Major Richardson, to the everlasting grief of her faithfully attached husband. After a few days' illness at St. Catharine's on the 16th of August, 1845.

One must assume, therefore, that Maria Caroline was Richardson's second wife, that Jane Marsh died between 1825 and

---

[5]Since I have not been to the United Kingdom since this research was instituted, I am indebted to various of my students and friends for locating these documents. I express my gratitude here to Messrs. Hugh Peacock, Allan Donaldson, F. Algar, Dr. W. K. Lamb, Col. C. P. Stacey, and Major Bateman.

1837, and that Richardson's second marriage occurred during this same period. I base the assumption about the dates on the facts that Richardson brought a wife with him to Canada early in 1838, and that we have such full knowledge of his life in Canada after 1838 that we should be sure to know about the death of Jane and the re-marriage to Maria Caroline had these events occurred in Canada. Diligent search on the part of many people has, however, failed to unearth any record of either the death of Jane or the marriage to Maria Caroline. The only missing part of the jigsaw puzzle that has come to light is the identity of Maria Caroline. Her obituary in the *Gentleman's Magazine* reads as follows:

On August 16, at the residence of the Rev. Mr. McDonough at St. Catherine's, Maria Caroline, wife of Major Richardson, Superintendent of Police on the Welland Canal, the second daughter of William Drayson, Esq., of Brompton, near Chatham, Kent.[6]

We know, then, that Richardson was twice married, in August of 1825 to Jane Marsh of Leamington, Warwickshire, and later to Maria Caroline Drayson of Brompton, Kent, and that his second wife died at St. Catharine's on August 16, 1845; but we do not know when his first wife died, or when he married for the second time.

Apart from his marriage to Jane Marsh, the only exact knowledge we have of Richardson between 1818 and 1835 is that he published three books and one pamphlet. The first book, *Tecumseh*, is a verse narrative of Indian warfare in the manner of Byron's *Childe Harold*. If he had hoped to emulate Byron in waking up to find himself famous, he must have been gravely disappointed. The only review of *Tecumseh* which I have succeeded in tracing states curtly: "We can only say that the feeling which prompted it is better than the execution. The notes are exceedingly interesting."[7] Whether the author of this brief review was being serious or sarcastic, the fact is that the notes to *Tecumseh are* more interesting than poem itself. Some of them give us glimpses of Richardson's boyhood, and one of them is an early example of his penchant for the sensational:

[6]*Op. cit.*, New Series, XXIV: 665 (July-December, 1845).
[7]*Literary Gazette*, No. 604, p. 519 (August 16, 1828).

To the propensity of this tribe for human food the Author can personally attest. Strolling through the Indian encampment an evening or two after the action of the Miami on the 5th of May, 1813, he, in company with another officer, suddenly found himself among a party of Minouminies who were seated round a large fire above which was suspended their untempting meal. At the surface of the boiling water appeared an offensive scum, and each warrior had his own particular portion attached to a small string, one end of which hung over the edge of the vessel immediately opposite. They stated with evident satisfaction, that it was an American, and extended their invitation to the Author and his companion, who to conceal their loathing, while declining the honour, were prudent enough to dress their countenances in a forced smile, which but ill-accorded with the state of their feelings. It would have been unwise to have manifested disgust.

That the Indians may have been joking seems not to have occurred to Richardson: he was never distinguished by his sense of humour. And the subject of cannibalism had a peculiar fascination for him; he often alluded to it, most nauseatingly in *The Monk Knight of St. John.*

Richardson's literary ambitions were not easily daunted. If he could not succeed in verse, he would try prose; if British readers were not interested in tales of Indian bravery, they might be intrigued by revelations of French vice. Accordingly, he set to work on a novel of fashionable dissipation in the French capital—*Ecarté, or the Salons of Paris.* This book certainly brought him notoriety, if not fame. Its anticipated revelations were heralded before publication in *The Athenaeum* of February 25, 1829; it was praised by some reviewers as an instrument of virtue, and damned by others as an instrument of vice; it served as the text for a long and earnest sermon in *The Westminster Review* on the evils of gambling. *The Literary Gazette,* which had so curtly dismissed *Tecumseh,* could damn but not dismiss the book; in typical self-righteous style, it fulminated:

This is another of those detestable publications whose only tendency can be to deprave the mind of even the most superficial and thoughtless readers. It is not easy for us to describe it, certainly not to expose it, without polluting our pages with obscene extracts. . . . Unfit to be seen beyond the precincts of the stews, the profligate manners of which it describes, *Ecarté* is merely less pernicious in consequence of the contemptible talent of its would-be libertine and licentious author . . .[8]

This hostile review, which Richardson explains as the consequence of a threat by William Jerdan, publisher of the *Gazette*, to damn the next book published by Henry Colburn, served Richardson as the occasion for one of his many quarrels. Here is his own version of the affair, as given in a footnote to *Eight Years in Canada*:

On the very next day after the ill-natured and threatened critique had gone forth to the public, there was an evening reunion of literary people at Mr. Redding's—the author of the 'Beckford Papers' etc.—at which were present Harrison Ainsworth, Thomas Campbell, Silk Buckingham, the author of 'Tremaine', Charles Ollier, and a number of other distinguished writers of the day. . . . Late in the evening. . . . Jerdan made his appearance. . . After conversing a short time with those who were most intimate with him, he came up to me, a personal stranger and said "he should be very happy to have the pleasure of taking wine with me" . . . I rose from a tabouret on which I had been sitting near the feet of the mistress of the house, and exchanging a significant glance with her, observed that Mr. Jerdan did the author of *Ecarté* too much honour in inviting him to drink wine with him, but that nevertheless I should be most happy to accept his proposal. Jerdan stared, drew up his eyebrows, seemed for the first time conscious of a *mal entendu*, bowed stiffly, sipped his wine, and then turned to converse with somebody else.

Such personal feuds were the stuff of life to Richardson; from this time forward there was scarcely a moment when he was not involved in a controversy with somebody. Some of his enemies he attempted to wound in his next publication, published like *Ecarté* anonymously—*Kensington Gardens in 1830*—Canto I of a projected satirical narrative poem modelled on Byron's *Don Juan* and brought out as a pamphlet by Marsh and Miller in 1830.

A measure of fame, as distinct from notoriety, came to Rich-

[8]*Op. cit.*, March 28, 1829, p. 208.

ardson in 1832 with the publication of his most ambitious novel, *Wacousta*. Reviewers on both sides of the Atlantic were almost uniformly favourable to the book. The London *Satirist* stated, "The perusal of this novel has afforded us more satisfaction than anything of the kind which has fallen within the range of our reading in many a long day",[9] and *The Athenaeum* concluded a three and a half column review with this measured judgment:

The merits of this novel consist in the spirit of its historical pictures, which possess, at least, the consistency of truth. The writer displays no ordinary share of graphic power, and has the rare talent of "rendering a fearful battle in music." His descriptions of scenery are well executed, but unfortunately they are rare. The story itself is not very consistent or very probable, but it maintains its interest to the end.[10]

American reviewers, while criticizing some improbabilities in the plot, also wrote at length of Richardson's gift for vigorous narration, powerful scenes, and vivid descriptions. And the novel was apparently popular with the general public, for six editions were published within the first eight years, and subsequent editions in 1851, 1868, 1888, 1906 and 1923.

After such a success, Richardson might have been expected to settle down to the life of a popular novelist. But his restless temperament could not long remain content with any one kind of life. Literary fame was not enough; he still yearned for martial glory. For sixteen years he had been vainly longing for active service; in 1834 an opportunity offered and he seized it eagerly.

Civil war broke out in Spain between the legitimate monarch, Queen Isabella, and the pretender to the throne, Don Carlos. The British Government, while remaining officially neutral, sanctioned the recruitment of a British Auxiliary Legion. Richardson enlisted, was promoted to a captaincy, and later to a majority at the storming of San Sebastian, and was created a Knight of Saint Ferdinand by the Queen of Spain. Since he also wrote no less than four books about the campaign, it would

---

[9]This review is quoted in H. J. Morgan's *Bibliotheca Canadiensis*; I have been unable to trace the magazine itself.
[10]*Op. cit.*, Dec. 29, 1832.

appear at first glance that Richardson had finally found a full
measure of satisfaction for his soaring ambition. Unfortunately
his own haughtiness and pugnacity again betrayed him. While
convalescing in London from his wound, and shortly after issuing his *Journal of the Movements of the British Legion* (1836)
in which he defended the Legion and its commander, General
Sir De Lacy Evans, against the hostile criticism of the Tories in
the House of Commons, Richardson heard that he had been
passed over by General Evans in a list of promotions and decora-
tions. He promptly added a section to the book bitterly attacking Evans as a cowardly and incompetent commander, and
reissued it in 1837 as *Movements of the British Legion with
Strictures on the Course of Conduct Pursued by Lieutenant-
General Evans.* Never one to drop a quarrel lightly, Richardson
followed this up with a second attack, *The Personal Memoirs
of Major Richardson as connected with the singular oppression
of that officer while in Spain by Lieutenant-General Sir De Lacy
Evans,* published in Montreal in 1838 after Richardson had
returned to Canada. The final assault was made in a satirical
novel in which Evans is the thinly-disguised villain—*Jack Brag
in Spain,* never published in book form but published serially
in the early eighteen-forties in Richardson's Brockville newspaper, *The New Era.*

The ramifications of this quarrel and its aftermath are too
complex to detail here. In retrospect, the whole affair has a
comic opera air. When Richardson returned to Spain in 1837 a
military Court of Inquiry was held to "investigate and report
upon the conduct of Captain Richardson, 6th Regt., for having
while in England thrown out imputations in print, and in letters
addressed to the Military Secretary, calculated to cast discredit
on the conduct of the Legion in the glorious action of the 5th
of May." Richardson managed to shift the subject of the inquiry
from the nature of his remarks to the nature of his conduct in
battle, and as there never was any doubt about his personal
bravery he managed to win a favourable verdict—but at the cost
of whatever vestiges of popularity he retained with his fellow
officers. Back in London, the affair was brought up several times
in debates in the House of Commons, where the government's
Spanish policy was a subject of intense controversy. Some members favoured direct participation on the side of the legitimate
Queen; others felt that even to allow the volunteer Legion to

participate was a dangerous precedent. Since the first edition of Richardson's journal of the campaign defended the Legion, and the second edition tended to discredit it, he found himself quoted by both sides, and there was much confusion as to which book was being quoted. In the debate of April 17, 1837, for example, we find Mr. O'Connell trying to clarify the issue as follows:

The gallant officer opposite, in the course of his speech, had talked disparagingly of the 10th Regiment, upon the authority of one Richardson, whose book was really two books; the one written when he was in favour with General Evans, and therefore all in his praise, the other written after he had been dismissed the service, and, of course, all against him.[11]

When the "gallant officer" referred to, Sir Henry Hardinge, interjected that Richardson had nothing but praise for Colonel O'Connell, the latter said "he should be sorry to receive praise from such a quarter as Mr. Richardson. If he was not mistaken, all the officers of his regiment refused to speak to him." The debate dragged on intermittently for months, and as late as March 13, 1838, after Richardson had left for Canada, Sir Henry Hardinge was still trying to make clear which edition of Richardson's chronicle he was quoting.[12]

Embroiled in such fruitless controversies, Richardson must have welcomed the news of the 1837 Rebellions in Upper and Lower Canada. His resolution to return to his native land is expressed with Miltonic gravity: "Canada being the land of my birth which, while a mere youth, I had left with my regiment in 1815, I naturally felt some solicitude for its welfare, and as the news which reached England by every packet was of a nature to induce the belief that my services might be available in her defence, I resolved to embark forthwith."[13] He embarked at the London Docks on February 18, 1838.

The John Richardson who returned to Canada in February, 1838, was a vastly different being from the ambitious young ensign who had set sail for Europe in 1815. He was now almost forty-two years old, a major, a holder of a decoration from the

---

[11]*Parliamentary Debates*, 3rd series, vol. XXXVII, p. 1385.
[12]*Ibid.*, Vol. XLI, p. 847.
[13]*Eight Years in Canada* (Montreal: 1847), p. 6.

Spanish queen, an acquaintance of almost all the literary men of London, and a successful novelist. Although his successes had been by no means unmixed with failures, he had some reason for pride in his achievements, and a substantial basis for the expectation that he would be received in his native country with respect if not with deference.

Once again, then, he set forth with high hopes. He had secured a commission from the London *Times* to act as their Canadian correspondent at a salary of £300 a year, and he had furnished himself with a letter of introduction to Sir Francis Bond Head from the Secretary of Colonies, Lord Glenelg.[14] His dream was to secure an influential public position in his native country. Like all his dreams, it was destined to frustration— frustration which was in large part brought about by his own tactless pugnacity.

The first disappointment came in New York, where he found Bond Head *en route* for England. The returning governor, obviously in a state of nervous agitation, said curtly that he could do nothing about the letter from Lord Glenelg recommending Richardson for an official appointment, and handed it back with the suggestion that Richardson try it on Sir George Arthur. Thus Richardson received the first of many rebuffs from Canadian governors, a succession of whom, for the next ten years, he was to bombard with requests for official posts and pensions.

Proceeding by coach and steamer to Canada, Richardson paid a brief visit to his native Queenston, went on to Toronto, Montreal, and eventually to Quebec where he met the newly arrived Lord Durham. The meeting was a fateful one for Richardson. The two men, similarly haughty and impetuous, were mutually attracted, and Richardson, who had hitherto held the most reactionary views about the Canadian situation, was temporarily converted to the more progressive ideas of Durham. Richardson's first two despatches to the *Times* had been correctly conservative, but now he began sending despatches which favoured Durham and Durham's proposals. Naively, he expressed the hope that the editor of the Thunderer would accept his information as the work of an honest reporter: "I know your object is to obtain facts, and that if in the attempt to elucidate these I should occasionally clash with your own views

---

[14]*Eight Years in Canada* (Montreal: 1847), p. 6.

on the subject, I shall at least have the credit of sincerity and impartiality."[15] The editor gave ample warning of his disapproval by appending a note to the despatch, stating: "The writer of these letters is an occasional correspondent: it will be seen that he is a sort of partisan of Lord Durham." No more of Richardson's despatches were printed, and his appointment as correspondent was cancelled. When he informed Durham of this, the latter wrote to Richardson on October 18, 1838 as follows:

It is indeed most disgusting to see such proof of malignity in those who ought to value truth and fair dealing as the best means of informing the public, of which they profess to be the best possible instructors.

Your course has been that of a man of honour and integrity, and you can hardly regret the dissolution of a connexion which it appears could only have been preserved by the sacrifice on your part of truth and justice—by the *suppressio veri*, if not the *assertio falsi*.[16]

Such praise was a salve to Richardson's injured dignity, but he needed more tangible help. Now that he had lost his position with the *Times*, he was desperately in need of an alternative source of income. He hoped, of course, that Lord Durham would find a means of rewarding his services, and Durham did indeed, through his secretary Charles Buller, promise to do what he could. But Durham's sudden resignation, illness, and early death put an end to these hopes, and Richardson had to begin anew, at the age of forty-two, the task of building a career. For the next seven years, as letters in the Public Archives of Canada testify, he made repeated overtures and petitions to successive governors, begging that his services to Canada as writer and soldier be recompensed by an official appointment or a pension.

The most elaborate of these petitions was addressed to Lord Sydenham on July 20, 1841. Never one to affect a modesty he did not feel, Richardson began by asserting that: "Your Excellency's Petitioner is generally known and acknowledged as the only Author this country has produced, or who has attempted

[15]"Lord Durham's Administration", *The Times*, Tuesday, Sept. 18, 1838, p. 5.
[16]This letter appears as Appendix 8 of *Eight Years in Canada*.

to infuse into it a spirit of literature."[17] He went on to detail his literary activities, his military services, and the services rendered by members of his family, and ended by requesting that he be granted a pension from the Civil List. On this long and beautifully written petition, we can still read Sydenham's hastily scribbled note: "Reply. There are no funds for such a purpose." Such was to be the melancholy fate of all Richardson's petitions until 1845.

Meanwhile, Richardson sought to make a living in his native country by the exercise of his pen. In the fall of 1838, after his dismissal from the *Times*, he remained in Montreal to see his *Personal Memoirs* of the war in Spain through the press. He is also said to have written a pamphlet, the only surviving copy of which is housed in the library of McGill University, entitled *Sketch of the late Battle of the Wind Mill near Prescott*. An unsigned pencilled note on the title page of this pamphlet states, "This was written by Major Richardson who edited the few numbers of the Prescott, Ont. *Sentinel* which were printed." He also, in characteristic fashion, became involved in a quarrel with some officers of the Grenadier Guards, issued at least five challenges to duels, and was "posted" by the Guards for alleged cowardice when he refused to accept a challenge because the messenger was not, in his opinion, a gentleman.[18]

Perhaps because Montreal was too uncomfortable for him as a result of such feuds, Richardson went to Amherstburg early in 1839, hoping to settle in the town where so much of his boyhood had been spent. Unable to find a house in Amherstburg, he rented one in nearby Sandwich, and there he completed his third novel, *The Canadian Brothers*, a lively and patriotic tale of the War of 1812. He returned to Montreal early in 1840 to see this book through the press, and after a few weeks there set out for Sandwich driving a new sleigh and a team of spirited black horses. In typical fashion, he had neglected to consider that the sleighing season was almost over, and when he reached the town of Brockville he was stranded by lack of snow. While making arrangements there for a carriage, he saw a large house and extensive grounds which took his fancy, and impulsively

---

[17]Public Archives Mgg.G 20, Vol. 4, No. 415.
[18]For an account of this affair see the column "All Our Yesterdays" by A. E. Collard, Montreal *Gazette*, November 12, 1955. For Richardson's version, see his *The Guards in Canada; or The Point of Honour* (Montreal: 1848).

bought this "Rock Cottage" at twice its market value. Presumably to meet this payment, he sold his commission in the British Army during the early summer.

At first Richardson found Brockville a dull and dispiriting place; moreover his pugnacious temperament soon got him into trouble with the local inhabitants. He became involved in a quarrel with a certain Colonel Williams at a private card party, and when Williams alluded to Richardson's alleged cowardice in the affair of honour in Montreal, Richardson displayed placards throughout the town accusing Williams of slander; another duel was narrowly averted.[19] He also objected bitterly to the habit of the male youths of the town of bathing in the nude near his house. In a long tirade in the August 19, 1842, issue of his paper, *The New Era*, Richardson verbally lashed such offenders:

There is an unblushing depravity, a shameless immorality, among a certain class of beings in Brockville, such as we never knew to be equalled in any town in Europe. . . . We shall make it a point to take down the names of all persons found bathing within view of our premises, after sunrise, whether in or out of the limits, and this list we shall submit to the magistrates at the next Session.

This attack was contained in the final issue of *The New Era*; the first issue had appeared in June, 1841. Richardson wrote and printed the paper himself, using a press he had specially imported from New York for the purpose. He commented on Canadian and foreign news, ran as serials his *Recollections of the West Indies, Jack Brag in Spain*, and *The War of 1812*, and sought to promote the sales of his other books by quoting laudatory reviews of them and soliciting subscriptions. It was, then, a kind of personal house organ of its editor and publisher—and very unlike the lofty journal he had advertised in his grandiloquent Prospectus:

A journal essentially Literary, and of a moderate, or *juste mileau* tone of politics, having for its object the ultimate good and prosperity of the Country, without undue or slavish bias towards any party, is a desideratum which cannot be more

---

[19]See the pamphlet *Major Richardson's Reply to Colonel Williams' Gasconarde* (1840), a copy of which is in the Queen's University Library.

seasonably hailed than at a moment when these stupendous Provinces, emerging from the comparative night in which they have hitherto been enshrouded, are about to take their initiative among Nations. Hence the project of *The New Era* or *Canadian Chronicle,* which the educated of all classes of society, and especially the more intellectual portion of the community, as well as the advocates of a consistent and good government are now called upon to support.

Since the support was not forthcoming in sufficient force, Richardson dropped the paper in August, 1842, to devote himself to another grandiose project—completing his history of the War of 1812, of which the part printed in *The New Era* was only the first of three projected sections, in order that it might be used as a textbook in Canadian schools. He printed the first part in book form from the *New Era* plates, and then applied to the government for a grant to enable him to complete the remainder. The Assembly voted him £250 for this purpose, but the sale of the First Series was so disappointing that Richardson did not have the heart to proceed with the work. He argued, rather unconvincingly, that the grant had been a reward for previous labour rather than an aid to future publication.

Again Richardson turned to newspaper publishing, and early in 1843 founded in Kingston *The Canadian Loyalist or Spirit of 1812*.[20] *The New Era* had been relatively non-partisan in its political reporting and it had failed; this new paper was pro-Tory, and violent in its denunciations of the Lafontaine-Baldwin ministry and of Francis Hincks; no doubt Richardson hoped in this way to gain readers and to assure himself of preferment when and if the Tories succeeded to office. This, of course, was the outcome, in the summer of 1844, and Richardson almost immediately suspended the paper, confidently expecting patronage.

Richardson had to wait almost a year for preferment—but it did finally come, on May 20, 1845, when he was appointed Superintendent of Police on the Welland Canal. At last he had the public position for which he had been vainly petitioning for seven years. It was not a very lucrative post—the pay was only

[20]According to *British Authors of the Nineteenth Century,* edited by Kunitz and Haycraft (New York: 1936), p. 521, this paper is also recorded as the *Native Canadian.* I have been so far unable to trace any surviving copies of it under either name.

ten shillings a day—nor a very influential one, but Richardson resolved to make the most of it. Unfortunately his own belligerence ruined yet another opportunity. Within two weeks of his appointment he dismissed "several insubordinate and useless characters".[21] Within a month he requested the Chief Engineer on the project to cancel a holiday granted the workmen for July 4, and when asked to give reasons for his request haughtily replied: "I certainly am not aware that I am compelled to give any reason to any person employed on this Canal, the superintendence of which is confided to my judgment and discretion." A fortnight later he was inquiring from the Governor-General what rights he, Richardson, had to punish those constables who disobeyed his orders; and a week later he reported to the Governor that a neighbouring magistrate had sworn out a warrant for the Superintendent's arrest, and that Richardson had actually been arrested by one of his own ex-constables! In the light of such revelations of troublesomeness, it can have afforded the Governor little comfort to be assured of Richardson's efficiency in drilling his men to a high pitch of military precision. "In the meantime," Richardson reported on November 8, 1845, "I have my men regularly drilled to the use of the Broad sword, and taught such cavalry movements as may be useful on the limited ground on which they would in all probability be required to act."

As a man with more commonsense would have expected, Lord Metcalfe was more impressed by Richardson's feuding than by his drilling. On January 17, 1846, the following letter was despatched to Richardson by Mr. D. Daly, the Provincial Secretary:

I have the honor, by command of the Administration of the Government, to acquaint you that His Excellency, in Council, has had under consideration the subject of the Police Force on the Welland Canal, and the question whether such Force may not with propriety be discontinued, and that His Excellency has been pleased to direct that your services and those of the Force under your command be dispensed with from and after the 31st of the present month.

---

[21]This, and the following quotations relating to Richardson's employment as Superintendent of Police is taken from the pamphlet *Correspondence (submitted to Parliament) Between Major Richardson, Late Superintendent of Police on the Welland Canal and the Honorable Domineck Daly, Provincial Secretary* (Montreal: 1846).

Richardson did not take his dismissal without protest; he complained bitterly that the notice was too short, and that his Force was still needed. All his protests were, of course, in vain. No doubt intelligence had reached the Governor to the effect that were the pugnacious major to remain in command, violence was likely to erupt. In fact it did erupt in spite of his dismissal; at midnight, on January 31, Richardson wrote to the Provincial Secretary from his home in Allanburgh:

I have to acquaint you, for the information of His Excellency the Administrator of the Province, but with sentiments of unmitigated disgust, that this night has been characterized . . . by a scene of outrage and confusion, and intended personal insult to myself—still the servant of the Government—which can have no parallel even among uncivilized nations.

These atrocities I shall later detail to you: sufficient be it for the present, to observe that more than thirty shots were fired opposite my house, which is situated on the Canal, accompanied by fierce shouts and yells, and that not only Canaliers but discarded Policemen, of my own, were of the number of the scoundrels.

Throughout these exchanges of letters, Richardson never revealed the slightest sense of doubt in the complete correctness of all his actions. His pride perhaps reached its apex on March 12, when he wrote from Montreal to the Provincial Secretary in part as follows:

As I am by no means prepared to forego my claim to an honorary rank which has been acknowledged by Her Majesty herself, and by the Commander in Chief of the British Army, in several written communications from His Grace, at the caprice of any of Her Majesty's Colonial Subjects, however exalted their local distinction, I enclose and with the seal unbroken, the letter you have done me the honour to send to me, with a view to its being properly addressed.

And yet, six days after sending such an insulting reply to the Provincial Secretary, Richardson had the effrontery to dispatch a long memorial to Earl Cathcart, Lord Metcalfe's successor in the Governorship, detailing all his woes and laying further claims:

That your memorialist however seeks not as a mere favor, but claims from the Government as a due . . . that he be placed in some situation of trust and emolument not inferior to that which he has recently filled, or receive a gratuity from the Government whose summary proceedings have seriously affected his private pecuniary interests.

The Governor's reply to this memorial, dated March 20, is curt, restrained, but very apt:

In reply I am to state that His Excellency considers that it would be useless to direct that the unfitness of the manner, in which you have expressed yourself towards the members of His Excellency's Government, should be pointed out to you, since your own sense of propriety has not prevented you from expressing yourself in the way you have done.

Thus, in rioting and ignominious wrangling, ended Richardson's single tenure of public office in Canada.

By this time, 1846, Richardson was fifty years old, a widower (his second wife, Maria Caroline, having died during the first weeks of his Superintendency of Police), and a lonely and embittered man. He had tried and failed twice as a newspaper publisher; he had had a brief taste of public office and had found it bitter; he had sold his army commission to meet his debts; he had tried to sell his books to his countrymen and had found only a handful of buyers; and he had alienated the appointed governor from whom, rather than from the elected assembly, he had always sought favours. He remained in Canada until 1849, writing and publishing *Eight Years in Canada* and *The Guards in Canada* in the interval, but more and more he found himself casting envious glances over the border which as a boy he had defended against the Yankee invaders. Several times during his second stay in Canada he had visited the United States, and had found that his books were better known and more highly esteemed there than at home. Like many another Canadian writer after him, Richardson decided that fame and fortune could be won much more readily abroad.

Once more then, but for the last time, Richardson set out on a new adventure with high hopes. In New York City, it must have seemed to him at first that his long-deferred dreams were to come true. In the space of three years he was able to publish four new novels—*Hardscrabble, Waunangee, The Monk Knight of St. John*, and *Westbrook*—and to issue new editions of *Wacousta, Ecarté*, and *The Canadian Brothers* (under the new title of *Matilda Montgomery*). He was something of a celebrity in the great American metropolis, as he had formerly been in London, a man whose name could add lustre to a newspaper. Thus we find this passage in the biography of "Frank Forester" (H. W. Herbert), a prominent Anglo-American journalist of the mid-century:

When *The Sachem* was commenced by the same parties who had essayed the establishment of *The Era*, an editorial position was reserved from motives of friendship for Herbert, although the paper had been designed to serve as a species of Native America organ. Nevertheless, its projectors contemplated the employment of the best available talent in the production of an unrivalled literary paper, regardless of national prejudices. . . . As literary associates to Herbert were conjoined Major Richardson, author of *Wacousta*, a popular Indian romance; William North, author of *The Slave of the Lamp*, and a poet of no mean order. . . .[22]

But it was not long before Richardson's pugnacity got him into further trouble. Shortly after the passage just quoted comes this revealing sentence: "After the contribution of several excellent articles and a few historical sketches, Herbert retired from the paper, in consequence of a misunderstanding with Major Richardson and Mr. North, upon some political question connected with the rule of England in Canada."

Indeed, although much remains to be discovered about this final phase in Richardson's career, it seems certain that it was no less troubled than the earlier phases had been. The new books were all mere potboilers—*The Monk Knight of St. John* in particular is the 1850 equivalent of the most lurid and erotically perverse of today's pocketbooks—and they were published by the notorious firm of Dewitt and Davenport in fifty-cent paperback editions which brought their author meagre financial return.

---

[22]*The Life and Writings of Frank Forester* (H. W. Herbert), edited by David W. Judd (London, n.d.).

He died, supposedly of erysipelas complicated by malnutrition, on May 12, 1852, at his lodgings at 113 West 29th Street, New York City. Legend has it that he sold his Newfoundland dog, Hector, a few days previously in order to buy food. His obituary notice, as it appeared on May 14 in the New York *Journal of Commerce*, is more matter-of-fact:

Died—On the 12th inst. Major John Richardson, late of H. B. M. Gordon Highlanders aged 53 (55) years. His friends are invited to attend his funeral, without further invitation, from the Church of the Holy Communion, corner 6th Avenue and 20th Street, this day at two o'clock, p/m.

Haughty and belligerent to the last, Richardson declared near the end of his life that he had no desire to be ranked among Canada's future men of genius or to share any posthumous honour reserved for them. A man of genius, in a literary sense, he certainly was not; but he was, according to his lights, a man of honour. He was a Hotspur who forever sought, and found, trouble; a romantic whose dreams always outran reality and who was capable of infinite self-pity and infinitesimal self-judgment; a colonial whose insecurity and sense of inferiority led him to distrust and despise his fellow-colonials; a man who did in many ways serve his native country but whose consciousness of those services robbed them of much of their lustre. His chief lack was a sense of humour, a sense of proportion; his chief virtue was that he was never, in any circumstances, merely dull.

Sir Charles G. D. Roberts*

A scant eighteen years ago, there appeared from
the hand of the late P. D. Ross, a review in the Ottawa *Journal*
which read in part as follows:

Sir Charles George Douglas Roberts is a very great Canadian.
If anyone should care to say that he is the greatest living Canadian, there is good argument for it. . . . Since his earliest maturity, more than sixty years ago, he has been pouring forth a flood
of distinctive Canadian literature—poems, novels, nature stories,
historical and general writing. The total production has come
to more than forty volumes. Who can measure what effect this
has had for good on Canadian life and thought? . . .[1]

In the same year, 1943, the late Professor Pelham Edgar wrote
that "the poetry of Roberts . . . is destined to endure all the
fluctuations of taste and time. Here is no question of the ephemeral, but of the inevitable, once said and said forever."[2] A
series of such tributes could easily be listed, going all the way
back to the eighteen-eighties when Roberts, still in his early
twenties, was already recognized as the leading man of letters in
the young Dominion. When Roberts was knighted for his services to Canadian literature, in June, 1935, congratulatory
letters poured in to him from all corners of the country: from
fellow-writers such as Morley Callaghan, Mazo de la Roche,

---

*A lecture delivered at Carleton University, Feb. 4, 1961 and published in
Our Living Tradition, Fourth Series (1962).
[1]From a review of Elsie Pomeroy's biography of Roberts, *Ottawa Journal*,
July 10, 1943, p. 17.
[2]"Sir Charles G. D. Roberts and His Times," *University of Toronto Quarterly*,
XIII: 124 (October, 1943).

E. J. Pratt, and Duncan Campbell Scott, from political leaders such as Robert Borden and William Lyon Mackenzie King, and from a host of ordinary men and women who saw in Roberts the very living embodiment of Canadian literature. To give just one more example, when in 1939 the young left-wing poet Dorothy Livesay wanted to rally Canadian writers to write honestly and directly about the life of contemporary Canada, she chose to address "An Open Letter to Sir Charles G. D. Roberts," then an old man in his eightieth year, stating, "I address myself to you because you are a pioneer Canadian and a pioneer poet among us; because you have the tradition and the culture of our country at heart; and finally because your voice has not sunk to a whisper, but has come out boldly with the changing times. . . . Because you have given so much we can still look to you to give more."[3]

Today, less than twenty years after Roberts' death, it seems that his reputation, which for sixty years seemed unassailable, is in danger of collapse. He still keeps a place in A. J. M. Smith's recently published *Oxford Book of Canadian Verse,* but he has only eight pages allotted to him as against ten for Isabella Valancy Crawford, twelve for Duncan Campbell Scott, twenty-three for E. J. Pratt, and eleven for Earle Birney. And even this modest allotment has been challenged by reviewers of Smith's anthology. Millar MacLure, in a recent review in the *Tamarack Review,* has written contemptuously that whereas "Lampman is a good old cheese, Roberts and Carman belong on captions in the New Brunswick Museum".[4] George Woodcock, in the *Canadian Forum,* recently complained that "it is laborious, except perhaps in nostalgia for the Edwardian afternoon, to read through as much of the Confederation poets as most anthologists, Dr. Smith among them, give us. Technical proficiency may begin with these writers, but the first really original presence among English Canadian poets is still E. J. Pratt."[5]

A similar situation exists with respect to Roberts' prose. None of his novels have been recently re-printed, and his *History of Canada* does not even linger, as it well might, in the form of selections in school readers. Only his short stories have some surviving vogue: a selection of them, under the title of *The*

[3]*Canadian Bookman,* XXI: 34-5 (April-May, 1939)
[4]*Tamarack Review* No. 17: 64 (Autumn, 1960).
[5]*Canadian Forum* V. 40: 180 (November, 1960).

Last Barrier and Other Stories, edited by Professor Alec Lucas, recently appeared in McClelland and Stewart's New Canadian Library, and an example of them is to be found in all of the recent anthologies of Canadian prose. One such anthology, Robert Weaver's *Canadian Short Stories* in Oxford's World's Classics series, is very recent, and it is significant of the probable trend that in one early review of that book the Roberts story is dismissed as being unworthy of inclusion. If Roberts' poetry does not survive, I think it very unlikely that his prose will.

Are we, then, to conclude that Roberts' place in our living tradition is now a dubious one at best? Was his work indeed ephemeral, over-praised and essentially hollow? To answer this question will be the purpose of the remaining part of this lecture. But to answer it properly, and certainly to answer it in the terms of the title of this series, means setting Roberts in perspective, examining the traditions out of which he grew and the extent to which, if at all, these traditions may still be said to be living.

I say traditions rather than tradition, for Roberts was in fact the product not of a single tradition but of several. There was first of all a family tradition. Whenever Roberts had occasion to mention the influences which affected him, he always gave first place to his father, Canon George Goodridge Roberts. In some brief manuscript autobiographical notes preserved in the Hathaway Collection in the library of the University of New Brunswick, Roberts has written: "What started? Brought up on father's knee—good poetry read to me—Tennyson, Longfellow, Byron—read for the music as often far over our head. About 8 or 9 made up mind was going to be poet. At 9 read Paradise Lost—it was a great Fairy story to me." His first book of poems, *Orion* (1880), was dedicated to his father, and he drew a very sympathetic portrait of him in his novel *The Heart That Knows* (1906).

Canon Roberts' interest in literature and scholarship is not surprising, for there was a family tradition of learning. The canon himself was a graduate of the University of New Brunswick, and served for many years as a degree examiner in Classics and French at that university. His father, in turn, the poet's grandfather, was a graduate of Oxford who was headmaster of the Fredericton Collegiate School for nearly half a century and acting Professor of Classics at the university during 1872-1873.

The poet's great-grandfather was also an Oxford graduate, and a scholar who compiled a Latin grammar and did a great deal of historical writing. When we add to all this the facts that the allied families of Goodridges and Gostwicks numbered many scholars and writers among their number, and that Roberts' mother, Emma Bliss, traced her ancestry back to a prominent New England family which had intermarried with the Emersons, we can see that young Charles Roberts was predisposed by heredity and family environment to some kind of scholarly or literary career.

Even the most sanguine, however, might not have expected quite such a literary flowering as actually occurred in Charles' generation and in the generation that followed it. In addition to the work of Charles himself, there was in his own generation the poetry of his sister, Elizabeth Roberts MacDonald, the novels, short stories, and verse of his brother Theodore, and the extensive magazine writing of his brother William Carman Roberts. The productivity has continued into the present generation. The son of Elizabeth Roberts MacDonald, Goodridge MacDonald, is a practising Canadian poet of minor but real distinction; the eldest son of Charles, Lloyd, is a well-known poet and broadcaster; Theodore's daughter Dorothy is a good poet and the author of some fine short stories; and his son Goodridge is one of the best Canadian painters. Certainly there is no question but that in this respect Sir Charles Roberts is very much part of a *living* tradition. That it is a real, meaningful tradition, and not a mere accident of birth, can be seen by looking at the paintings of Goodridge. In their combination of tenderness and strength, in their loving particularity of detail, in their strong sense of design, in their subtle colouring, and in their combination of visual accuracy and spiritual insight, they have much in common with the best of his uncle's poems.

The second tradition with which I should like to deal is the provincial and civic tradition. I link the two, because it was largely the city of Fredericton, the capital of New Brunswick, that influenced Roberts, but not exclusively so. He was born near Fredericton, spent his early boyhood at Westcock near Sackville, and returned to Fredericton at the age of fourteen. After his education had been obtained at the Fredericton Collegiate School and the University of New Brunswick, he taught for a year at Chatham on the Miramichi, returned to Fredericton as principal of the York Street School, and apart from a brief three-month interval in Toronto as editor of *The Week,* remained there until he became a professor at King's College, Windsor, in 1885. There was another brief interval of life in Fredericton in 1895 and 1896, so that altogether Roberts spent some twelve of his most formative years in the little capital city.

Now Fredericton, though a very small city of some seven thousand persons in Roberts' day, had much to offer to a young poet. For one thing, it had a literary tradition which went back virtually to its foundation. The first Provincial Secretary of New Brunswick was the lively Tory satirist Jonathan Odell, who from Fredericton sent out poems which found their way into the leading periodicals of England such as *The Gentleman's Magazine.* A little later, in the early decades of the nineteenth century, Julia Catherine Beckwith wrote in Fredericton the first novel to be published by a native English-Canadian: *St. Ursula's Convent, or The Nun of Canada* (1824). In the eighteen-sixties, Fredericton was the home for several years of Juliana Horatia Ewing, one of the most famous Victorian authors of children's books such as *The Peace Egg, Lob-lie-by-the-fire,* and *Jackanapes.* In the eighteen-eighties, Fredericton was the home not only of the three writing Roberts' that we have mentioned but also of the poets Bliss Carman, Francis Sherman, and Barry Stratton. In the early years of this century, Fredericton had to be content to be known as the birthplace of writers who were no longer in residence, but in the nineteen-twenties a new literary generation developed: Dorothy Roberts wrote her early poetry there, her father Theodore returned to live there (he was still living there in 1944 when I first went to Fredericton) and Alfred Bailey and Malcolm Ross began to write their poetry and prose while students at the university. The literary tradition of Fredericton has continued up to the present. In 1945 Alfred Bailey and others founded *The Fiddlehead,* a magazine of verse which is still flourishing and in which a group of new young poets, including Elizabeth Brewster, Fred Cogswell, Robert Rogers and, most recently, Alden Nowlan, published most of their early work. In 1952, Brigadier Michael Wardell, an associate of Lord Beaverbrook, established in Fredericton the University Press of New Brunswick, and he has published a number of books by local authors and others and has established a magazine, *The Atlantic Advocate,* which is doing much to enrich the cultural and political life of the Atlantic Provinces. It has been said that there are more poets per square mile in Fredericton than in any other area of Canada, and I can well believe it. It is interesting to note that in his introduction to *Writing in Canada,* the report of the Canadian Writers' Conference held at Kingston in 1955, F. R. Scott was able truthfully to say "with few exceptions, the writers all came from the five cities of Vancouver, Toronto, Kingston, Montreal, and Fredericton."[6] To be included in this list may not have meant much to the metropolises of Toronto and Montreal, but it meant a great deal to the comparatively tiny city of Fredericton; and it provided external authority for my claim that in Fredericton at least the Roberts tradition is a living one.

That Roberts was conscious of the literary tradition of Fredericton is clear from an essay on that city by him which I recently found in typescript in the U.N.B. library. So far as I know, this essay was never published.[7] In it Roberts mentions Juliana Horatia Ewing and declares that Fredericton "intellectually and socially wields an influence out of all proportion to her size." But the chief thing which this essay reveals is Roberts' keen awareness of the physical beauty of Fredericton. He writes in part as follows:

Fredericton lies on a point of deep-soiled intervale, eighty-four miles above the mouth of the river Saint John. About her the great river draws a broad and gleaming crescent. Behind her rises a rampart of wooded hills. Opposite to her wharves flow in two lovely tributary streams, the Nashwaak and the Nashwaaksis, offering ceaseless enticement to the lovers of birch and paddle. And into the Nashwaak itself, just above the bridge that spans its mouth, empties a lilied, slow-winding, greenly shadowed brook, dear to those who go canoeing just two in a canoe. This is fitly known as "Lovers' Creek." . . . A little above the city the river is thickly sown with islands, level and grassy, enringed with trees, and holding out the most tempting invitations to all who would go camping.

Undoubtedly the sheer physical beauty of Fredericton did much to inspire the poetry of Roberts, Carman, and their friends. As

[6]*Writing in Canada,* edited by George Whalley (Toronto: Macmillan, 1956), p. 10.
[7]It is to appear, however, in the February, 1961, issue of *The Atlantic Advocate.*

A. J. M. Smith has put it, "The Fredericton of the seventies
. . . appears like an enchanted city, with its elm-shaded streets,
its generously proportioned old homes, its Cathedral, and the
college on the hill, while the river winding through the town
and the wooded slopes behind brings the forests and an echo of
the sea almost to people's very doorsteps."[8]

But there was a quality in the social life of Fredericton which
also put its stamp upon Charles Roberts. Settled first by United
Empire Loyalists, Fredericton retained in the days of Roberts,
and indeed retains to this day, many of their values and attitudes. Some, if not all, of these values were admirable. From
the very first, the Loyalists showed their interest in education
by the early establishment of the College of New Brunswick,
and this interest in culture and the things of the mind gave to
Fredericton an intellectual quality rare indeed in a pioneer
country. The Loyalist founders stood, also, for the values which
we associate with the aristocratic tradition: they vowed to make
the infant province of New Brunswick "the most gentlemanly
on earth," and they clung tenaciously to courtesy, gentility, and
good breeding in their social relationships. The social life which
revolved about the Cathedral, Government House, the Garri-
son, the University, and the Legislative Assembly reminds us
rather of that of Bath or of some other eighteenth-century re-
sort of fashion than of a pioneer community surrounded by
untracked forests. First-hand testimony of this is provided by
Sir George Parkin (of whom more later) who in 1920 wrote to
Dr. L. W. Bailey: "My wife and I often speak of the immense
advantage we gained from living in such surroundings as we
had in the Fredericton of our early days. There was an old-
fashioned courtesy and dignity, a real interest in the things of
the mind and spirit, which seem to have somewhat disappeared
in the rush of life and supposed progress of later times."[9] As
one who is proud to call Fredericton his adopted home, I should
like to say that I do not believe this atmosphere has been altogether lost. I encountered it the moment I arrived in Fredericton, and have cherished it ever since: gentleness, courtesy, a
genuine respect for learning and literature.

---

[8]The Founders' Day Address, University of New Brunswick, February 19,
1946.
[9]Quoted in *Sir George Parkin* by Sir John Willison (London: Macmillan, 1929),
pp. 14-15.

Now all this left a deep mark on Roberts. In the autobiographical notes to which I referred earlier, Roberts wrote under the heading of "purpose": "to write good literature, but underlying it to make for chivalry." In all his work we see evidence of the chivalric values: through it all shine his dignity, restraint, compassion, courtesy, and courage. I never met Sir Charles Roberts, but I did come to know his younger brother Theodore well, and at the risk of sounding dreadfully old-fashioned I am prepared to say that Theodore Roberts was every inch a gentleman. His tall, erect figure, his soft but pleasing voice, his grace of manner, his complete absence of pomposity, his readiness to encourage a young writer, his unfailing gentleness and courtesy: these I shall always remember as embodying at its best the social tradition of Fredericton. Again I say the tradition is a living one, for almost all the same qualities are exhibited by Theodore's son, the painter Goodridge Roberts.

I feel that at this point I may be in danger of sentimentality, of exaggerating the good qualities of the city which has sometimes sarcastically been called "The Celestial City." Let me, by way of light relief if nothing else, quote two less flattering references to Fredericton. The first is a glimpse of the city as it was when Roberts was still in residence, and comes from the pen of an anonymous U.N.B. undergraduate writing in the *University Monthly* in March, 1882. After paying Fredericton a number of compliments, he went on, "Its streets are well laid out, but its sidewalks are either not up to the standard or else entirely wanting. . . . The water in Fredericton, for the most part, is not fit to drink, and the sooner means are devised and arrangements made for the supply of better water to the city, the sooner will Fredericton rise from its present lethargic state to an active and live town." Civic pride urges me to point out that Fredericton now has an excellent water system! The other unflattering reference is much more recent, and comes from the pen of the young Toronto poet, Raymond Souster:

FREDERICTON

So this is "the poets' corner
Of Canada"—Bliss, Sir Charles
And Francis Joseph Sherman,
All born, all Latin'd and Greek'd here.

> Not one of them
> With anything really to say,
> But dressing it up, faking it,
> So that they fooled quite a few in their time.

> And I can understand why.
> Outside of the noble river
> Which none of them bothered to write about,
> This city has little to commend it,
> And couldn't help but in time
> Drive a man to drink or lousy poetry.

> Which vices are no doubt being practised
> At this very moment today.

Well, I like Souster's poems very much when they are poking fun at his native Toronto, but I must say that he shows a remarkable inability to see the true nature of Fredericton!

From the civic tradition I turn now to the academic tradition of Roberts. It is in this connection that native and adopted sons of New Brunswick feel that least justice has been done to them by Upper Canadians. In his *Colony to Nation*, Professor A. R. M. Lower let fall the unfortunate remark that "curiously enough it was the sterile soil of New Brunswick which bred the Roberts family and their relative Bliss Carman";[10] Elsie Pomeroy in her biography of Roberts dismisses his school and university years with a tribute to Parkin and a few anecdotes; and Professor Pelham Edgar expressed what we may call the orthodox Toronto sneer most explicitly when he wrote, "Of the formal education received both at the collegiate school, and during his three years (1876-1879) at the University of New Brunswick, there is not a great deal to be said. The staffs were not noteworthy in the scholarly sense, and we may assume that the standards were not, on a comparative estimate, high."[11] The most succinct and accurate comment on that is that nothing could be further from the truth.

There are actually three New Brunswick institutions of learning which can legitimately claim some significant part in the moulding of Charles Roberts: Mount Allison University, the

[10]*Op. cit.*, (Toronto: Longmans, 1946), p. 414.
[11]"Sir Charles G. D. Roberts and His Times," *University of Toronto Quarterly*, XIII: 119 (October, 1943).

Fredericton Collegiate School, and the University of New Brunswick. Mount Allison's part was a small but nevertheless a significant one: when Roberts' father was rector of Westcock, Charles showed a juvenile talent for painting, and arrangements were made for the boy to take classes at Mount Allison from Professor Gray. From these classes, I presume, we may trace the very strong sense of design which is such a conspicuous feature of Roberts' descriptive poems. At the Fredericton Collegiate School, of which his grandfather had been so long the headmaster, and which had and has for generations been the chief feeder of the University, Roberts had the good fortune to come under the influence of George R. (later Sir George) Parkin.

So much has been said of Parkin's influence upon Roberts and Carman that I do not need to dwell upon it here. Parkin was himself a graduate of the University of New Brunswick, getting his degree in the year of Confederation, and in an autobiographical fragment he thus described the education he received there in the sixties: "Our President, Brydone Jack, trained in the severe school of the Scottish universities, taught us mathematics; Montgomery Campbell, fresh from his fellowship at a Cambridge college, brought us the inspiration and culture of an ancient English university; Professor Bailey, a student under Agassiz at Harvard, filled us with the enthusiasm for natural science which he had caught from his famous master; Baron d'Avray, a Jerseyman of French descent, with all the delicate courtesy of his race, combined a refined taste in English literature with a perfect mastery of French. Three years of work spent under such able and inspiring teachers went far to remedy the worst defects of earlier education and at least opened the doors for wider knowledge."[12] In 1871 Parkin was appointed headmaster of the Collegiate School upon the resignation of Roberts' grandfather, but after two years he obtained leave of absence and spent the year 1873-1874 in Oxford. At Oxford Parkin listened to Ruskin's lectures on art, to Dean Stanley's sermons on liberal theology, to T. H. Green's lectures on philosophy and Bonamy Price's lectures on political economy; he read the new poetry of Tennyson, Rossetti, Arnold and Swinburne; and he was elected Secretary of the Oxford Union, an almost unique honour for a first year man. It was a

---

[12]Quoted in *Sir George Parkin*, by Sir John Willison (London: 1929), p. 13.

Parkin fresh from such exciting experiences that Roberts and Carman had as their teacher—no wonder that Carman called him "a fascinating teacher, this intense and magnetic personality." Carman goes on:

I don't remember that my lessons in the old school were ever drudgery. Often we would not cover more than a few lines in the hour. A reference might occur which would bring up a side issue in history or mythology, and then we must see how some modern or contemporary writer had treated the same theme. One of the class would be sent running to Parkin's rooms to fetch a book. Tennyson, perhaps, or Rossetti, or Arnold, or another, and we must listen to his poem on the subject. These were wonderful hours of growth, though we never dreamed of our incomparable good fortune. . . .[13]

Parkin, of course, went on to greater things—to the principalship of Upper Canada College, the secretaryship of the Rhodes Trust, and to the authorship of several books of history and biography—but it is doubtful if he did anything more permanently valuable than stimulate the youthful imagination of Roberts and Carman.

But Parkin's great influence upon them has, somewhat unfairly, overshadowed the influence of the professors at the University of New Brunswick to which, in due course, the poets passed. That university, projected as far back as 1785 by the Loyalist founders of the province, had struggled along for almost a century when Roberts entered it. Although it was still a small university, it had weathered its worst storms in the eighteen-fifties and, following its reorganization as the secular provincial university in 1859, it had begun to move steadily forward. That its standards were not low, as the late Dr. Edgar would have it, is attested by the brilliant series of graduates who emerged from it in the sixties, seventies, and eighties—men such as James F. McCurdy, for many years Professor of Oriental Literature in the University of Toronto, James Mitchell and William Pugsley, both of whom became Premiers of New Brunswick, George E. Foster, a member of the Federal Cabinet for over twenty years, Archdeacon W. O. Raymond, John Douglas Hazen, later premier of New Brunswick and Minister of

---

[13]*Ibid.*, p. 36.

Marine and Fisheries in the Federal cabinet, and Walter C. Murray, who became the first president of the University of Saskatchewan. Another proof of the university's vitality in these years is the outstanding record of its seniors in the examinations for the Gilchrist Scholarship, and by the success of its graduates in winning prizes at Oxford, Edinburgh, Harvard and other great centres of learning.

Fortunately, we have first-hand testimony of the influence the little university exercised upon its students. I have already quoted Parkin's testimony. Here is what his classmate, George E. Foster (later Sir George Foster) said of its influence upon him:

On the whole, I incline to the opinion that the course of training received was quite as beneficial to the undergraduates as would have been possible at one of the larger universities. Under its ministry I pursued my way from the preliminary instruction of the school to a wider and ever-widening field of knowledge in Classics and Mathematics, of both of which I was fond, and of Natural Science, a hitherto unknown field in which I found especial attractions. . . . The grounding and stimulus received at my Alma Mater I can trace through my whole life as a resourceful and sustaining foundation.[14]

Most fortunately, I am able to give you a first-hand account of Roberts' own sense of debt to the University of New Brunswick. For the first time recently I discovered in our library archives a signed typescript of a talk on U.N.B. in the 1870's given by Sir Charles himself on February 5, 1942. Since I do not think the talk has ever previously been published, I shall give it in full:

Looking back across the years I realize ever more and more clearly that, for my temperament at least, it was a great piece of good fortune to have been educated at what was then a small college, the University of New Brunswick,—a small college, indeed, but one with a definite atmosphere of its own and a distinctly formative tradition. The handful of Freshmen who gathered each September on the Terrace and eyed each other with suspicious curiosity consisted for the most part of more or

[14]*The Memoirs of the Rt. Hon. Sir George Foster* by W. Stewart Wallace, (Toronto: Macmillan, 1933), p. 24.

less raw material, somewhat leavened by four or five youthful
matriculants from the Collegiate or High Schools of Fredericton, Saint John or Saint Stephen. These were speedily drawn
under the influence of a very attenuated staff—a president and
four professors each responsible for several subjects of the curriculum. This influence, exerted unconsciously but all the more
potently for that, and accepted with equal unconsciousness by
its recipients, worked upon us with remarkable efficiency, so
that long before the year was out these very "verdant" Freshmen had all insensibly taken on the College stamp. In my own
case, as I remember, we were an unruly and turbulent class,
not easy to assimilate; but it soon came about, somehow, that
unsuspectingly we were ruled, and liked it. In the true sense of
the word we were being educated, rather than merely lectured
at. We were being securely grounded in fundamental things, and
we were being specialized not at all. At the end of our course we
found ourselves prepared to choose understandingly our own
individual careers and with some confidence to embark upon
them. . . .

My own personal debt to this small college that then was is
incalculable. It confirmed and increased that love for Greek and
Latin literature which had been first inspired by my father in
private lessons and later nourished by Dr. Bridges and Dr.
Parkin at the Collegiate School of Fredericton. Greek, Latin
and English Literature (but Homer and Milton especially) were
the formative influences to which I have chiefly owed whatever
there may be of excellence, if any, in my own literary output.
In the intimate teaching of this small college stress was laid
upon the beauty and wisdom of these literatures rather than
upon the dry bones of grammar and rhetoric which, of necessity, underlay them. In other words, the teaching I received was
inspirational before it was mechanical.

In these few lines I am paying grateful tribute not by any
means to small colleges in general but to this small college
as I experienced it. And my appreciation of this small college
that was does not in the least conflict with my admiration of,
and my unbounded aspiration for, the great and distinguished
University which it is coming to be.

Who were the "president and four professors" to whom
Roberts refers? The president was still William Brydone Jack,
professor of Mathematics, Natural Philosophy and Astronomy.
Jack, a native of Dumfriesshire, had such a brilliant record in

mathematics and physics at St. Andrews that, on his graduation as Master of Arts in 1840, he was offered the professorship of physics at New College, Manchester, as successor to the great physicist, Dr. John Dalton. He chose rather to come to the tiny King's College, Fredericton, where he lectured for forty-five years and from 1861 to 1885 served as president. He was especially interested in astronomy, and was among the first to make use of telegraphy in determining longitude. His work in this connection was of great service to Sir William Logan in his construction of the geological map of Canada.

The professor of Chemistry and Natural Science was Loring Woart Bailey, grandfather of the present Dean of Arts at U.N.B., Dr. Alfred G. Bailey. Loring Bailey was a member of the famous class of '59 at Harvard, and had Charles W. Eliot as his tutor in mathematics, Louis Agassiz as his instructor in biology, and Longfellow as his professor of modern literature. After graduating from Harvard, Bailey was appointed an assistant in the Department of Chemistry under Professor Josiah P. Cooke; and from Harvard he came directly to Fredericton, where he remained for over half a century. In his lifetime he published scores of scientific papers, and he was at various times offered professorships at Bowdoin, Colby, Vassar, and McGill.

The professor of English Language and Literature and Mental and Moral Philosophy in Roberts' time was Thomas Harrison. Harrison was a native of Sheffield, New Brunswick, who for some reason had passed up the nearby provincial university to attend Trinity College, Dublin. There he compiled a brilliant academic record, graduating with honours in Mathematics and Natural Philosophy. When in 1885 he succeeded Jack in the presidency of U.N.B., Harrison took over the lecturing in Mathematics. Of his ability to teach English we know nothing directly: we can only guess that it was of a high order from this comment in the *University Monthly* of February, 1883:

The Argosy [the student newspaper at Mount Allison University] contains an article against the want of an English course at Sackville. If the students of Sackville attain their object they will look back upon the days spent in the study of English literature as among the most interesting and most profitable of their college course. It is the study above all others in the

University of New Brunswick in which students take an interest. In this department more students find an incentive to study than in any other branch of the course.

The professor of Classical Literature and History was George Eulas Foster, to whom I have already referred. Another native of New Brunswick, he graduated from the provincial university in 1867, taught school for a few years, and in 1872-1873 studied at Edinburgh and Heidelberg. At Edinburgh he had Sellar as his professor of Latin, Blackie as his professor of Greek, and Masson as his professor of English. Under Masson he won a much-coveted prize in English Literature. In September, 1873, Foster returned to Fredericton as professor of classics in U.N.B. He was soon greatly in demand as a public lecturer, and his skill in this respect took him, after six years, into politics. For over twenty years he was a member of the Federal Cabinet; he was on several occasions acting Prime Minister of Canada; he was Canada's representative at the Peace Conference and at the League of Nations; and his reputation for oratory was such that he was frequently called "the Demosthenes of Canada."

Of the fourth professor, Francis Philibert Rivet, professor of French Language and Literature, I have been able to discover nothing. But what I have said of the four men above indicates beyond serious doubt, I believe, that the professors under whom Roberts studied at the University of New Brunswick were scholars of real distinction. They represented between them the universities of St. Andrew's, Trinity College, Dublin, Harvard, Heidelberg, and Edinburgh, and at all these great international centres of learning they had acquitted themselves brilliantly. They served a small provincial university, but they were far from being provincial mediocrities themselves. *The University Monthly* was probably quite correct when, in reply to charges of weakness made by Toronto's *Varsity*, it stated flatly, "A more capable staff of instructors is not to be found in any other institution of a like nature in Canada."[15]

Before leaving this subject of Robert's academic tradition, I should like to point out that the Roberts tradition at the University of New Brunswick is still very much alive. All of his books, and many of his letters and manuscripts, are preserved

---

[15]*Op. cit.*, April, 1885.

in the University Library; his works have been the subject of two M.A. theses in recent years; his portrait hangs in the reading room of the library and was the subject of a recent poem by Elizabeth Brewster; a monument to Roberts, Carman, and Sherman stands on the campus in front of the old Arts Building; and there was recently established the Roberts Prize for the best short story submitted each year by a student of the university.

In June of 1883 Charles G. D. Roberts, a young man of only twenty-three, delivered the Alumni Oration at his alma mater. His title was "The Beginnings of Canadian Literature," and the few names he was able to educe—Charles Heavysege, John Reade, John Hunter Duvar, C. P. Mulvaney, "Fidelis" and "Seranus" in poetry, for example—are evidence of the virtual vacuum which he had set himself to fill. In assessing Roberts' place in the national tradition, it is only proper to remind ourselves that when he came on the scene he was virtually alone. Roberts' contemporaries were aware of this. Archibald Lampman wrote:

Almost all the verse-writing published in Canada before the appearance of *Orion* was of a more or less barbarous character. The drama of *Saul* by Charles Heavysege and some of Heavysege's sonnets are about the only exceptions which can be made to this statement. Mr. Roberts was the first Canadian writer in verse who united a strong original genius with a high degree of culture and an acute literary judgment. He was the first to produce a style strongly individual in tone, and founded on the study of the best writers.[16]

There is no denying Roberts' importance in our literary history. He it was above all others who started the Group of the Sixties, and within a decade of the date of his Alumni Oration made Canadian poetry known and respected throughout the English-speaking world.

By saying this I do not mean to imply that Roberts was better than Carman, or Lampman, or Scott. I deprecate all attempts to rank these four poets. There was no rivalry between them: in all the letters and critical articles of the four that I have

---

[16]"Two Canadian Poets: A Lecture by Archibald Lampman," *University of Toronto Quarterly*, XIII: 411 (July, 1944).

188/Essays in Canadian Criticism

read I have never found the slightest evidence of jealousy among them. They all agreed that Roberts was their leader, in the sense that he first published his poems in the great magazines of North America and in book form, but he was the first among equals. We must, I think, consider the Confederation Group as a group, noting differences between them, but not seeking to select one or two as "masters" and discussing the others as also-rans. All four of them had in common the great distinction that, in contrast with all the colonial versifiers who had preceded them, they looked clearsightedly at the Canadian landscape and the Canadian people. They shared the further distinction that they took the craft of poetry seriously. They all wrote a quantity of mediocre verse, but they all wrote a few poems which were as different from the verse of Sangster and Mair and Duvar as chalk is from cheese. To suggest, as some recent critics have, that anthologies of Canadian verse should virtually begin with Dr. Pratt is absurd. I yield to no one in my admiration for Dr. Pratt, but to begin the study of Canadian poetry with him would be to ignore some of the finest poems we have yet produced or are likely to produce for many decades. Surely only prejudice or ignorance could lead anyone seriously to assert that we should jettison Carman's "Low Tide on Grand Pré," Duncan Campbell Scott's "Piper of Arll," Lampman's "Heat," or Roberts' "Tantramar Revisited."

In calling this group the Confederation Poets, as Malcolm Ross has done in his recent, admirable selection of their work in the New Canadian Library, we are drawing attention to an important part of their inspiration: the new national feeling that resulted from the union of the provinces in 1867. As a boy, Roberts derived a sense of national pride from his father. Miss Pomeroy tells us:

From the first suggestion of Confederation his father had been an ardent supporter of the idea, and had talked about it to his young son. Never did the boy forget his father's enthusiasm when the Union was about to be achieved. Standing out clearly in his mind was a drive through the Dorchester Woods in the early summer of 1867, when his father expatiated on the great event of that time, dwelling particularly upon the leaders' vision which was responsible for the Union, and upon their faith in its ultimate outcome, a great united Canada "which would stretch from sea to sea." Soon Dorchester Church came into view, but before dismissing the subject, the Rector added, "In the building of this young nation I hope my son will grow up to play his full part. . . ."[17]

Charles Roberts never lost this sense of national purpose. In his Alumni Oration he urged upon the university a more conscious concern with Canadian life and Canadian literature: "Where do we want a more vivid realization of the fact that we have a country, and are making a nation; that we have a history, and are making a literature; that we have a heroic past, and are making ready for a future that shall not be inglorious? In our universities, if they would not lose their birthright." His poem "Canada" expresses, if somewhat too rhetorically, his faith in Canada's destiny, and his *History of Canada* is full of pride in Canada's past and of high hopes for Canada's future.

But the most permanently valuable expressions of Roberts' love of country were not these direct ones, but the stories and above all the poems in which this love was given indirect expression. This brings us, rather belatedly perhaps, to Roberts' actual writings. We have seen the traditions that shaped him— a scholarly family, a beautiful city and province, a group of inspired teachers, an outburst of national excitement—now we must ask whether the results of all these influences were of any permanent value.

Of Roberts' prose, I do not intend to say much. Roberts himself said that he lived *by* prose *for* poetry, and there is in his prose a commercial, journalistic quality that is quite lacking from the best of his verse. His *History of Canada* (1897) has an excellent treatment of the early part of our story, an adequate account of the early nineteenth century, a scrappy and desultory account of the decades after Confederation, and a somewhat rhetorical conclusion in which Roberts weighs the respective advantages of Annexation, Independence, and Imperial Federation and comes out in favour of the last. I could not conscientiously recommend anyone to read the whole book today, rather than, say, the histories of Creighton and Lower, but I do think that some of his descriptions of early episodes in our history might be included in school textbooks. Indeed, there is a certain

---

[17]*Sir Charles G. D. Roberts, A Biography*, by Elsie M. Pomeroy (Toronto: The Ryerson Press, 1943), p. 10.

juvenile quality about most of Roberts' prose. His historical novels, such as *The Forge in the Forest* (1896), *A Sister to Evangeline* (1898), *Barbara Ladd* (1902), and *The Prisoner of Mademoiselle* (1904), are costume melodramas that might still enliven the imaginations of teen-age boys, but have little appeal to the mature reader. Even his more serious novels, such as *The Heart of the Ancient Wood* (1900) and *In the Morning of Time* (1919), which were Roberts' own favourites and were declared by Pelham Edgar to be of "enduring fascination," seem merely quaint today.

Only the short stories among his prose, I believe, have any chance of permanent survival. And even here, we must eliminate all those stories which deal with human, as distinct from animal, life. The stories of human life that cause one to hesitate before dismissing them—such, for example, as "The Perdu" or "The Blackwater Pot"—make their claim to attention by their accuracy and suggestiveness of natural description: but their characters are so stereotyped, so one-dimensional, that, rather reluctantly, one has to discard them. Roberts had literally no power of creating credible human beings. In the best of the animal stories, however, this weakness is not apparent, and here the brilliantly accurate descriptions and compelling atmospheric effects are sufficient. Stories such as "The Young Ravens That Call Upon Him" and "The Heron in the Reeds" have a kind of classic simplicity which makes them, within their admittedly narrow limits, virtually invulnerable. "The Young Ravens That Call Upon Him" especially, with its camera-eye technique, its subtlety of atmospheric detail, its structural juxtaposition of eagle and ewe, and its constant restraint of utterance, strikes me as a classic. The final two paragraphs, in which the repose of the eagles is contrasted with the agony of the ewe whose lamb the eagle has snatched away, are worthy of reading as an example of what Roberts could do in stories of this sort:

In the nest of the eagles there was content. The pain of their hunger appeased, the nestlings lay dozing in the sun, the neck of one resting across the back of the other. The triumphant male sat erect upon his perch, staring out over the splendid world that displayed itself beneath him. Now and again he half lifted his wings and screamed joyously at the sun. The mother bird, perched upon a limb on the edge of the nest, busily rearranged her plumage. At times she stooped her head into the nest to utter over her sleeping eaglets a soft chuckling noise, which seemed to come from the bottom of her throat.

But hither and thither over the round bleak hill wandered the ewe, calling for her lamb, unmindful of the flock, which had been moved to other pastures.

What really captures our interest in these animal stories, apart from their realistic portrayal of the cruelty and terror which dominate the natural world, is their accuracy of observation and their strong sense of design. These, too, are the best qualities of Roberts' poetry. Much nonsense has been talked about "mere nature description" in poetry, as if anyone with the time and the will could write it. The fact is that really to see a scene, and still more the ability clearly to record one's observations, is a very rare capacity indeed. Most of us go through life with our eyes half closed, and it is the poet and the painter who do our seeing for us. Even poets, as a reading of Goldsmith, Sangster and Mair will indicate, have a tendency to see a scene through the eyes of other poets, rather than through their own. When Roberts' "Tantramar Revisited" appeared in *The Week* in 1883, it was the first poem published in Canada to see a part of the Canadian landscape as it really was:

Skirting the sunbright uplands stretches a riband of meadow,
Shorn of the labouring grass, bulwarked well from the sea,
Fenced on its seaward border with long clay dikes from the
    turbid
Surge and flow of the tides vexing the Westmoreland shores.
Yonder, toward the left, lie broad the Westmoreland marshes,—
Miles on miles they extend, level, and grassy, and dim,
Clear from the long red sweep of flats to the sky in the distance,
Save for the outlying heights, green-rampired Cumberland
    Point;
Miles on miles outrolled, and the river-channels divide them,—
Miles on miles of green, barred by the hurtling gusts.

Miles on miles beyond the tawny bay is Minudie,
There are the low blue hills; villages gleam at their feet.
Nearer a white sail shines across the water, and nearer
Still are the slim, grey masts of fishing boats dry on the flats,
Ah, how well I remember those wide red flats, above tide-mark,
Pale with scurf of the salt, seamed and baked in the sun!

Well I remember the piles of blocks and ropes, and the net-reels
Wound with the beaded nets, dripping and dark from the sea!
Now at this season the nets are unwound; they hang from the
    rafters
Over the fresh-stowed hay in upland barns, and the wind
Blows all day through the chinks, with the streaks of sunlight,
    and sways them
Softly at will; or they lie heaped in the gloom of a loft.

That is descriptive poetry of a high order. The epithets are not the conventional "verdants" and "pensives" of Sangster, but each has been chosen deliberately to suggest the exact nature of the scene before the poet's eyes. "Labouring," for example, is calculated exactly to summon up the picture of that long marsh grass of the Tantramar country, which is constantly in slow, troubled motion from the winds that blow off the bay. "Turbid" catches exactly the twisting, muddy tumult of the incoming Fundy tide, stirring up the red mud of the flats and river channels. "Barred by the hurtling gusts" was a phrase the accuracy of which I did not appreciate until I had seen the Tantramar marshes and the peculiar way in which gusts of wind, by bending the grasses over in parallel strips, do cause a series of darker bars of colour to move over the meadows.

But of course it is not merely the accuracy of the individual details that distinguishes this poem. There is also the way in which these details are arranged into a series of patterns or designs, and these designs in turn into the structure of the whole poem. The poem begins with a reference to the poet's own losses at the hands of time, and then turns to the Tantramar, which he declares to be unchanged. He then describes the Tantramar scene from his vantage point on a hill-top, beginning with the road that leads down to the plains beside the sea, the houses and orchards that dot them, the marshes that extend along the edge of the bay, and on to the distant blue hills on the far shore: leading one's eye from the near scene to the far horizon. Then he begins to reverse the process: the white sail brings us back across the bay, the fishing boats and nets bring us back to the mud flats at the water's edge, fresh-stowed hay suggests the meadows and the farms, and so on. Finally, he completes the design by bringing our attention back to himself, and his awareness that even here, if he looked closely, he would find the hands of chance and change at work.

Another distinctive element in the poem is its metrical ingenuity. The poem is written in the classical elegiac metre, in alternate dactylic hexameters and pentameters which had been recently employed by Clough, Arnold and Longfellow. It was probably Longfellow's *Evangeline* that provided Roberts with his metrical model, but the charge of derivativeness has little weight if, as I believe is the case here, the imitation surpasses the model. Here are a few lines from *Evangeline*:

Far in the West there lies a desert land, where the mountains
Lift, through perpetual snows, their lofty and luminous
    summits.
Down from their jagged, deep ravines, where the gorge, like a
    gateway,
Opens a passage rude to the wheels of the emigrant's wagon,
Westward the Oregon flows and the Walleway and Owyhee.
Eastward, with devious course, among the Wind-river
    Mountains,
Through the Sweet-water Valley precipitate leaps the Nebraska.

Surely these lines are relatively clumsy and cumbrous and monotonous. They show little of Roberts' power to modulate the movement of the rhythm to suit the material with which he is dealing. Notice, for example, how Roberts, in the passage we have already quoted, uses the first long, unpunctuated line "Skirting the sunbright uplands stretches a riband of meadow," with its repeated "r's" and its short vowels, to suggest length and light, and then breaks the next line, "Shorn of the labouring grass, bulwarked well from the sea," in half to give, first, the effect of the short, clipped grass and, second, the effect of the dike blocking the sea. The music and rhythm of Roberts' poem has a quality which is all his own. It is not the cumbrous, sing-songy music of Longfellow, nor the soft, sad, austere music of Arnold, nor the lilting melody of Carman, nor the slow, wistful, meditative music of much of Lampman: it is a grave, masculine, striding song, a trifle heavy perhaps, at moments a little bit too deliberate, but on the whole striking a very happy balance between over-facility and awkwardness. A more facile rhythm would have been quite inappropriate to the somewhat harsh and forbidding Tantramar country, a more hesitant one would not have captured the flow of wind over grass and sea.

Many of the qualities found in "Tantramar Revisited" occur again in the best of Roberts' sonnets. Here, for example, is "The Potato Harvest":

> A high bare field, brown from the plough, and borne
>   Aslant from sunset; amber wastes of sky
>   Washing the ridge; a clamour of crows that fly
> In from the wide flats where the spent tides mourn
> To yon their rocking roosts in pines wind-torn;
>   A line of grey snake-fence, that zigzags by
>   A pond and cattle; from the homestead nigh
> The long deep summonings of the supper horn.
> Black on the ridge, against that lonely flush,
>   A cart, and stoop-necked oxen; ranged beside,
>   Some barrels; and the day-worn harvest-folk,
> Here, emptying their baskets, jar the hush
>   With hollow thunders. Down the dusk hillside
>   Lumbers the wain; and day fades out like smoke.

In that sonnet the painterly quality in Roberts is very evident: the colours are all exactly specified, and the eye is led from the hill and sky by the crows and the snake fence to the farmstead in the octave, and again from the hill to the house by the wagon in the sestet. The whole picture has the clarity and homely charm of a Breughel, together with Breughel's strength and firmness of structure. But complementing the pictorial pattern is a pattern of sounds: the clamour of the crows, the mourn of the tides, and the comforting call of the supper horn in the octave are balanced by the thunder of the potatoes into the barrels and the lumbering noise of the homecoming wagon in the sestet. A moment of activity has been fully captured; and the sense of the completion of a cycle is suggested by the beautiful closing phrase, "and day fades out like smoke."

There are a dozen such sonnets in which Roberts catches with loving and yet quite unsentimental fidelity the rural life and landscape of the Maritime Provinces. Most of them are to be found in what is undoubtedly his finest volume, *Songs of the Common Day* (1893). In that volume he had the happy inspiration of recording the procession of the seasons in his native environment in a sonnet sequence. One wonders what source those critics who dismiss Roberts' poetry as completely derivative would educe for this sonnet sequence. Sonnet sequences aplenty were found in Elizabethan England, and Rossetti's *House of Life* provided a more recent example: but these sonnet sequences dealt with love, not with the humble occupations of everyday life. The idea of the celebration of rustic life probably came to him from Virgil, but the idea of celebrating it in a series of sonnets seems to have been original.

I am so fond of Roberts' sonnets of everyday life that I am tempted to linger over them. In justice to him, however, I must draw your attention to others of his poems which I feel deserve a place in our living tradition. He wrote in "Marsyas" a fine poem on a classical theme, and in "Grey Rocks and Greyer Sea," "Epitaph for a Sailor Buried Ashore," "Epitaph for a Husbandman," and above all in "Ave" a group of moving elegies. The elegy, with its quiet dignity of tone, was peculiarly well suited to Roberts' talent. I am less fond of his mystical poems, which have been widely praised but which seem to me vague and rhetorical. "In the Wide Awe and Wisdom of the Night" is probably the best of them, and even it concludes with a rhetorical flourish which is more remarkable for its sound than its sense:

> And knew the Universe of no such span
> As the august infinitude of Man.

I do not think that Roberts' directly patriotic poems will survive either: one can admire their sincerity, admit that they once played their part in stimulating a slowly developing sense of Canadian nationhood, and yet believe that they are too pontifical, too solemnly vainglorious, to suit the modern temper. I should prefer, before concluding, to quote one or two relatively unknown poems by Roberts that seem to me to have qualities worth preserving. "The Brook in February" has a child-like innocence which I find much more attractive than Roberts' more pretentious philosophical and political verses:

> A snowy path for squirrel and fox,
>   It winds between the wintry firs.
> Snow-muffled are its iron rocks,
>   And o'er its stillness nothing stirs.

> But low, bend low a listening ear!
>> Beneath the mask of moveless white
> A babbling whisper you shall hear
>> Of birds and blossoms, leaves and light.

"Monition," in contrast, is a deft little poem of warning, and evokes very briefly and suggestively a sense of doom:

> A faint wind, blowing from World's End,
>> Made strange the city street.
> A strange sound mingled in the fall
>> Of the familiar feet.
>
> Something unseen whirled with the leaves
>> To tap on door and sill.
> Something unknown went whispering by
>> Even when the wind was still.
>
> And men looked up with startled eyes
>> And hurried on their way,
> As if they had been called, and told
>> How brief their day.

There is not time for "The Iceberg," the minor masterpiece of Roberts' later life, but I can find a moment for one of my own favourites, "Philander's Song," which reminds us that Roberts at heart was not a solemn man, for all his sense of dedication, but a gay lover of life and love:

> I sat and read Anacreon.
>> Moved by the gay, delicious measure
> I mused that lips were made for love,
>> And love to charm a poet's leisure.
>
> And as I mused a maid came by
>> With something in her look that caught me.
> Forgotten was Anacreon's line,
>> But not the lesson he had taught me.

It was almost exactly seventy years ago, on the evening of February 19, 1891, in a public lecture in this city of Ottawa, that Archibald Lampman paid his personal tribute to Roberts' influence. It is a famous and oft-quoted passage, but the coincidence of time and circumstance emboldens me to quote it yet again:

As regards Mr. Roberts' work, I have always had a personal feeling which perhaps induces me to place a higher estimate upon it in some respects than my hearers will care to accept. To most younger Canadians who are interested in literature, especially those who have written themselves, Mr. Roberts occupies a peculiar position. They are accustomed to look up to him as in some sort the founder of a school, the originator of a new era in our poetic activity. I hope my hearers will pardon me, if I go out of my way to illustrate this fact by describing the effect Mr. Roberts' poems produced upon me when I first met with them.

It was almost ten years ago, and I was very young, an undergraduate at college. One May evening somebody lent me *Orion and Other Poems,* then recently published. Like most of the young fellows about me I had been under the depressing conviction that we were situated hopelessly on the outskirts of civilization, where no art and no literature could be, and that it was useless to expect that anything great could be done by any of our companions, still more useless to expect that we could do it ourselves. I sat up all night reading and re-reading *Orion* in a state of the wildest excitement, and when I went to bed I could not sleep. It seemed to me a wonderful thing that such work could be done by a Canadian, by a young man, one of ourselves. It was like a voice from some new paradise of art calling to us to be up and doing. A little after sunrise I got up and went out into the college grounds. The air, I remember, was full of the odour and cool sunshine of the spring morning. The dew was thick upon the grass. All the birds of our Maytime seemed to be singing in the oaks, and there were even a few adder-tongues and trilliums still blossoming on the slope of the little ravine. But everything was transfigured for me beyond description, bathed in an old-world radiance of beauty [by] the magic of the lines that were sounding in my ears, those divine verses, as they seemed to me, with their Tennyson-like richness and strange, earth-loving, Greekish flavour. I have never forgotten that morning, and its influence has always remained with me.[18]

---

[18]Reprinted in *University of Toronto Quarterly,* XIII: p. 410 (July, 1944).

Fifty years later, Professor Pelham Edgar wrote:

The future will recognize even more than we are willing to do
that Roberts was a pivotal figure, a musical hinge around which
our poetry first began to revolve. Our younger poets of today
may not recognize their debt, for it is the time-honoured privi-
lege of youth to repudiate its own ancestry and overleap the
generations; but in the long perspective of history the pervasive
quality of Roberts' influence will be recognized at its true
importance.[19]

For my own part, I place myself with Lampman and Edgar
rather than with those more recent critics who would consign
Roberts to the New Brunswick Museum. The type of poetry he
wrote is out of vogue today, but vogues in poetry change almost
as quickly and quite as surely as vogues in women's hats. He
made us aware of the poetic possibilities in our own scenery
and in our own customs; he wrote always in honesty and sincerity and with high purpose; he was himself a craftsman and
he inspired others to be craftsmen; from first to last he encouraged the young poets around him, with no sense of envy or
rivalry and with no thought of reward. I have not made extravagant claims for his literary merit, nor have I gone out of
my way to emphasize his weaknesses. He did have many weaknesses; in particular, as if he felt that single-handedly he must
create Canadian literature in all its branches, he tried to do
too much, became a kind of literary jack-of-all-trades. But by
virtue of his influence on others, and by virtue of the few truly
excellent poems he himself wrote, he certainly deserves a place
in our living tradition.

---

[19]*University of Toronto Quarterly*, XIII: p. 117 (October, 1943).

Canadian Literature in the Fifties*

LET me begin with a word of apology—and a word of reproach. It is far too early to assess the literature of the last decade, and I apologize for my temerity in attempting it. What I say must be tentative in the extreme, and I am sure that I shall live to regret it. But you set me the task—and I must reproach you for doing so. If I mislead you, it is not my fault but yours.

When I began to think about Canadian literature of the nineteen-fifties my opinion was that it was merely a continuation of the literature of the forties, with a few more or less interesting modifications. Further study has convinced me that the decade marked a watershed in our literary history. In it many of the writers and tendencies that had dominated the scene for roughly a quarter of a century came to an end, and an almost entirely new generation of writers came to the fore. This was equally true in all the major departments of our writing— in poetry, fiction, criticism, biography, and the essay. Only the drama, that orphan in the Canadian storm, remained virtually static.

To consider first that form—poetry—in which our literary imagination has always most significantly expressed itself, the poets who dominated the thirties and forties in Canada were E. J. Pratt, A. J. M. Smith, A. M. Klein, F. R. Scott, Leo Kennedy, Robert Finch, Earle Birney, P. K. Page, Patrick Anderson, and Anne Marriott. Now most of these poets did publish one volume of verse in the fifties, but in most cases it came rather nearer the beginning than the end of the decade, it marked a decline rather than an advance in their work, and

*An address delivered at a symposium at Bishop's University, March 18, 1961.

199

in some cases it gave every indication of being their last. Pratt's *Towards the Last Spike* appeared as early as 1952; although it had some merits it did not approach the level of his best work; and as Pratt is now almost eighty years old and in poor health it is unlikely that he will publish a further volume. A. J. M. Smith's *A Sort of Ecstasy* appeared in 1954; almost without exception the best poems in it were reprinted from his 1943 publication, *News of the Phoenix*; and the paucity of poems which Smith has subsequently published in magazines suggests that the anthologist and the critic have largely submerged the poet. A. M. Klein published no poetry at all in the decade and seems to have lapsed, most unfortunately, into silence. F. R. Scott is the only poet of the group who published as many as two volumes of verse in the decade—*Events and Signals* in 1954 and *The Eye of the Needle* in 1957—but the first of these only barely sustained the level of his earlier volume, *Overture* (1945), and the second consisted almost entirely of reprints. Knowing Scott's energy at first hand, I should be the last to write him off as a poet, but I shall be pleasantly surprised if his future output shows any significant development. Although I had some correspondence in 1953 with Leo Kennedy about a possible new book of verse by him, the book has never appeared, and I assume that he has abandoned the craft. Robert Finch's only book of verse, *The Strength of the Hills*, appeared in 1948, and since that time he does not seem even to have published verse in the magazines. The occasional piece of magazine verse by Earle Birney does still appear, but his last volume appeared in 1952 and all indications are that his major preoccupations are now prose fiction and scholarship.[1] P. K. Page published *The Metal and the Flower* in 1954; some critics regarded it as an advance over her previous work, but my feeling was that it was a relatively spiritless imitation thereof; this suspicion has been confirmed by Miss Page's subsequent desertion of poetry for painting. Patrick Anderson, whose dazzling poetry lit up our literary sky in the war and immediate postwar years, made a single appearance in the decade in 1953 with *The Colour as Naked*, but has since become a writer of prose travelogues. Another poet who was well known in the thirties and forties,

---

[1]Here, of course, time has proved me quite wrong. Birney has published two excellent books of verse in the sixties. [Editorial note, 1969]

Anne Marriott of *The Wind our Enemy* (1939), also lapsed into virtual silence in the fifties.

Actually this list of poets who gave up the craft in the fifties could be augmented. Alfred G. Bailey, whose *Border River* was one of the most accomplished and distinctive books of 1952, has been too preoccupied by administrative duties at the University of New Brunswick to write any poetry in recent years; and a similar fate seems to have overcome Roy Daniells, author of *Deeper into the Forest* (1948), at the University of British Columbia. Charles Bruce is another poet whose Muse seem to have deserted him: since *The Mulgrave Road* in 1951 he has turned his attention to fiction. A similar switch from poetry to prose has been made by Ronald Hambleton, whose *Object and Event* appeared in 1953: his only recent publication has been the novel *Every Man Is an Island* (1959). James Wreford is another poet who had some reputation in the forties but who gave up the craft: he has not been heard from since 1950, when he published *Of Time and the Lover*.

With so many poets giving up poetry, it would seem that Canadian verse in the fifties went into a period of decline. Such, fortunately, was not the case, partly because a few poets who had begun to write in the forties sustained or augmented their reputations in the fifties, and more particularly because a whole new generation of poets made its appearance.

In the ranks of those who sustained or augmented their reputations, we may number Irving Layton, Miriam Waddington, James Reaney, Dorothy Livesay, Raymond Souster, and Louis Dudek. Irving Layton is certainly the poet who made the most dramatic impact in the decade. Known only as a minor figure in the Montreal Group in the forties, he published in the fifties no less than twelve volumes of verse, and established himself as the leading poetic voice of the country. His work steadily advanced in depth, scope, and skill, and his *Red Carpet for the Sun* (1959) was not only the best single volume of verse published in Canada during the decade but also probably the best published in English anywhere. The achievements of the others were less spectacular but still satisfying. Miriam Waddington's *The Second Silence* (1955) and *The Season's Lovers* (1958) maintained the acute social observation and intelligent compassion of her earlier work, and added a new dexterity of technique and a greater maturity of feeling. James Reaney, whose *Red Heart* was such an exciting first book of verse in 1949, was the most exigent of the group, publishing only the single volume, *A Suit of Nettles*, in 1958. Opinion is divided about this book—Northrop Frye and others praised it extravagantly, and it won the Governor-General's Award, whereas Louis Dudek called it "a crashing disappointment"—but there is no disputing the fact that, for good or ill, it is unforgettable. I find parts of it irritating, parts of it dull, and parts of it brilliantly comic. Of all the Canadian poets, Reaney seems to me to have the most distinctive angle of vision—the vision of the terrible child who delights in turning things inside-out and upside-down.

A less exciting but more consistent poet is Raymond Souster. Entirely unaffected by the new cult of mythopeia in the academies, he has gone on etching his sadly comic or comically sad engravings of the modern urban scene. He published five books in the decade, and gives every indication of continuing to write in the same quiet but oddly fascinating vein for several decades to come. Without the energy of Layton or the wit of Reaney, he has an honesty and sincerity that may well outlast their more spectacular talents. His *Selected Poems* (1956) belongs in any selection of the ten most memorable Canadian books of verse of the decade.

Louis Dudek began the fifties as the leader of this group of "proletarian" poets which included Layton and Souster; by the end of the decade his companions had outdistanced him in poetry, although he had to some extent compensated for this decline by his increasingly significant literary criticism. He published seven books of verse, but the successive books did not develop significantly in either technique or philosophy. His great temptation is facility, and in his two poetic travelogues, *Europe* (1955) and *En Mexico* (1958) this fault betrayed him into long passages of dull meditation. His poetic gift seemed increasingly to define itself as a capacity for ironic social comment and literary parody, as seen in his *Laughing Stalks* (1958).

It is not altogether clear whether Dorothy Livesay belongs in this group of poets who sustained their reputations in the fifties, or in the group who virtually abandoned poetry in the decade. Apart from two small chapbooks published in 1950 and 1955, her claim to belong in the more favourable grouping must be based on her *Selected Poems*, published in 1957. The later poems in this book seemed to indicate a capacity for growth beyond the rather shrill left-wing poems which brought her fame in the thirties, but she has published very little since 1957, and her work with the United Nations in Paris and elsewhere may preclude the writing of more verse.

A more secure hope for Canadian poetry can, however, be based upon the early work of the many new poets who made their appearance in the fifties. For the first time in Canadian literary history, there has been no interregnum between the poetic generations. The new names are so numerous that a mere listing of them could not fail to lead to confusion. Attempts to group poets into "schools" are notoriously danger-ous, and not particularly useful if the schools themselves are numerous. In a recent heroic but rather futile attempt at such grouping, Louis Dudek came up with no less than seven schools: the inactive older poets, the active older poets, the English Traditionalists, the Migrants, the Survivors of the Forties, Les Jeunes of Yesterday, and Les Jeunes of Today. I think I can do a little better than that, reducing the multitude to three main schools and a few loose fish.

The first and most vocal school is that of the mythopoeic poets, the school of Reaney. This group has the advantage of having Northrop Frye as its godfather and sponsor, and of being made up mainly of academics. This latter point may not seem to be an advantage, until one realizes that almost all the channels of literary communication in this country are con-trolled by the academics. These advantages have led, in my opinion, to an over-valuation of this group of poets. Their work at its best is undeniably clever, sophisticated, and brilliant as all get-out—but at its worst it is too self-consciously literary and coy. The chief figure in this group, of course, apart from Reaney himself, is Jay Macpherson, whose *The Boatman* (1957) was, next to Layton's *Red Carpet*, undeniably the most exciting single book of verse in the decade. Miss Macpherson's verse has elegance, wit, allusiveness, technical virtuosity, and charm, as well as enough mythological references and cross-references to sink any ship that did not have such a skilful boatman to handle it. But at the same time one cannot avoid the nagging suspicion that this is literature about literature rather than literature about life. How deep are the roots of this poetry in Miss Mac-pherson's own experience? Has she ever gone to bed with a snake?

One feels similar qualms about the other members of the

group: Anne Wilkinson, Eli Mandel, Wilfred Watson, Daryl Hine, and Margaret Avison. And one's qualms are by no means quieted by several of the recent utterances of Mr. Reaney, who seems to come dangerously close to saying that the way to write a poem is to pick a myth at random and weave a garland of verse around it. Is not this just a new version of the fallacy Henry James found in George Eliot's novels—that they were written not out of observation but out of a desire to preach a moral homily?

Much as I admire Frye as a critic and Reaney as a poet, I must say that there is an atmosphere of mutual admiration about their recent utterances that I find slightly suffocating. Mr. Reaney, for instance, wrote as follows in a recent issue of *Poetry* (Chicago): "Besides E. J. Pratt the one even greater literary fact in the Canadian poetic landscape is the criticism of Northrop Frye . . . Up in Canada the general reaction on the part of poets . . . is that here is something that can completely change your life [Reaney seems to have undergone the change of life frequently in recent years—he talks about having his life changed in almost every review he writes], here is a vision that maps out for the poet a symbolic language with the precision with which it was once mapped out for him by the Renaissance mythographers . . . One can hardly be a poet in Canada without feeling the two books *Fearful Symmetry* and *Anatomy of Criticism* brooding over one's literary programme. In each book there are literally hundreds of designs for poems, *all from literature itself*, but never seen with such clarity before. Instead of groping his way from lyric to lyric [as Donne did, or Yeats, or Hardy?] here at last the poet can see what fields there are to plow and what to sow . . . So this is what the Canadian literary landscape looks like to me: a giant critical focus with some mythopoeic poets trying to live up to it." Well, I must confess that I am temperamentally too irreverent to take that kind of thing altogether seriously, especially when I turn to Frye's criticism in "Letters in Canada" and read "I have glanced at the critical issues raised by *The Boatman* because it seems to me a conspicuous example of a tendency that I have seen growing since I began this survey eight years ago. With the proviso that 'professional' in this context has nothing to do with earning a living [*that's* fortunate], the younger Canadian poets have become steadily more professional in the last few years, more concerned with poetry as a craft with its own traditions and discipline . . . The more amateurish approach which tries to write up emotional experiences as they arise in life or memory has given way to an emphasis on the formal elements of poetry, on myth, metaphor, symbol, image, even metrics."

This is a large subject, and I have space for only two brief comments. The first is that if poetry is now being led by criticism, rather than vice versa, I suspect that it is true for the first time in English literary history and for that very reason a rather dubious proceeding. The poets who were writing when Dr. Johnson was at the height of his reputation were gradually undermining the very neo-classical critical structure which he was busily erecting, Hardy, Housman, and Yeats wrote their early poetry without reference to the critical theories of Matthew Arnold, and when T. S. Eliot was advocating the poetry of impersonality young Dylan Thomas was writing some of the most intensely subjective verse of all time. My second observation is that if to write poetry out of one's own emotional experience rather than out of books of literary criticism is an amateurish proceeding, there have been some excellent amateur poets over the centuries. Yeats, for example, knew a great deal about mythology, but almost every single one of his poems can be related to some crisis in his own life or in the life of his native Ireland. Yeats uses myth to illuminate and universalize his own experiences, but the basic stuff of his poetry is what in memorable phrase he calls the foul rag and bone shop of his heart.

The other two schools of contemporary Canadian poetry have in common a determination to make their poetry out of the life about them, although they may use myth as Yeats does to give that life shape and meaning. The schools to which I refer may, for the sake of convenience, be labelled the School of Layton and the Fiddlehead School. These two schools are differentiated one from the other in that the Layton (or Montreal) School writes primarily of an urban environment, usually though not always in an aggressively modern idiom and style. The Layton School includes the holdovers Layton, Dudek, and Souster, plus Alfred Purdy, Henry Moscovitch, Leonard Cohen (the most promising of the lot, apart from Layton himself), Milton Acorn, George Ellenbogan, and an assortment of still younger poets in and about McGill and Sir George Williams. The Fiddlehead School, which has found a focus since 1945 in *The Fiddlehead* magazine at the University of New Brunswick, includes Fred Cogswell, Elizabeth Brewster, Robert Rogers, Alden Nowlan (who in his mid-twenties is probably the most promising of *this* group), Robert Gibbs (a young Saint John poet who has been quite undeservedly ignored by most Canadian critics), and (by general similarity of style and outlook rather than by geographical proximity) George Johnstone and John Glassco. It is my personal conviction, or, if you will, prejudice, that it is with these two groups, rather than with the more obviously scintillating Reaney group, that the real future of Canadian poetry lies.

These then are the three schools into which contemporary Canadian poetry can be grouped. There are, however, a few loose fish who do not obviously belong with any of the groups: R. A. D. Ford and Douglas LePan, the last survivors, albeit very accomplished ones, of what might be called the genteel or academic school of Canadian verse; George Walton, Ronald Everson, and Goodridge MacDonald, older men who continue to write occasional verse of some distinction; Ralph Gustafson, better known as an anthologist but whose poetry seems to grow more youthful and irreverent as its author's age and dignity increases; and the three young poets D. G. Jones, Marya Fiamengo, and Ronald Bates, who do not seem to have quite made up their minds with which of the three existing schools to throw in their lot.

To turn from Canadian poetry to Canadian fiction is to enter an entirely different realm of discourse. Whereas there are almost fifty poets who demand and deserve serious reading, there are less than a dozen novelists who even aspire to anything beyond light entertainment. A similar situation does exist in the novel of the fifties as in the poetry, however, in that most of the excitement was provided by newcomers.

Of the novelists whose reputation was established when the decade began, only Morley Callaghan and Hugh MacLennan in any sense augmented their reputations, and they only to a limited degree. Morley Callaghan's only novel of the period was *The Loved and the Lost* (1951), and although it was highly praised for its symbolism and intricate structure it retained the basic weakness of Callaghan's earlier novels: a lack of ethical definition, a fuzziness of theme. It was the long-delayed publication of his collected short stories, in 1959, that demonstrated Callaghan's claim to an honoured place in our literary history. His gift is for detached moments of insight into character and emotional states, and it displays itself to much better advantage in the short story than in the novel.

Hugh MacLennan's *Each Man's Son* (1951) and *The Watch That Ends the Night* (1959) were more successful as wholes than any of his previous novels, and the latter book in particular was flatteringly reviewed as one of the most significant novels of our time. In spite of the almost unanimous chorus of praise, doubts persist of the permanence of MacLennan's status as a novelist. His novels are too discursive and reflective, too given to long passages of exposition and commentary. His real forte is for the essay, as his two collections *Thirty and Three* (1954) and *Scotchman's Return* (1960) amply demonstrate. There is a spontaneity and verve in most of his essays which is singularly lacking in his novels. His novels when they are not ruminative too often degenerate into sentimentality or melodrama.

A few of the older novelists barely held their own in the decade, writing in the manner to which their readers had become accustomed. This was true, for example, of Mazo de la Roche, who produced in the ten years four more instalments in the Jalna saga. In *A Boy in the House* (1952) she did produce one novel of a different sort and achieved an intensity now quite lacking from the Jalna chronicles. W. G. Hardy, in *The Unfulfilled* (1951) and *The City of Libertines* (1957), served up his usual mixture of sex, scholarship, and sermonizing. Will R. Bird produced four more historical novels about Yorkshire immigrants to Nova Scotia. E. A. McCourt, in *Home Is the Stranger* (1950), *The Wooden Sword* (1956), and *Walk Through the Valley* (1959), gave us three more novels of the West which mingled realistic observation of scenery and manners with melodramatic action and inconsistently motivated characters. Thomas Raddall, after giving promise in *The Nymph and the Lamp* (1950) of becoming a more realistic novelist of contemporary life, relapsed in *Tidefall* (1953) and *The Wings of Night* (1956) into melodrama. More significant, but lacking that final touch of distinction which makes the difference between the first- and second-rate, were the three books of fiction published in the decade by Hugh Garner:

Cabbagetown (1951), *Present Reckoning* (1951) and *The Yellow Sweater and Other Stories* (1952). Unlike most of the writers in this group, Garner does keep his eye unswervingly on the life about him, but his style is loose and cumbersome.

The passing of the old order was most clearly apparent in the number of established novelists who ceased to write in the fifties, or who produced work markedly inferior to their previous novels. Frederick Philip Grove's death in 1948 removed from the scene the most considerable fictional talent of the inter-war period; Irene Baird, whose *Waste Heritage* (1939) was the only serious contemporary attempt to portray the Canadian depression of the thirties, published no fiction in the fifties; Laura Goodman Salverson apparently reached the end of a long career as a writer of historical romances in *Immortal Rock* (1954); Philip Child, whose humane novels were among the most interesting produced in Canada in the forties, also apparently abandoned the art; and Sinclair Ross and Joyce Marshall, both of whom had written very promising first novels in the previous decade, produced, in *The Well* (1958) and *Lovers and Strangers* (1957) respectively, second novels which were gravely disappointing.

Fortunately, however, there were many new novelists who more than made up for these losses. Ethel Wilson, who had made her début just before the beginning of the decade with *Hetty Dorval* and *The Innocent Traveller*, continued to demonstrate in *The Equations of Love* (1952), *Swamp Angel* (1954) and *Love and Salt Water* (1956) that mixture of innocence and sophistication, compassion and irony, delight and apprehension, which makes her work so distinctive and fascinating. Not a major talent, Mrs. Wilson is one of those agreeable minor writers who make of their limitations a virtue, and work with great refinement within a narrow range. Robertson Davies, who had some reputation as a critic and essayist in the forties, turned to fiction in the fifties and produced three witty novels: *Tempest-Tost* (1951), *Leaven of Malice* (1954) and *A Mixture of Frailties* (1958). These novels had their roots in the early work of Aldous Huxley and Evelyn Waugh, but the application of their satirical and serio-comic technique to the Canadian scene resulted in something fresh and exciting. None of his novels was completely successful—like Huxley, he tends to use his characters as personal mouthpieces and to waver between

low and high comedy—but each marked an advance on its predecessor and each made some significant commentary on the
plight of the Canadian imagination.

A third novelist who had just the beginnings of a reputation
in 1950, David Walker, also contributed richly to the fiction of
the fifties. The two talents he had demonstrated respectively in
Geordie and *The Storm and the Silence*, humour and suspense,
were exhibited in the new decade in *Digby* (1953) and *The
Pillar* (1952) and *Harry Black* (1956). I personally prefer the
humour of *Geordie* and *Digby*, but Walker always writes with
professional skill and authority.

Mrs. Wilson, Mr. Davies and Mr. Walker had some standing
when the decade opened; the most exciting development of the
fifties was the appearance of several young novelists who made
their début in the decade. The most prolific of the group was
Mordecai Richler, who published four novels between 1954
and 1959: *The Acrobats, Son of a Smaller Hero, A Choice of
Enemies,* and *The Apprenticeship of Duddy Kravitz*. Richler
obviously has abundant energy; he also has a quick eye for
physical and social detail, a retentive ear for dialogue, and a
sharp nose for the pretentious and phoney. His novels scintillate
with eccentric characters, comic situations, and satirical comments. Their lack, so far, is a significant positive theme to
unify the discrete episodes: his novels are collections of brilliant
fragments. But when he looks at the Canadian urban scene, he
sees it far more clearly and honestly than any previous novelist.

Canadian novels of the past had fallen almost exclusively into
three groups: historical romances, regional idylls, and, chiefly
in the work of Grove, Ostenso, and Stead, realistic studies of
life in the rural West. Morley Callaghan was almost the only
novelist prior to the fifties to deal realistically with the life of
our cities. Perhaps the most interesting development in the
fifties was the tendency, which we have just seen to be demonstrated by Richler, to recognize the fact that the environment
of most Canadians is now urban. Historical romances almost
disappeared from the scene: the only new novelist who essayed
the form with any measure of success was Suzanne Butler with
her *My Pride, My Folly* (1953) and *Vale of Tyranny* (1954).
Rather than the romantic past, historically-minded novelists
tended to record the contemporary scene in fictional form, as
in Lionel Shapiro's *Sixth of June* (1955), Herbert Steinhouse's

Ten Years After (1958), or Colin McDougall's *Execution* (1958).

Regional idylls were similarly out of favour, the only practitioners with any claim to seriousness being Luella Creighton (*High Bright Buggy Wheels,* 1951; *Turn East, Turn West,* 1954) and Basil Partridge (*The Penningtons,* 1952; *Larry Pennington,* 1954; *Chaplet of Grace,* 1956). A new sub-species of novel began to replace the traditional regional idyll—the more or less sophisticated comedy of manners. Jan Hilliard's *A View of the Town* (1954) and *Dove Cottage* (1959) and John Cornish's *The Provincials* (1951) and *Olga* (1959) were examples of this new tendency.

But the significant trend was towards realistic and symbolic studies of city life; for so long the exception, these novels became the rule. Douglas Sanderson in the flawed but memorable *Dark Passions Subdue* (1952), explored guilt and perversion among the bright young students of Montreal; Norman Levine, in *The Angled Road* (1952), described with cruel honesty the experience of growing up in Ottawa; Adele Wiseman, in *The Sacrifice* (1956) and John Marlyn, in *Under the Ribs of Death* (1957), portrayed the problems of European immigrants struggling to acclimatize themselves in the bustling frontier city of Winnipeg.

Perhaps the most deft and certainly the most moving of all these novelists of city life, however, was Brian Moore. His first two novels, *The Lonely Passion of Judith Hearne* (1955) and *The Feast of Lupercal* (1957), were set in Belfast, but in *The Luck of Ginger Coffey* (1960) he turned to Montreal for a setting. We can only hope fervently that Moore will continue to live and write in Canada, for he seems to have all the gifts that a novelist requires: a sympathetic yet by no means mawkish understanding of people, especially of people in distress, a capacity to create scenes of great tension which yet persuade us of their authenticity, a sense of humour conjoined with a sense of pathos, a sense of place and of time, and—something that Richler so far lacks—an underlying positive philosophy of life. All his novels proclaim his faith in the power of the human spirit to endure in spite of its tendency to err and falter.

Moore, then, is at least potentially a major novelist. The same may be said of Richler, of Wiseman, and even, though less confidently, of Marlyn. Never before has Canada had so many as four young novelists of such early achievement and promise.

Nor does that exhaust the list of possibilities. Ernest Buckler, though he has been disappointingly silent since the appearance of *The Mountain and the Valley* in 1952, may again write in tenderness and anguish of life in rural Nova Scotia. Margaret Hutchison, in *Tamarac* (1957) and Sheila Watson in *The Double Hook* (1959) have both written first novels combining a sensitivity of feeling with dexterity of technique. Phyllis Brett Young, author of *Psyche* (1959) and *The Torontonians* (1960), may correct her tendency to romanticize basically realistic material: at the moment she seems too anxious to please the ladies' lending libraries.

In both poetry and fiction, then, the fifties was a period of new beginnings. In expository prose the same was true. Canadian literary criticism, which in the twenties and thirties consisted almost exclusively of extravagant praise of native mediocrity, became at least honest and incisive and, at best, in the work of Northrop Frye, brilliantly creative. Canadian biography took on a new sense of style and excitement in the work especially of Donald Creighton and William Kilbourne. The Canadian essay, as exemplified variously in Farley Mowat's *People of the Deer* (1952), Hilda Neatby's *So Little for the Mind* (1953), Father Raymond Coccolo's *Ayorama* (1955), and A. R. M. Lower's *Canadians in the Making* (1958), became more controversial and illuminating.

And the same sense of excitement could be found in the literary environment: here too new beginnings were the rule. The establishment of the Canada Council in 1957 made possible a system of grants to writers which should make it far more easy for their projects to reach completion. New literary magazines such as *Yes, Combustion, Tamarack Review, Delta, Prism, Alphabet, The Waterloo Review,* and *Canadian Literature* provided the writers with a far wider range of outlets than they had ever had before. The first Canadian book club was organized late in the decade, and will undoubtedly enlarge the domestic market for books. The Canadian Writers' Conference, held at Kingston in the summer of 1955, helped to give the writers a new sense of common purpose. More and more the universities were recognizing the existence of an indigenous literature—a fact which was perhaps most clearly symbolized by the publication of R. E. Watters' *Check List of Canadian Literature* (1959) and the initiation of the cooperative writing venture, *Literary History of Canada,* under the general editorship of Carl F. Klinck.

All these are auspicious developments. Yet one must end on a note of caution. Canadian literature is still in a state of promise rather than of solid achievement. If there were gains in the fifties, there were also losses. The decade saw the demise of Alan Crawley's *Contemporary Verse* and John Sutherland's *Northern Review.* It also saw the dissipation of the idealism and sense of common purpose which marked the war and post-war years, and which gave to the poets of the *Preview* group, for example, such a sense of comradeship. The prolongation of the Cold War, the increasing contrast between the material prosperity of the West and the restless hunger of the under-developed nations of Africa and the East, the posturings of Mr. Dulles and Mr. Khruschev: these things made Canadian writers confused and frustrated, accounted probably in large part for the retreat into the literature of literature on the part of so many of our poets. But the one solidly reassuring fact is that in spite of these frustrating circumstances a large number of promising new writers have appeared. If the sixties fulfil the promise of the fifties, we may be able ten years from now to look backward with pride. At the moment it is more fitting to look forward with hope.

Contemporary Canadian Poetry*

T<small>HE</small> contemporary Canadian poet certainly cannot complain of neglect. Anthologized in books and magazines and on the radio, cheered on campuses and in coffee bars, bemedalled and befellowed by the Canada Council, featured on Fighting Words and fawned upon by ambitious academics, he is the white-haired boy of all our festivals, the rival of Richard and Mahovlich, the Paul Anka of the classes. No wonder that there are so many aspirants for the laurels, so many new poets blossoming that the critic finds himself swooning with the heady mixed perfumes of their flowers.

The latest—or, to be safe, since so much is appearing so fast these days, one of the latest—exhibitions of their products is *Poetry 62*, a joint anthology of English- and French-Canadian poets edited by two young poets, Eli Mandel and Jean-Guy Pilon. (It is worth noting in passing that our poets are far from bashful: most of the anthologies are edited by poets, of poets, and, one sometimes suspects, for poets. At least Mr. Mandel has had the unusual modesty not to anthologize himself; but Monsieur Pilon is here.) It is one of the best shows we have had—lively, various, eclectic, and provocative.

The book's format is one of several recent indications that The Ryerson Press is taking on a new lease of life: the dust-jacket is eye-catching without being pretentious, the binding is strong and the cover plain but well designed, the paper is of agreeable weight and texture and the typography is clear and pleasing. In short, the book has been conceived as an aesthetic object and not as just another product.

Getting to the book's contents, one first encounters a rather

---

*Published in *The Canadian Forum*, April, 1962.

forbidding epigraph: a passage of pompous mumbo-jumbo about art, excised from Edgar Wind's *Pagan Mysteries in the Renaissance*. This, of course, is all part of the show, the trumpets sounding at Stratford, the frenzied guitar solo before the poet emerges from the shadows to orate across the coffee tables. A pity that this particular trumpet has such an uncertain sound.

Next, Mr. Mandel steps forth as master of ceremonies. He flatters us by addressing us as rebels. "The tyrant, then, like the conformist, hates poetry, for poetry is the antithesis of un-consciousness . . . Terror of the organization man, its vitality suggests to him chaos . . . Fearing its huge demands for compre-hension, he longs for the single stupidity of hate." This is excellent stuff: it makes clear at once that in reading this book one belongs to the elect, is the automatic foe of tyranny and conformity. But isn't there, Mr. Mandel, such a thing as the conformity of the coffee houses? And what about the con-formity of the academy?

Mr. Mandel goes on to make the justifiable assertion that "the most striking feature of contemporary Canadian poetry is its range of activity," but rather disappoints us by failing to be more specific. A brief essay by Mr. Mandel on what he considers to be the most interesting features within this wide range would have been most welcome. In short, I wish that he hadn't played it so safe in this preface: attacking conformity and asserting breadth of range is remaining altogether too much in the shelter of agreement.

Only at one point does Mr. Mandel abandon his caution: he asserts that in this poetry "one senses a gathering of forces for the performance of some unprecedented and enormously sig-nificant drama of the mind." Now this is very strong language indeed, and raises expectations in the reader that the poems which follow quite fail to fulfil.

In trying to assess so many poets in the comparatively short space of a review, one inevitably looks about for short cuts. One of the most convenient is the method of Matthew Arnold, that of touchstones. This is far from an infallible critical approach, but it is particularly useful in the Canadian context. Our literary society is small and ingrown, most of our poets are known personally to each other and by the critics, and external comparisons are needed to give us perspective.

As touchstones of greatness, two passages of English poetry come to my mind. Here are the opening lines of Donne's fourteenth Holy Sonnet:

> Batter my heart, three person'd God; for you
> As yet but knock, breathe, shine, and seek to mend;
> That I may rise, and stand, o'erthrow me, and bend
> Your force, to break, blow, burn and make me new.

And here are the opening lines of Yeats' "Byzantium":

> The unpurged images of day recede;
> The Emperor's drunken soldiery are abed;
> Night resonance recedes, night-walkers' song
> After great cathedral gong;
> A starlit or a moonlit dome disdains
> All that man is,
> All mere complexities,
> The fury and the mire of human veins.

In those two passages, I do indeed sense "a gathering of forces for the performance of some unprecedented and enormously significant drama of the mind." What do they have in common? First of all, they suggest that the poet is on top of his material and in full command of his method: each poet knows exactly what he wants to say, and he says it clearly, forcefully, and with an involved but not capricious intensity which exploits all the varied resources of language. Secondly, the poet in each case is speaking of something which is of critical importance to himself, which is indeed a matter of his own personal salvation. Thirdly, this matter is of immediate critical importance not only to himself but to his contemporaries. And lastly, it is a matter of universal, indeed of eternal, significance.

Now if we turn from Donne and Yeats to *Poetry 62* we find little which even approaches this level of poetic achievement. Of course we should not expect to do so, because most of the poets in this anthology are still young, and Donne and Yeats wrote their passages in the late phases of their careers. But we might expect to find foreshadowings of this mature authority, as we find them in the early poems of Yeats and Donne. Are there any such foreshadowings in *Poetry 62*?

In what follows I shall be chiefly concerned with the English-speaking poets in the anthology, for I am not really competent to judge the French. I should like to say, however, that my imperfect knowledge of French does permit me to get enough out of the French poems in the book to feel that some of them come closer to the ideal standard than all but a very few of the English poems. Such lines as these, from Alain Grandbois' "Mirages", have something of the calm majesty, the verbal richness, the imaginative resonance of "Byzantium":

Ce calme fleuve refoulant rageur vers sa source
Faisceaux O gravitations solaires astrales
Contre les barreaux contre les murs de glace
Et les vents portaient les grands oiseaux . . .

And I find a similar eloquence in Pierre Trottier's "Terre D'Exil" and Luc Perrier's "Au nombre de mes joies sans nombre."

The first English-speaking poet in the anthology is Wilfred Watson. In some of his earlier poems, notably "The Windy Bishop" and "Canticle of Darkness," Watson did occasionally approximate the touchstones, but the long poem by which he is represented here seems to me to fail on all four counts. The meaninglessness repetitions, the frequent digressions, the often functionless echoes of and allusions to Eliot and other poets, and the refusal to speak plainly—all these suggest that Watson is far from being in command of either his material or his method. It is difficult to believe that he personally is deeply concerned with the theme of his poem, a satire upon pseudo-scholarship in the English Departments of Canadian universities in general and the University of Toronto in particular. If this is indeed a serious concern to Mr. Watson, it can safely be said that it is not a major worry of his Canadian contemporaries. As for its universal validity, it has none. Of all the subjects crying out for satire in Canada today, I should put pseudo-scholarship very near the bottom of the list. The poem is not even remotely tuned to the facts: Canadian professors of English are *not* very productive of scholarly articles; the most productive scholars (one thinks of Woodhouse and Frye) are definitely not out to win promotion or impress the president; most of the articles which are produced are the result of

specific requests from editors or chairmen of programme com-
mittees, or the products of genuine intellectual excitement on
the part of their authors.

Personally (although I could be biased) I should consider
pseudo-poetry in Canada a more legitimate target for satire
than pseudo-scholarship.

Margaret Avison is represented by three characteristic poems
in which she celebrates epiphanies, moments of escape from the
bondage of time and space. In her poems one does encounter
the resonance of real poetry, in lines such as these:

> Beyond the manly and autumnal
> arcades of calendared knowing
> swings the implicit instant.
> Clusters and cones of
>   light, leaf-shelved
> topple dimension down.

Miss Avison's work impresses one also by its integrity: her
vision is distinctive, her attitude is consistent and sure; Alfred
Purdy, on the other hand, seems to be still very much of a
chameleon in both method and matter. In "Mind Process Re
a Faucet" he vacillates from the grave dignity of the opening
lines through pointless archaism ("a lovesome sound god
wot?") to careless slang ("Mind that gets bloody tired") and
meanders around the subject without ever really coming to
grips with it. In "Likes and Opposites" he has gone back to the
manner of the early Auden, but cannot achieve Auden's cryptic,
epigrammatic cleverness. His third poem is an irritatingly
formless and diffuse commentary on the poetic theory of Louis
Dudek. Mr. Purdy can do better than this: he is misrepresented
in this anthology.

Milton Acorn comes off rather better. There is nothing in
his six poems to make Donne and Yeats turn over in their
graves, but these last three lines from his first poem—

> I don't know if hate's the armour of love;
> what side he joined, or if he joined: but
> when he learned to hate those dreams ended—

and the whole of "Nature" at least have something approaching
the mature intensity of a master.

Ronald Bates is one of the minor surprises of the volume. His first book, *Wandering World*, struck me as a rather flaccid volume, but there are some excellent passages in this group of his poems. "Fairy Tale" and "Linear A," especially, show him to be the master on occasion of a sharp and taut descriptive line and of a truly imaginative vision. Technically he has improved enormously; I am not sure that he yet has found a truly significant theme in which he is urgently involved.

James Reaney poses a more difficult problem. He does not even attempt here (in a long poem about the past and present of Winnipeg) the kind of direct, impassioned statement that we find in the touchstone passages of Yeats and Donne. This of course suggests one of the limitations of the touchstone method, and prompts the observation that there is an oblique as well as a direct kind of poetry. Reaney's approach is oblique, his tone is wry, and his effects are charming (though also, at times, terrifying). Rather than attacking his subject from above, he is busily pinching away at its soft underbelly. He is easily the most deft artist among the English-speaking poets represented here. These lines may have little resemblance to Yeats and Donne, but they are a touchstone of their own kind:

> Red Orange Green Arrows Side Streets No Parking
> A car with a headache, it looks like a shark,
> Glittering, really rather beautiful; demonic engine
> Humming to the children and the old ladies—Come here,
> Under my wheels and I'll toss you. Glittering
> Hard merciless cars.

With Phyllis Gotlieb we are back to a more direct, traditional kind of verse. The strength of her work, like the strength of Raymond Souster's, is that it obviously grows out of personal observation and conviction. Like Souster's also, her poems proceed easily and effortlessly, but almost always end in a final furious sprint that stirs our admiration. To go back to our external touchstones, it is no mean compliment to say that Miss Gotlieb's "Hospitality" might have appeared in one of Yeats' last volumes without seeming out of place.

I shall be frank and admit that Kenneth McRobbie eludes me completely. His work seems to embody all the fashionable tricks of the beat generation—parentheses that begin and never end, the evasion of syntax, unregulated images of desolation—

but none of the weird compulsive power that people like Ginsberg occasionally achieve. Here, I suggest, we witness at first hand the conformity of the coffee bar.

D. G. Jones, on the other hand, is definitely moving towards a personal mode of utterance and towards the kind of assured ease exhibited by Yeats and Donne. His two long poems here are well-chosen—they are two of the best in his recently published *The Sun Is Axeman*—and impress us with their sincerity, clarity, and capacity to combine the personal and the universal. Jones is obviously sensitive to both the interior and exterior landscape, and he shifts from one to the other, and makes each reflect and sharpen the image of the other, with delightful deftness. A genuine and distinctive personality emerges from the lines, and Mr. Jones is obviously a young poet to watch with eager anticipation. Such lines as these, taken from "In This Present Mood", come as close as any in the volume to the quality of the touchstones:

> May our
> Bodies be a gift
> Which we can give
> Without excess of pride,
> Which we receive
> Without excess of greed.
> And may our flesh
> Be food for that
> Deep emptiness
> Which like a hunger
> Troubles our brief lives.

John Paul Harney is a poet I had not noticed before, and I commend Mandel's perceptiveness in discovering and including him in this volume. His work here is lively, vigorous, coarsely alive, if a trifle obvious and self-conscious. He reminds me somewhat of Irving Layton, with his frank earthy celebration of life in general and sex in particular. Since he has only just turned thirty, he is obviously another young man to watch.

Alden Nowlan is a poet I have been watching for some years now, and it is good to see him represented by five poems here even if the poems are definitely not from his top drawer. Only "The Dog Returned from the Woods" and "Beets" have the concise irony of Nowlan's best work, but they are among the most unforgettable poems in the whole book.

Leonard Cohen is also off form. Presumably all his best recent work had gone into *The Spice-Box of Earth,* and these four tentative poems were left-overs. Only the slightly humorous "For Marianne" has any adhesive power.

Daryl Hine's contributions are similarly disappointing. "An Allegory of Sleep" displays his technical virtuosity and his capacity for an almost suffocating sensuousness, but even it impresses one as a literary exercise rather than as the product of deep feeling. Hine at the moment seems to be obsessed with myths for their own sake, and to have forgotten that when Spenser and Milton and Yeats resorted to myths they used them to clarify and deepen their own problems and prophecies.

John Robert Colombo is also still groping, but groping to more purpose. In "Riverdale Lion" he has at least looked observantly at his own environment, even if the comment to which the observation leads him is a rather trite one. "Passion" is a clever trifle, and "All Our Edens Are Lost and Never Regained" is too fussy and mannered—though it is by no means a negligible effort at a fresh treatment of the old theme of the omnipresence of death. "Lines for the Antichrist of the Establishment" tries to say something in an elaborate, "literary" way that would have been much better said more plainly, but his last poem, "Prologue to Paradise," really redeems the group by its imaginative power and sheer rhetorical splendour.

To sum up, this anthology is not, as it might at first glance appear to be, just another item in the growing list of anthologies of Canadian verse. By selecting his poetry arbitrarily, without much concern for inclusiveness or the Smith or other canons, Mandel has enabled us to have a fresh view of contemporary Canadian poetry. Without the overshadowing presence of the big trees such as Pratt, Birney, Layton and Souster, we are able to see the younger and smaller growths with a new clarity—and what we see is often very pleasing. If the fully successful poems are few and far between, it is I suspect because their authors have forgotten that great poems have the qualities that were listed above in connection with the passages from Yeats and Donne. The rewards of being a poet in Canada today are so numerous and beguiling that there is a grave temptation to write poetry for the sake of the rewards rather than out of the sheer agony or ecstasy of personal experience. But the rewards are far from being wholly undeserved.

The Young Writer in Canada*

I SUPPOSE that the popular line to follow in approaching this subject would be to launch a full-scale attack on our cultural environment. One might have a marvellous orgiastic release from flaying once more our materialism, our lingering colonialism, our prudery, our hypocrisy, and our muddled mediocrity. However, I have chosen to leave such pleasures to others. Instead, I am prepared to argue that in most respects our present environment is at least relatively favourable to the young writer, and that if we do not in this or the next generation produce a literature worthy of the name the bulk of the blame will lie upon ourselves rather than upon our public.

I say relatively favourable because there has never been and will never be an environment fully satisfying to the writer. We think of Elizabethan England as an environment for the writer as nearly perfect as could be imagined, and yet this is what Ben Jonson thought of it: "Poetry, in this latter age, hath proved but a mean mistress to such as have wholly addicted themselves to her, or given their names up to her family." If we compare our cultural environment with that of the contemporary United States, United Kingdom or even France I do not think the comparison is one from which we need suffer. I remember Phyllis Webb, at the Canadian Writers' Conference in Kingston in 1955, educing statistics to prove that even from the standpoint of sales, the small book of poetry or the quality first

*A paper given at the Student Conference on Creative Writing in Canada at Hart House, University of Toronto, February 25, 1962, and published in *Queen's Quarterly*, Summer, 1962. As an historical note, it might be added that the paper was discussed by a panel on which the author was joined by Jay Macpherson, Irving Layton, and Pierre Elliott Trudeau.

novel did rather better in Canada than in either Britain or the States. And just the other day the poet Louis Dudek was telling me that he would much rather be a poet in Canada today than in the United States, because here it is so much easier to get a fair hearing. The grass always looks greener on the other side of the fence, and we have been deluding ourselves for too long in thinking that there is something inherently more favourable in the cultural environments of other countries.

Certainly if we compare the present situation in Canada with the recent, and still more with the distant, past, the phrase "relatively favourable" becomes something of an understatement.

Even if we go back only ten years, to the early months of 1952, think what a change there has been. Then the Canada Council was only a dream in the minds of the members of the Humanities Research Council and Social Science Research Council. The only literary magazines (apart from the university quarterlies which are and were media primarily for scholarly rather than creative writing) were *The Canadian Forum* and John Sutherland's *Northern Review*; now we have a string of magazines from coast to coast, with new ones springing up almost overnight. In 1962 the Governor General's Awards were still administered by the Canadian Authors Association, and did not carry the handsome monetary prizes they do today. There was no Canadian Readers' Club in 1952, to bring selected books by Canadians to the many areas of this country which have no proper bookstores.

Go back twenty years, to 1942, and the comparison is even more distinctly in our favour. To think of the situation as it existed then is to realize how much the Second World War and its aftermath did to enhance our interest in Canadian writing. In 1942 A. J. M. Smith's *Book of Canadian Poetry* had not yet appeared, nor E. K. Brown's *On Canadian Poetry*: and I should like here and now to record my personal gratitude for those two books which, appearing side by side in 1943, did perhaps more than anything else to convince me and many others that Canadian literature was a legitimate subject for responsible critical scrutiny. In those early years of the war the C.B.C. had not yet launched its activities on behalf of Canadian writing: there was no "Stage" series, no "Critically Speaking," and no "Anthology," no programme of Canadian short stories nor reading of Canadian verse.

But turn to the more distant past, and I feel we must blush at our temerity in complaining and admit that if Canadian writers are in danger of being killed today they are only in danger of being killed by kindness. Think of the situation in 1881, when the poverty of our cultural environment was such that the young Archibald Lampman, in the garden of Trinity College, went into ecstasies at the knowledge that Charles Roberts' *Orion* had been written in Canada by "a young man, one of ourselves." The very idea that any Canadian could write a respectable book of verse came with the force of a divine revelation to Lampman—and yet within little more than a decade he himself, Bliss Carman, Charles Roberts, Duncan Campbell Scott and William Wilfred Campbell had managed to bring a whole corpus of Canadian poetry to the attention of a fair segment of the English-speaking world. This they accomplished merely by their own personal dedication—with no aid from the Canada Council, C.B.C., or Canadian publishers (for even the latter were then non-existent, or virtually so, and all these young poets had to find publishers in Boston, New York, or London).

It would perhaps be labouring the obvious to go back a full hundred years, to 1862, when there was no Canada and no anything—except poor old Charles Sangster struggling along alone with no peers (and *his* peers would not have had to be very accomplished), no magazines, no current of ideas to sustain him, nothing at all to encourage him but his own incredible and perhaps deluded belief that his poems somehow *mattered*, were somehow worth the ruination of his physical and mental health.

So there is no doubt at all that the situation of the young Canadian writer today is much better than it ever has been, and little doubt that it is as good as his situation would be anywhere in the world. But of course his situation is not perfect. Let us now abandon our historical point of view, and look closely at the young writer's actual present environment, trying to discern where it is favourable and where it is in need of improvement.

To begin at the beginning, the chances are that the young writer comes from a home in which there are few books and little reading. We are one of the worst book-buying publics in the world and, whether this be cause or effect or a bit of both, we have very few bookstores to serve as show-windows for our literary wares. Our library situation is little better: we still have no real National Library, although I believe it is presently a-building and although it already functions as adequately as its energetic chief, Dr. W. Kaye Lamb, can make it; our university libraries are grossly inadequate in comparison with those of the United States and the United Kingdom; only our largest cities, with a few notable exceptions, have adequate public libraries. Not to grow up with good books is a very severe handicap to any writer: it means that in most cases his style will be formed only by the approved pablum that finds its way into the school curriculum.

This brings us to the school situation, which is about as bad as it could be. A child whose first acquaintance with reading is with the inanities of the "Dick and Jane" series can scarcely be blamed if he decides that literature is for little morons. Nor is the picture notably brighter in the higher grades. Our public and high school "readers" are diluted with mediocre selections; they have little Canadian content and what Canadian content they do have is more likely to be Pauline Johnson and Audrey Alexandra Brown, say, than P. K. Page and Jay Macpherson. I recently had some experience with editing a possible high school literature textbook, and I found that although I had been assured in advance that the authorities were determined to raise the standards and confine the book to genuine masterpieces, when the chips were down objections were raised to all the more difficult selections — to Chaucer's *Canterbury Tales,* Spenser's *Faerie Queene* and Milton's "Lycidas", for example. Compare the kind of reading diet that an English student entering Oxford or Cambridge has had, with the diet enforced upon the Canadian student entering U.B.C. or U.N.B., and you have one comparison that is definitely not in our favour.

A similar gulf lies between the standards of literary teaching in the two countries. The English educational system has allowed itself to be taught by the "new criticism" that the real thrill of literary study comes from the detailed, independent appraisal and analysis of the form and meaning of the words on the page; but I am afraid that in most of our schools literature is still taught as a form of virginal rapture ("Isn't that beautiful?") or of mnemonic discipline ("Learn the first fifty lines by heart, including the punctuation.") Too often the teaching of English is allocated to the physical education instructor in the hours when he has nothing better to do, or to some elderly virgin whose favourite author is the late lamented Alfred, Lord Tennyson. I hasten to say that there are many honourable exceptions to this rule—but it *is* the rule.

If and when the young writer surmounts these hurdles, and reaches the university, he at once finds himself in a much more favourable cultural environment. This is no doubt why, whereas most English students begin to be poets in their last years at school, Canadian students scarcely ever write anything worthwhile until they are in their second or third year of college. Now, at last, the young writer does strike literature of real quality and teaching of a high standard (though not always, because of our frequent practice of palming off freshmen on inexperienced graduate teaching fellows, of as high a standard as it should be).

Even in the nineteenth century, our universities were the chief training centres of our poets and other writers. Roberts and Carman were never tired of paying tribute to their teachers at the University of New Brunswick, and Lampman owed much to his courses at Trinity. Today the universities are much more consciously concerned with the nurture of the young Canadian writer. Most of our universities have courses in Canadian literature, which if they do nothing else at least draw the student's attention to the possibility of writing in Canada, and to the dearth of really *good* writing, a dearth which he then may be stimulated to redress. Many of our universities now also have courses in Creative Writing. I teach one such course myself, but I am fully aware of its dangers and limitations. In spite of the dangers, I do feel that such courses have value, if only to demand of the talented but often unduly optimistic young writer that he either "put up or shut up." These courses are most valuable, however, not in producing writers (who to a large extent are born rather than made) but in producing disciplined, practical critics and sympathetic, knowledgeable teachers. If there are dangers in Creative Writing courses, there are dangers in more orthodox and traditional parts of the university curriculum in English. Ideally, a university course in English should make one "heir of all the ages," should enable one to feel the continuity of tradition and the individual talent, to think of Chaucer and Donne and Milton as being in a sense as contemporary as Eliot, Thomas, and Truman Capote. Unfortunately, this ideal is seldom realized in practice, and the student all too often falls prey to one of the following delusions.

The first delusion may be labelled literary faddism. Each generation has its fad. From 1910 to 1930 it was wit and brittle cynicism, the sort of thing typified by *Smart Set*, Michael Arlen, the early novels of Aldous Huxley and even, at a higher level, the early poems of T. S. Eliot (in Canadian terms, you will find a great deal of this sort of thing in the pages of the *McGill Fortnightly Review*). From 1930 to 1950 the fad was social realism and social protest, as in the novels of John Dos Passos and the poems of the Auden-Spender group in England. Since 1950 the fad has been mythology and symbolism. If the young writer realizes that these fads are only fads, and that really creative writers have no truck nor trade with them except as they happen to coincide with their own independent purposes, he will be all right; but too often he surrenders, speaks of "writing in the modern idiom," and merely turns out imitations in the currently fashionable mode.

The second delusion we may call the conformity of non-conformity. We are all armoured today against the conformity of the organization man, but we are more vulnerable to the conformity of the coffee-house, and the conformity of the academy. I shall not labour the point, but merely content myself with quoting a sentence from Emerson that I believe should be the motto of any young writer worth his salt: "Let the single man plant himself indomitably on his instincts, and there abide, and the whole world will come round to him."

Then there is the delusion which we may describe as literary snobbery. It takes many forms. It may take the form of assuming that there is some superiority inherent in being a student of English literature rather than a student of Mechanical Engineering. When I see this kind of snobbery at work I am inclined to favour Irving Layton's choice of academic specialty: the author of *The Bull Calf* holds a Bachelor of Science in Agriculture. One other form of literary snobbery I shall mention finds expression in the lifted eyebrow at any reference to Canadian literature. To these students, Canadian literature is second-rate axiomatically; not because they have read it and assessed it to be such, but because to dismiss it in favour of the study of some fifth-rate English metaphysical wit is generally considered better academic form.

A fourth trap into which a university education may lure the young writer is that of pseudo-sophistication. The student comes to know so much about literary history, literary theory, and literary technique that he either fails to write at all (why should the young eagle deign to stretch his wings?) or writes prettily or wittily but without genuine conviction.

There are many other academic traps, but the only other one I shall mention is premature fame. It is relatively, almost ridiculously, easy to make a name for oneself today in Canada as a poet—and only slightly more difficult as a novelist. It may happen, I believe it has happened, that a young writer makes this name for himself as a student and never recovers from the resultant swelled head. To those who rightly fear this trap, I merely recommend a reading of Milton's so-called "digression" on fame in "Lycidas."

Let us suppose that the young writer somehow evades all these traps, begins to write at university, gets his early efforts published in the university literary magazine, and now wants to continue his literary career. What are his chances in this country today? When I was a student in the late nineteen-thirties, they were slim: the depression was on, Canadian publishers had very short annual lists, the only Canadian literary magazine was *The Canadian Forum*. In spite of that, some of us managed to continue as writers: Northrop Frye, George Johnstone, Alice Eedy, and Margaret Avison were all contributors to *Acta Victoriana* during my period of connection with it. Today, your chances are infinitely better and I am sure many of you will continue to write.

First of all, you have a great variety of literary magazines to which to send your early efforts: *Prism* in Vancouver, *Tamarack* in Toronto, *Alphabet* in London, *Delta* and the new *Black Magazine* in Montreal, *Fiddlehead* in Fredericton, not to mention old standbys such as the *Forum, Queen's Quarterly,* and *Dalhousie Review*, and new magazines whose founding is being rumoured. Each of these magazines has its own special bias, its own limitations, but between the lot of them any work of real merit should be able to find a taker.

If your contributions are accepted with any regularity by any or all of these magazines, you have a very good chance of being picked up for some kind of reading by the C.B.C., or for republication in one or other of the anthologies of prose or verse which are being issued with increasing frequency by Canadian publishers. If by these or other means you acquire some solidity of reputation, you run a very good chance of applying successfully for a grant from the Canada Council.

If by means of such a grant, or by independent work in your spare time, you manage to complete the manuscript of a book, you have a much better chance than ever before of having it published in this country. Since you have already discussed the relations of writer and publisher, I shall merely point out here that Canadian publishing houses today are much more receptive to new writers, and eager to present their work in attractive form, than ever before. If your work is too limited in appeal to attract the commercial houses, you have a variety of non-commercial presses to approach, including Raymond Souster's Contact Press, Jay Macpherson's Emblem Books, and British Columbia's Klanak Press.

Once your book is published, you can be sure of much more attention from reviewers than ever before in Canada. It is true that most of our newspaper book pages are of low quality, their reviews often being written by people who have not the necessary background of knowledge or taste, but in the literary magazines we have mentioned, in the university quarterlies, and, if you are lucky, on the C.B.C.'s "Critically Speaking," you will be given informed and sensitive criticism. We do however lack, I admit, one strong critical weekly or monthly in which we could be sure of finding intelligent reviews of all significant Canadian books. *The Canadian Forum* comes closest to this ideal, but it has some strange omissions; *Canadian Literature* tries to be comprehensive, but is hampered by quarterly publication. The *University of Toronto Quarterly's* "Letters in Canada" is also of great value, but often over a year has elapsed between the publication of a book and its review there. Some magazine in Canada roughly equivalent to the *Times Literary Supplement* in London or the *Saturday Review* in New York would be a great boon to our literature. It is altogether too difficult to find out what *is* being published in Canada today.

Even if your book is reviewed favourably and at length, its sales will not be large—hardly even large enough to pay you the minimum wage for the hours you have expended upon it. But this should not surprise or dismay you. Seldom in any country have serious writers been able to live solely by their pens. Chaucer was a high government official, Donne a clergyman, Bacon a busy lawyer and judge. It should not cripple the Canadian writer's talent to work in a university, the C.B.C., or the Civil Service. If he is really determined to write, he will somehow find the time and energy to do so. That phenomenal literary success in the material sense is almost non-existent in this country is probably a good thing—look what success did to the author of *Mr. Roberts*, to William Saroyan and to Scott Fitzgerald. There is something vicious and soul-destroying about success in America.

For the first time, then, we have an adequate series of links of communication for our writers, though there are still weak links in the series. The three weakest links in my opinion are the schools, the newspaper reviews, and the general public. We need much better teachers and curricula of English in our schools, much higher standards of information and sensitivity in our newspaper book pages, and we need much greater depth in our reading public. The truly literate public in this country is a very thin red line—and almost pathetically vulnerable.

But a series of links of communications is not in itself enough. Our writers must have something to communicate, and the skill with which to do so.

There is no lack of material in this country—in fact there is an abundance of material. Older and more "literary" countries such as England and France have had their cities, towns and countryside treated over and over again, so that a new writer must search hard for a new angle or a new technique. But so little has been written about the life of this country that it is virtually virgin territory, and even a traditional treatment of it would be new and valuable. In spite of the glimpses of that city in Ethel Wilson's novels, and in Earle Birney's poetry, no one has yet really captured the quality of life in contemporary Vancouver; Sinclair Ross and Patricia Blondal have barely indicated what rich material exists in the small towns of the prairies; Grove and Ostenso and Stead gave us some memorable pictures of the rural life of the West in the nineteen-twenties, but who will write the novel of contemporary life in rural Saskatchewan? As for the cities of the West, no one to my knowledge has yet seriously tackled Edmonton, Calgary, or Saskatoon, and

John Marlyn in *Under the Ribs of Death* and Adele Wiseman in *The Sacrifice* have shown what scope Winnipeg offers but have by no means exhausted its material. Robertson Davies has written brilliantly of Kingston from one point of view, and Morley Callaghan and Raymond Souster with some poignancy of Toronto, but there is no convincing study of small town or rural life in Ontario (but merely, so far, a series of saccharine idylls). Much more use has been made of Montreal as literary material, in the poetry of Smith, Scott, Klein, Dudek, and Layton, and in the novels of Richler and Moore and Callaghan, but there is such variety in the life of that city, its face is changing so quickly, that it too still has much to offer. In the Maritimes, the scenery and to a lesser extent the society were limned in the last century by Haliburton and Howe, Roberts and Carman, but what novelist has yet caught the present posture of that area, fascinatingly wavering between a nostalgic pride in the past, a poignant sense of the depressed present, and the dawning hope of a new destiny in the future?

It is sometimes said that the Canadian environment is dull, and that it therefore is unsuitable material for the writer. One pertinent comment on that attitude would be that to the dull all things are dull. In my view, there is nothing dull about Canada: in contrast with the countries of Western Europe, including the United Kingdom, it has the excitement of being confident that its future will be greater than its past. And even if it is dull, great literature, and great satire in particular, can be made of dullness. Why don't those who complain of Canada's dullness write the contemporary analogue of Pope's *Dunciad*? Why don't those who complain of her smug complacency write the analogue of Swift's *Modest Proposal*? Why don't those who complain of our conformity, materialism and hypocrisy write the analogue of Butler's *Erewhon*?

I am convinced that the material exists, and that the channels of communication exist. What is needed in this country if our literature is to flourish is that the writer look in his heart and write.

That sentence would make a dramatic ending for my remarks. But it would be an evasion of certain other hard facts. Looking into the heart is not really enough. The writer must have natural talent, and that is a rare gift. Moreover, he must be ready to cultivate that talent by unremitting study and toil.

Because it is relatively easy nowadays to get published in this country, we are in danger of taking literature too lightly, of building a premature reputation upon shaky foundations. The writer who wants his work to survive must study the great masters of the past, and be ready to measure himself always by the achievements of Donne and Yeats, Austen and Hardy. What did these masters have in common? They were all passionately interested in their immediate environment, and convinced of its importance. Jane Austen might easily have concluded that there was nothing of permanent interest in the lives of English villagers in the early nineteenth century, Yeats that Ireland was a provincial backwater best left to stink and stagnate. Secondly, they were all ready to study and to learn from the tradition that lay behind them: Donne from medieval theology and philosophy, Yeats from Swift and Burke and Blake, Austen from Fielding and Burney and the eighteenth-century essayists, Hardy from Greek tragedy and Shakespeare. Thirdly, they were ready to break with such aspects of their tradition as were no longer relevant—Donne with the mellifluousness of the Spenserians, Austen with the sentimental ruralism of Goldsmith and Mackenzie, Hardy with the didactic meliorism of George Eliot and Charles Dickens, Yeats with the patriotic piety of nineteenth-century Irish verse.

In addition, these writers were all masters of a technique which they had developed and sharpened by prolonged practice. They were never content: each of them developed through a series of tentative efforts to the firm mastery of their maturity. But although they had, then, a measure of humility, a continuing self-discontent, they did have a basic confidence in themselves. In the great works of their maturity, as in Donne's *Holy Sonnets*, Yeats' *Last Poems*, or Hardy's *Tess*, they speak with authority and assurance, are possessed of a vision which is distinctive and deserved.

But you may well ask me why I choose such extra-Canadian examples. Is the young Canadian writer justified at least in complaining that his task is made more difficult by the lack of a usable literary tradition in his own country? To some extent, he is. It does make it more difficult to be self-confident when so little undeniably excellent work has been done by his predecessors. But a usable tradition need not be a tradition of greatness. There is some inspiration to be gained from a knowledge that

Thomas Chandler Haliburton was able to make the emergent society of colonial Nova Scotia interesting to readers in the United Kingdom and the United States who scarcely knew or cared that Nova Scotia existed, that Charles Sangster went on revising the manuscripts of his poems when his hands were so crippled by arthritis and neurasthenia that he could only hold a pen for a few minutes of the day, that Frederick Philip Grove wrote his flawed but intermittently powerful novels in shacks on the prairies in winter, and went on writing a whole dozen of them though for thirty years he could not find a publisher for even one, that Morley Callaghan is still today turning out good novels when all the young writers who were his contemporaries in the nineteen-twenties have stopped writing altogether or have turned, like John Dos Passos, to mediocre pot-boilers. The history of writing in this country is a record of a few partial triumphs and many complete failures—and the partial triumphs have always been won against terrible odds. But it is not pollyanna-ism to suggest that gradually the partial triumphs are becoming less partial and more frequent, and that the odds are becoming a little less overwhelming. Surely it is legitimate to take some comfort today from the successes that have been achieved by prose writers such as Mordecai Richler, Brian Moore and Norman Levine and by poets such as Irving Layton, James Reaney, and Leonard Cohen? Or, if you want a contemporary example of the survival of a talent in the face of odds as great as any writer ever faced, take the case of Alden Nowlan, whose poems and short stories have been drawing increasingly favourable attention, but who left school in his native Nova Scotia in Grade V, has worked ever since at a variety of energy-consuming jobs, and who has been living during his last creative five years in the little library-less, bookstore-less village of Hartland, N.B.

Of course it is true that there is much to deplore in our Canadian milieu. Our society does equate success with monetary and material success; we still do have something of a colonial inferiority complex in our constant self-depreciation and our childish pleasure over a congratulatory judgment from outside; our censorship laws are absurd and their means of application are dubious at best; we affect a superiority in race relations which we are far from deserving; we have failed to become a truly bilingual society and our two chief racial stocks are still two solitudes; we talk much of our need for higher educational standards but the talk is seldom translated into action. The point I have been trying to make is not that our society is anything like perfect, but rather that much more depends on the determination of the writer than on the quality of his environment. The young writer in Canada today should apply himself to his task with the dedication of a Donne, Yeats or Hardy, or of a Haliburton, Grove or Callaghan, and waste very little time worrying about the poverty or richness of his cultural milieu.

The Canadian Imagination*

THE Canadian imagination thus far is mainly a function of a landscape and a climate, and only secondarily of a society. When one thinks back over the history of Canadian art and literature, the images which come to mind are of great stretching plains, of brooding mountains and rocks, of swift, raging rivers, of stormy oceans and inland lakes, of acres of wind-heaped snow, of fiercely twisting trees—and amidst all this vastness and strength, man is but a dot, a temporary intruder, vulnerable but persistent.

The landscape and climate of Canada are so inescapably impressive that it was inevitable that the first efforts of Canadian artists should be to come to terms with them. The land is so various that in itself it offers an almost inexhaustible challenge. The variety of Canadian landscape and climate has never been properly understood abroad: the tendency has been to abstract the power of the one and the coldness of the other, to simplify Canada as Kipling did to "Our Lady of the Snows." But within Canada, in the space of a single year, is to be found almost every type of landscape and climate short of the fully tropical. The rocky coasts of Newfoundland are succeeded by the fertile river valleys and thickly wooded hills of Nova Scotia and New Brunswick, the rolling farmlands of Prince Edward Island, the inward sweep of the St. Lawrence River whose banks are divided into the long, narrow fields of the habitants of Quebec, the sprawling industrial and commercial cities of Quebec, Montreal, Kingston, Toronto, and Hamilton and the productive farmlands which still surround them, the great inland

---

*Introductory essay, Canadian issue of *The Literary Review* (U.S.A.), Summer, 1965.

lakes Ontario, Erie, Huron and Superior, the rocky, thickly forested areas of Northern Ontario, the busy wheat-marketing city of Winnipeg, the immense and fertile prairies and the prosperous and rapidly growing Western cities of Regina, Saskatoon, Calgary and Edmonton, then the great, baffling, beautiful ranges of the Rocky Mountains, the fruit-growing valleys, swift-flowing rivers and coastal mountains of British Columbia, and finally Vancouver Island, Newfoundland's western counterpart. There is, in other words, an extraordinarily rich mixture of the forbidding and the inviting, of strength and gentleness, of the vast and the enclosed, of power and grace.

There is a similar variety of climatic conditions. In January, Canada is virtually a land of ice and snow, where temperatures may dip as low as seventy-five degrees below zero and where prairie winds blow the snow into impassable mounds; but in July all the land is lush with grass and grain, flowers are blooming in the gardens, the temperature may reach a hundred degrees above zero, and the lakes are alive with boats and bathers.

It is these paradoxes which have so far given to Canadian art and literature its most distinctive qualities. Exhilaration succeeded by or coupled with apprehension—this is what we find expressed over and over again in the most distinctive products of the Canadian imagination. In Canadian painting, we find these responses in the sombre landscapes of Homer Watson, in the storm-tossed but harshly beautiful lakes and trees of Tom Thomson, J. E. H. MacDonald, and Arthur Lismer, in the vast distances and angular mountain shapes of the canvases of Lawren Harris and A. Y. Jackson. More recently, we find similar effects in the British Columbia paintings of Emily Carr, where trees spiral upwards to the sky with a fierce vitality that at once exhilarates and terrifies, or in the Georgian Bay landscapes of Goodridge Roberts, where a superficially calm pastoralism reveals on closer inspection a sickening awareness of transience and decay, or in the muted canvases of Jean-Paul Lemieux, in which stark, haunted figures of men stride across grey limitless plains like ghosts upon the wastes of Time.

In Canadian literature this paradoxical awareness of the glory and terror of the natural environment is everywhere. Bliss Carman who, for all his over-facility and his uncertainty of taste, is still the Canadian poet best known abroad, catches this quality again and again—in "The Windflower," "A Sea Child," and perhaps most successfully in "Low Tide on Grand Pré," a few stanzas of which I should like to quote:

> The sun goes down, and over all
>   These barren reaches by the tide
> Such unelusive glories fall,
>   I almost dream they yet will bide
>   Until the coming of the tide.
>   . . .
> Was it a year or lives ago
>   We took the grasses in our hands,
> And caught the summer flying low
>   Over the waving meadow-lands,
>   And held it there between our hands?
>   . . .
> The night has fallen, and the tide . . . .
>   Now and again comes drifting home,
> Across these aching barrens wide,
>   A sigh like driven wind or foam:
>   In grief the flood is bursting home!

The other poets of that turn of the century generation—Charles G. D. Roberts, Archibald Lampman and Duncan Campbell Scott—were also at their best in capturing the peculiar mixture of excitement and menace found in the Canadian natural scene. Roberts achieves it in poems such as "The Solitary Woodsman," "Ice," and "Tantramar Revisited;" Lampman in "In November," "Heat," and "The City of the End of Things." The image of man dwarfed but spiritually indomitable amid a wilderness that at once frightens and fascinates is perhaps clearest of all in the Indian poems of Duncan Campbell Scott—"The Forsaken," "At Gull Lake," "Night Burial in the Forest," and "Night Hymns on Lake Nipigon."

This double vision is also to be found in the poetry of the late E. J. Pratt, perhaps the greatest poet yet to appear in Canada. His long narrative poems such as *The Roosevelt and the Antinoe, Brébeuf and His Brethren* and *Towards the last Spike* alternately exult in and lament at the strength of rock and sea, and set man in his physical frailty but spiritual tenacity to wrestle tragically or triumphantly with these natural forces.

Even in his shorter poems, such as "The Shark" and "The Sea-Cathedral," Pratt projects this vision of a world which at once repels and allures us.

Although the Canadian poets of the next generation, such as A. J. M. Smith, A. M. Klein, F. R. Scott, Dorothy Livesay and Earle Birney, who began to publish their work in the nineteen-twenties and thirties, were less exclusively interested in nature and man's response to it; even they often achieve their most memorable effects in suggesting the mixture of exhilaration and fear which the Canadian landscape arouses. Smith's "Lonely Land," for example, is a classic example of this double vision, and many of F. R. Scott's imagist-type lyrics about northern streams and rocks imply the same attitude.

And the poets of the most recent generation, whether they be primarily social realists such as Irving Layton, Louis Dudek, Raymond Souster, Fred Cogswell, Alden Nowlan and Alfred Purdy, or more introspective and mythopoeic creators such as James Reaney, Anne Hébert, Alain Grandbois, Margaret Avison and Eli Mandel, still draw much of their imagery from the protean Canadian landscape and weather.

Canadian imaginative prose has at its most successful and characteristic often evoked the same atmosphere and stated the same theme. Probably the greatest Canadian novelist so far to appear was Frederick Philip Grove, and his novels of prairie life, such as *Our Daily Bread, The Yoke of Life,* and *Settlers of the Marsh,* show us the struggle of men to come to terms with a perverse but beautiful environment. Grove's short story "Snow," in which a few neighbours set out in a blizzard to rescue a farmer and find him frozen under drifted snow, is perhaps the clearest expression of this motif in our fiction, although other examples are abundant. One thinks, for example, of the scene with the wolves in Callaghan's *They Shall Inherit the Earth,* or of the prairie dust storm in Sinclair Ross's short story "The Lamp at Noon," and of many scenes in the novels of Ethel Wilson and Hugh MacLennan.

As in poetry, there has recently been in our fiction a shift of emphasis away from man's conflict with and delight in nature. The intricacies of personal relationships, and of the individual's relations with society at large, tend now to be in the forefront. But, for a variety of reasons, Canadian society has seldom been projected as memorably as has Canadian landscape. In part it is that the landscape dwarfs the man, and makes of the average Canadian a relatively inarticulate, shy, practical man. In part, also, it is the lack of any clear sense of Canadian social identity.

The Canadian knows that he is not British, and not American; but exactly what he is, or what he wishes to become, he is uncertain. His society was born not in revolution but in counter-revolution, and he has fought no large-scale civil war. His society has evolved slowly from colony to nation by a series of almost imperceptible changes. What relatively minor crises there have been—the end of the French régime, the War of 1812, the rebellions of 1837, the Confederation of the colonies in 1867, the two World Wars—have quickened our responses, but none of them have stirred Canadians to their depths. Canadians tend therefore to be tentative, compromising and pragmatic in their approach to social and political questions, to be wary of dogma and enthusiasm. This makes them good international negotiators and pacifiers, and enables them to play a most useful role in the peace-keeping efforts of the United Nations. But it gives to their society, and therefore inevitably to the literature and art which attempts to reflect and interpret it, a certain dullness—unless, that is, one can be satisfied with a brilliantly successful effort to build bridges and railroads and dams across difficult terrain.

Another factor discouraging the dramatic portrayal of Canadian social development is the proximity of the United States and the waning but once powerful influence of the United Kingdom. Since these two neighbouring societies are more obviously interesting than Canadian society—that of the United States by virtue of its novelty and vitality, that of the United Kingdom by virtue of its antiquity and picturesqueness—the potential Canadian writer is beset by an inhibiting inferiority complex. Is the relatively drab society of a country such as Canada really worth writing about? Since publishers in the United States and the United Kingdom, upon whom until the last twenty years or so Canadian writers had to depend for publication, were in the habit of saying that ordinary Canadian life was not interesting to their readers, it is no wonder that most Canadian writers concentrated upon their landscape and its animal and vegetable life.

Those writers who nevertheless insisted upon writing of Canadian society tended to approach it from one of two points of view, and occasionally from a combination of the two. On the one hand they could accept the thesis that Canada was dull, but attempt to make that dullness lively by indulging in satire at its expense. This has always been the favourite, face-saving device of our writers, and we can trace a long line of successful satirists, beginning with Thomas Chandler Haliburton in the early nineteenth century and including in this century, most notably, Stephen Leacock, Robertson Davies, Roger Lemelin, Mordecai Richler, Andrè Langevin and Norman Levine in prose, and F. R. Scott and James Reaney in poetry.

Most of those writers who could not or would not be satirical at the expense of their country chose to become regionalists, to chronicle rather sentimentally the idiosyncratic manners and customs of small regions of the country so as to make a case for our distinctiveness. This approach produced the scores of regional idylls which combined to dominate our fiction in the first thirty years of this century, a genre of which the outstanding examples are the novels of Ralph Connor, L. M. Montgomery, Louis Hémon and Mazo de la Roche, the Yukon ballads of Robert Service and Tom MacInnes, and the habitant poems of W. H. Drummond. These writers were all commercially successful, since the quaintness of Canadian life was a saleable commodity. Almost by definition, however, their work fell short of greatness. They deliberately excluded from their work the more forbidding and frightening elements of human experience, and concentrated instead upon an idyllic atmosphere only occasionally ruffled by the gentler winds of chance and change. Most frequently of Presbyterian extraction, these writers were usually didactic in a conventional way, and they presented a sometimes endearing but certainly misleading image of Canadians as a group of clean-minded and strong-bodied men aided and abetted by virtuous and industrious women.

Only a small minority of writers escaped the horns of this dilemma—the dilemma, that is, whether to exaggerate the vices of Canada for satirical effect, or to exaggerate its virtues for sentimental effect. A few chose to confront the Canadian situation squarely, finding drama themselves in the stuff of Canadian life and trusting in their powers to persuade others of its interest. Outstanding among them were the chief Canadian novelists, Frederick Philip Grove, Morley Callaghan, Hugh MacLennan and Ethel Wilson, who, for all their differences in tone, style and theme, shared the basic conviction that Canadian life could be written about without apology or condescension. Associated with them were a few poets, beginning in the nineties with Charles G. D. Roberts and including most prominently the social realists of the forties and fifties such as A. M. Klein, Earle Birney, Irving Layton, Louis Dudek and Raymond Souster. Satire often is found in the writings of these men, both in prose and poetry, but it is not the essential nor the dominant element in their work.

A few others have escaped the dilemma by choosing to ignore the Canadian scene, and to concentrate upon universal themes and symbols. This effort has been especially apparent recently in the work of the mythopoeic school of poets centred in Toronto and associated with the critical theories of Northrop Frye; and Principal Douglas LePan, of University College, Toronto, has recently argued that this is the most hopeful path for future Canadian writers to follow. With this view I find myself in complete disagreement. Most literature which has universality, such as the novels of Hardy or the plays of Shakespeare or the poems of Milton, achieves this universality by the profound exploration of the central issues of its own place and time, and I am convinced that the Canadian works of imagination which will have universal appeal will be those which most searchingly explore Canada.

There is at the present time a great debate in progress in Canada, a debate between the two founding races, English and French, about the very basis of their continued existence together. This debate has brought us closer to a fundamental enquiry into our own identity and destiny than any previous event in Canadian history, and it may be that this confrontation, if we can survive it, will stimulate the Canadian imagination to the point where it can grasp not merely the protean paradoxes of its landscape and climate but also the core of its social and spiritual being.

The Phenomenon of Leonard Cohen*

I n referring to Leonard Cohen as a phenomenon, I am motivated by the quantity, quality and variety of his achievement. Still only thirty-three, Cohen has published four books of verse and two novels, and has made a national if not international reputation by his poetry reading, folk-singing, and skill with the guitar. The best of his poems have lyrical grace and verbal inevitability; his two novels are as perceptive in content and as sophisticated in technique as any that have appeared in English since World War II; and his voice has a magic incantatory quality which hypnotizes his audiences, and especially teen-age audiences, into a state of bliss if not of grace.

In this paper I intend to place the major emphasis on his second novel, *Beautiful Losers* (1966), which is certainly his single most impressive achievement, and in my opinion the most intricate, erudite, and fascinating Canadian novel ever written. But since *Beautiful Losers* is not an isolated achievement, but the culmination of Cohen's career to date, I shall begin by looking at his other books to see how they lead up to and enrich our understanding of it.

The title of Cohen's first book of verse, *Let Us Compare Mythologies* (1956), might have applied almost equally well to his latest novel, which is among other things an exercise in comparative mythology. From the very first, Cohen has been interested in mythology and magic, in the imaginative means which men at all times and in all places have devised to give interest, order, meaning and direction to their world. In *Let Us*

*Delivered as a Centennial Lecture at Sir George Williams University and at the University of Alberta in 1967, and printed, in modified form, in *Canadian Literature*, Autumn 1967.

Compare Mythologies he was chiefly concerned with the similarities and differences between the Hebrew mythology of his
family and the Christian mythology of his environment, but
by the time he wrote *Beautiful Losers* he had become much
more ecumenical. In the novel there are learned allusions to
the mythologies of the North American Indians, Egypt, Greece,
India, Christianity, Tibet, Judaism, and China, as well as to
the contemporary mythologies of the drug traffic, advertise-
ments, comic strips, movies, the hit parade, space travel and
radio and television serials.

The first poem in *Let Us Compare Mythologies*, "Elegy,"
exhibits a number of characteristics which recur throughout
his work:

> Do not look for him
> In brittle mountain streams:
> They are too cold for any god;
> And do not examine the angry rivers
> For shreds of his soft body
> Or turn the shore stones for his blood;
> But in the warm salt ocean
> He is descending through cliffs
> Of slow green water
> And the hovering coloured fish
> Kiss his snow-bruised body
> And build their secret nests
> In his fluttering winding-sheet.
>   (p. 15)

We see there his almost magical control and modulation of verbal melody, his sensuous particularity, the empathetic reach of
his imagination, and his fascination with situations which
mingle violence and tenderness to heighten the effect of both.
We also see emerge for the first time the theme of the quest—
here as usually in Cohen the quest for a lost or unknown God,
mysterious, elusive, but compelling. Cohen, like his racial ances-
tor Spinoza (to whom he frequently alludes), is a man drunk
with God. In "Prayer for Messiah" he writes:

> His blood on my arm is warm as a bird
> his heart in my hand is heavy as lead
> his eyes through my eyes shine brighter than love . . . .
>   (p. 20)

In an old blind man he sees a "City Christ":

> He has returned from countless wars,
> Blinded and hopelessly lame.
> He endures the morning streetcars
> And counts ages in a Peel Street room.
>
> He is kept in his place like a court jew,
> To consult on plagues or hurricanes,
> And he never walks with them on the sea
> Or joins their lonely sidewalk games.
>
> (p. 29)

Almost as prominent in *Let Us Compare Mythologies* as the religious theme is the theme of sex. Indeed in Cohen's work, as in more ancient mythologies, religion and sex are closely associated: this association reaches its culmination in *Beautiful Losers*, but it is embryonically present in this first book of verse. In "Song," for example, the sexual relationship is given a quasi-religious intensity, and the lover is invested with the qualities of a god or semi-divine hero:

> The naked weeping girl
> is thinking of my name
> turning my bronze name
> over and over
> with the thousand fingers
> of her body
> anointing her shoulders
> with the remembered odour
> of my skin
>
> O I am the general
> in her history
> over the fields
> driving the great horses
> dressed in gold cloth
> wind on my breastplate
> sun in my belly
>
> (p. 34)

These twin quests for God and for sexual fulfillment are motivated by the recognition of the individual's vulnerability, by an agonized sense of loneliness. Loneliness and the means of escaping it—sometimes tragic, sometimes pathetic, sometimes at least temporarily successful—form one of the basic and recurrent themes in *Beautiful Losers*. It is present in this first book of verse in "Summer Night," of which I quote the concluding lines:

> Through orchards of black weeds
> with a sigh the river urged its silver flesh.
> From their damp nests bull-frogs croaked
> warnings, but to each other.
> And occasional birds, in a private grudge,
> flew noiselessly at the moon.
> What could we do? We ran naked into the river,
> but our flesh insulted the thick slow water.
> We tried to sit naked on the stones,
> but they were cold and we soon dressed.
> One squeezed a little human music from his box:
> mostly it was lost in the grass
> where one struggled in an ignorant embrace.
> One argued with the slight old hills
> and the goose-fleshed girls, I will not be old.
> One, for his protest, registered a sexual groan.
> And the girl in my arms
> broke suddenly away, and shouted for us all,
> Help! Help! I am alone. But then all subtlety was gone
> and it was stupid to be obvious before the field and sky,
> experts in simplicity. So we fled on the highways,
> in our armoured cars, back to air-conditioned homes.
>
> (p. 55)

But thus to emphasize the serious and tragic aspects of *Let Us Compare Mythologies* is to ignore the wit and humour which here as in all of Cohen's work add variety and contrast to his vision. *Beautiful Losers* is, in one sense, a comic novel, a modern version of picaresque, and among the early poems are several examples of Cohen's comic gift: "The Song of the Hellenist," "When This American Woman," "These Heroics," "Folk Song," "Song," "Satan in Westmount," "Poem," and perhaps best of all, "The Fly:"

> In his black armour
> the house-fly marched the field

of Freia's sleeping thighs,
undisturbed by the soft hand
　　which vaguely moved
to end his exercise.

And it ruined my day—
　　this fly which never planned
to charm her or to please
should walk boldly on that ground
　　I tried so hard
to lay my trembling knees.

　　　　　　　　　　　　(p. 67)

　　Before leaving *Let Us Compare Mythologies* (which was clearly a remarkable book to be written by an undergraduate) I should like to remark on Cohen's descriptive power. The ability to write selective, impressionistic and evocative descriptions of persons and places has always been one of Cohen's strengths. Descriptions of sunsets have been written so often that one would doubt that even the most skilled craftsman would dare to attempt another, or that he would have any chance of achieving novelty of effect if he did. In "Prayer for Sunset," however, Cohen tried and succeeded:

The sun is tangled
　　in black branches,
raving like Absalom
　　between sky and water,
struggling through the dark terebinth
to commit its daily suicide.

Now, slowly, the sea consumes it,
leaving a glistening wound
　　on the water,
　　a red scar on the horizon;
In darkness
　　I set out for home,
terrified by the clash of wind on grass,
and the victory cry of weeds and water.

Is there no Joab for tomorrow night,
　　with three darts
　　and a great heap of stones?

　　　　　　　　　　　　(p. 49)

The poem also illustrates Cohen's erudition, particularly his intimate knowledge of the Bible. Not many poets today are so steeped in Holy Scripture as to recall the circumstances in which Joab killed the rebellious Absalom (see II Samuel XVIII: 14-17.)

The Spice-Box of Earth (1961) reinforces the themes of religious and sexual affirmation and their frequent identification in Cohen's work. The love play celebrated with such hypnotic tenderness in "You Have the Lovers" is compared to a ritual, and the loss of self-consciousness in the sexual union becomes a paradigm of a mystical epiphany:

> When he puts his mouth against her shoulder
> she is uncertain whether her shoulder
> has given or received the kiss.
> All her flesh is like a mouth.
> He carries his fingers along her waist
> and feels his own waist caressed.
> She holds him closer and his own arms tighten around her.
> She kisses the hand beside her mouth.
> It is his hand or her hand, it hardly matters,
> there are so many more kisses.
>
> (p. 33)

For Cohen, the state of sexual fulfillment is virtually synonymous with the state of grace: the fulfilled lover feels himself to be a part of a universal harmony. As he puts it in "Owning Everything":

> Because you are close,
> everything that men make, observe
> or plant is close, is mine:
> the gulls slowly writhing, slowly singing
> on the spears of wind;
> the iron gate above the river;
> the bridge holding between stone fingers
> her cold bright necklace of pearls.
>
> . . .
>
> With your body and your speaking
> you have spoken for everything,
> robbed me of my strangerhood,
> made me one
> with the root and gull and stone. . . .
>
> (pp. 38-39)

(Incidentally, we might notice in passing that the image of the necklace, in line 8 above, becomes one of the thematic symbols of *Beautiful Losers*.)

The identification of religion and sex is also seen in "The Priest Says Goodbye," where the priest is the lover and lust is said to "burn like fire in a holy tree," but its most conspicuous occasion is the poem "Celebration," where the act of fellatio becomes a "ceremony" and is likened to a phallus worship of the ancient Romans, and where the man's semen becomes a "blessing." The clearly affirmative tone of this poem surely gives the lie to those critics of *Beautiful Losers* who profess to find satire and disgust in the sexual scenes. An affirmation of all forms of sexual activity, however "perverse" in conventional terms, provided that they do not involve outright cruelty or murder, is surely an organic part of Cohen's philosophy:

> As the mist leaves no scar
> On the dark green hill,
> So my body leaves no scar
> On you, nor ever will.
>
> (p. 61)

> Beneath my hands
> your small breasts
> are the upturned bellies
> of breathing fallen sparrows.
>
> (p. 63)

But if tenderness and affirmation are present in *The Spice-Box of Earth*, so also are the darker themes of human vulnerability and loneliness and of violence and cruelty. Cohen is a romantic, but he is not the type of romantic optimist who ignores or denies the existence of evil. His compassion for human loneliness is memorably expressed in "I Wonder How Many People in This City":

> I wonder how many people in this city
> live in furnished rooms.
> Late at night when I look out at the buildings
> I swear I see a face in every window
> looking back at me,
> and when I turn away
> I wonder how many go back to their desks
> and write this down.
>
> (p. 12)

In "To a Teacher" he expresses his compassion for a former teacher who has succumbed to madness, and in "Song for Abraham Klein" he encourages that tragically silenced singer to resume his song and thus cure himself of melancholia.

Bitterness at the indignities and false guises imposed upon the Jews dominates "The Genius," and the bitterness of a betrayed lover "The Cuckold's Song." This latter poem is a good illustration of Cohen's versatility of both matter and manner. It begins in anger and modulates into wit and self-mockery; in style it substitutes, for Cohen's usual melodic grace, harsh colloquial diction and angry speech rhythms:

> If this looks like a poem
> I might as well warn you at the beginning
> that it's not meant to be one.
> I don't want to turn anything into poetry.
> I know all about her part in it
> but I'm not concerned with that right now.
> This is between you and me.
> Personally I don't give a damn who led who on:
> in fact I wonder if I give a damn at all.
> But a man's got to say something.
> Anyhow you fed her 5 MacKewan Ales,
> took her to your room, put the right records on,
> and in an hour or two it was done.
>
> . . .
>
> What really makes me sick
> is that everything goes on as it went before:
> I'm still a sort of friend,
> I'm still a sort of lover.
> But not for long:
> that's why I'm telling this to the two of you.
> The fact is I'm turning to gold, turning to gold.
> It's a long process, they say.
> it happens in stages.
> This is to inform you that I've already turned to clay.
>
> (pp. 47-8)

Cohen's descriptive gift in this book is perhaps best illustrated by "An Orchard of Shore Trees," which begins:

> An orchard of shore trees
> precise because of autumn

etches its branches
in the grey silk river

The edge of the sky
fills up with blue and soft sand

A barge bearing lights
    like the leaning faces
of motionless immortal sailors
trails behind
    a cat o' nine tails
made of dark chain
punishing the silken water . . .

                            (p. 15)

A particular premonition of *Beautiful Losers* found in *The Spice-Box of Earth* is the mechanical mistress of "The Girl Toy," which points forward to the Danish Vibrator of the novel. This poem is also one of the first indications of Cohen's fascination with machinery, which becomes a thematic motif in both of his novels. In the poem, as in the novels, Cohen's attitude towards the machine is ambivalent: it is at once frightening and alluring. A further point to be made about "The Girl Toy" is that in its allusions to Yeats' "Sailing to Byzantium" ("famous golden birds," "hammered figures") it is premonitory of the strong Yeatsian influences present in *Beautiful Losers*.

Such premonitions in the early poetry, however, fade into relative insignificance when we examine Cohen's first novel, *The Favourite Game* (1963). It positively bristles with allusions, images and thematic motifs which were to be more fully developed in the second novel. In fact *The Favourite Game*, which at first reading one is apt to dismiss as just another if somewhat superior version of the autobiographical novel of the young artist growing to maturity, becomes a much more richly resonant novel when it is re-read after *Beautiful Losers*. For example, the statement that Martin Stark, the "holy idiot" of *The Favourite Game*, "stuck his index fingers in his ears for no apparent reason, squinting as if he were expecting some drum-splitting explosion" (p. 191) is apt to be passed over on first reading as a mere omen of disaster, but in the light of all the discussion of the Telephone Dance in *Beautiful Losers* it becomes a powerful symbolic allusion to man's perpetual attempts to find connection with the cosmic rhythms. When we read that Wanda's face "blurred into the face of little Lisa . . . that one dissolved into the face of Bertha" (p. 192) we think of the transposition not merely in terms of nostalgia for Breavman's lost loves but in terms of the eternal principle of femininity which in *Beautiful Losers* sees Isis, Catherine, Edith, Mary Voolnd, the Virgin Mary, Marilyn Monroe and the blonde housewife in the car blend into one essential Woman or Universal Mother. The seemingly casual statement that "We all want to be Chinese mystics living in thatched huts, but getting laid frequently" (p. 192) becomes much more meaningful when read in the light of the "go down on a saint" motif in *Beautiful Losers,* and that novel's more fully articulated notion of the desirability of combining spiritual vision with physical ecstasy.

The quest motif, which we have seen to be adumbrated in the early poems, is more fully developed in *The Favourite Game,* but still remains embryonic in contrast with the much more intricate version of it that occurs in *Beautiful Losers.* Breavman's prayerful invocation of God in his journal entry (p. 199) is a sort of first sketch for the narrator's prayers in the second novel, and Breavman's wavering between that quest and greed for secular wealth and success is premonitory of the recurrent pattern of aspiration and rebellion through which the narrator of *Beautiful Losers* passes. Breavman also has a vision of the ultimate unity of all things which prefigures the narrator's visions of cosmic unity in the later novel:

Mozart came loud over the PA, sewing together everything that Breavman observed. It wove, it married the two figures bending over the records, whatever the music touched, child trapped in London Bridge, mountain-top dissolving in mist, empty swing rocking like a pendulum, the row of glistening red canoes, the players clustered underneath the basket, leaping for the ball like a stroboscopic photo of a splashing drop of water— whatever it touched was frozen in an immense tapestry. He was in it, a figure by a railing. (p. 205)

The idea that many forms of popular culture, and especially the hit tunes of the juke-box and the radio, are pathetic but not contemptible versions of this longing for union, this quest for harmony, is also sketched in *The Favourite Game* (see, for example, pp. 222-3), and then much more fully worked out in such sections as "Gavin Gate and the Goddesses" in *Beautiful Losers* (pp. 73-78).

A rather similar link between the two novels is their mutual concern with magic and miracles, and their joint acceptance of the movie as a contemporary form of magic. The most pervasive thematic motif in *The Favourite Game* is Breavman's conception of himself as a sort of magician, miracle-worker, or hypnotist. After Bertha, Breavman's childhood girl-friend, falls from the tree, Breavman says:

> "Krantz, there's something special about my voice."
> "No, there isn't."
> "There is so. I can make things happen."
>
> (p. 15)

After his father's death, Breavman performs a magic rite:

> The day after the funeral Breavman split open one of his father's formal bow ties and sewed in a message. He buried it in the garden, under the snow beside the fence where in summer the neighbour's lilies-of-the-valley infiltrate.
>
> (p. 26)

He also declares that "His father's death gave him a touch of mystery, contact with the unknown. He could speak with extra authority on God and Hell" (p. 27). He studies everything he can about hypnotism, and in one of the funniest scenes in the novel hypnotizes his mother's maid and has her make love to him (pp. 51-56). Breavman sounds very much like F. in *Beautiful Losers* when he tells the girl, Tamara, "I want to touch people like a magician, to change them or hurt them, leave my brand, make them beautiful" (p. 101). Again reminding us of F., and more especially of the narrator of *Beautiful Losers*, Breavman longs for a miraculous transfiguration of himself:

> In his room in the World Student House, Breavman leans elbows on the window-sill and watches the sun ignite the Hudson. It is no longer the garbage river, catch-all for safes, excrement, industrial poison, the route of strings of ponderous barges.

Can something do that to his body?

There must be something written on the fiery water. An affi-
davit from God. A detailed destiny chart. The address of his
perfect wife. A message choosing him for glory or martyrdom.

(p. 139)

When he is enjoying the love-affair with Shell, and writing the
love poetry which appeared in *The Spice-Box of Earth*, Breavman feels that he is creative because he is "attached to magic"
(p. 165). At the boys' camp, Breavman longs to be "calm and
magical," to be "the gentle hero the folk come to love, the man
who talks to animals, the Baal Shem Tov who carried children
piggy-back" (p. 187). But the closest approximation to the great
thematic passage about magic in *Beautiful Losers* comes in *The
Favourite Game* when Breavman watches the firefly and thinks
that it is dying:

He had given himself to the firefly's crisis. The intervals became longer and longer between the small cold flashes. It was
Tinker Bell. Everybody had to believe in magic. Nobody believed in magic. He didn't believe in magic. Magic didn't
believe in magic. Please don't die.

It didn't. It flashed long after Wanda left. It flashed when
Krantz came to borrow Ed's *Time* magazine. It flashed as he
tried to sleep. It flashed as he scribbled his journal in the dark.

(p. 194)

The firefly there is obviously a symbol of an ultimate light, is
a pulsing signal from the eternal rhythm, and its continued
life, as time (*Time*) is carried away, bespeaks the persistence of
Light. This symbolic method of writing, which only occasionally overrides the literal method in *The Favourite Game*,
becomes continuous in *Beautiful Losers*, which is a powerful
symbolist novel from beginning to end.

A special form of the magical theme is the emphasis Cohen
places on the movies as the chief contemporary expression of
the magical process. References to movies occur on almost every
page of *Beautiful Losers*, but the emphasis first becomes apparent in *The Favourite Game*. Near the beginning of that first
novel, Breavman watches a movie of his family in the course of
which "A gardener is led shy and grateful into the sunlight to

be preserved with his betters" (p. 10). Obviously the magical quality of movies alluded to here is their capacity to preserve mortals after death, to confer a sort of immortality. Later on, Breavman imagines himself and the girl Norma as they would appear in the camera eye:

The camera takes them from faraway, moves through the forest, catches the glint of a raccoon's eyes, examines the water, reeds, closed water-flowers, involves itself with mist and rocks.
"Lie beside me," Norma's voice, maybe Breavman's.
Sudden close-up of her body part by part, lingering over the mounds of her thighs, which are presented immense and shadowed, the blue denim tight on the flesh. The fan of creases between her thighs. Camera searches her jacket for the shape of breasts. She exhumes a pack of cigarettes. Activity is studied closely. Her fingers move like tentacles. Manipulation of cigarette skilled and suggestive. Fingers are slow, violent, capable of holding anything.

(p. 73)

Here what fascinates Cohen, as it will again in *Beautiful Losers*, is the magical capacity of the camera to transfigure reality, to intensify experience, and to suggest symbolic overtones by its searching examination of the details of fact. One source of Breavman's magical insight is that a "slow-motion movie" is "always running somewhere in his mind" (p. 99).

This in turn suggests another way in which *The Favourite Game* illuminates one of the themes of *Beautiful Losers*. In the later novel, F. tells the narrator (and since most of the narrative is in the first person, I shall hereafter speak of the narrator as "I") that "We've got to learn to stop bravely at the surface. We've got to learn to love appearances" (p. 4). On other occasions he directs "I" never to overlook the obvious (p. 10), to "aim yourself at the tinkly present" (p. 12), and to "Connect nothing . . . Place things side by side on your arborite table, if you must, but connect nothing" (p. 17). Subsequently, in a passage which out of context is rather obscure, he says:

Of all the laws which bind us to the past, the names of things are the most severe. . . . Names preserve the dignity of Appearance. . . . Science begins in coarse naming, a willingness to disregard the particular shape and destiny of each red life, and call

them all Rose To a more brutal, more active eye, *all* flowers
look alike, like Negroes and Chinamen.

(p. 40)

What the slow-motion camera does is to reveal the individuality
of things, the sensuous particularity of being. Cohen's belief is
that the truly magical view is not attained by looking at the
world through a haze of generality, or through the still frames
of scientific categories, but by examining as closely as possible
the particular streaks on the particular tulip. In this he resembles Wordsworth, who sought by close examination of the
familiar to discover the element of wonder in it. (If the juxtaposition of Cohen and Wordsworth seems odd, it might be useful to recall that at least once in *Beautiful Losers* there is an
obvious echo of Wordsworth's "Tintern Abbey"—"Five years
with the length of five years," [p. 145]). Hence it is that we get
such passages as the following in *The Favourite Game*, passages
in which the search for sensuous exactitude has been developed
into a fine art:

How many leaves have to scrape together to record the rustle
of the wind? He tried to distinguish the sound of acacia from
the sound of maple. (p. 66)

"If you tape their [birds'] whistles, Shell, and slow them
down, you can hear the most extraordinary things. What the
naked ear hears as one note is often in reality two or three notes
sung simultaneously. A bird can sing three notes at the same
time. (p. 169. See also *Beautiful Losers* p. 160)

There is another way in which the use of movies in *The
Favourite Game* points forward to *Beautiful Losers*. Breavman
says to his friend Krantz "we're walking into a European movie"
(p. 107), and proceeds to imagine himself as an old army officer
in such a film. This exemplifies another magical power of the
cinema: its capacity to enlarge our experience, to provide us
with vicarious living. This is what F. alludes to in *Beautiful
Losers* when he writes to "I", "You know what pain looks like,
that kind of pain, you've been inside newsreel Belsen" (p. 194).

Closely related to this matter of magic, and serving as a further link between *The Favourite Game* and *Beautiful Losers*,
are the games which figure so prominently in both novels. The

game is a kind of ritual which imposes order and pleasure on the minutiae of daily living, and is thus in itself a kind of micro-myth or semi-sacred rite. In *Beautiful Losers*, F. says, "Games are nature's most beautiful creation. All animals play games, and the truly Messianic vision of the brotherhood of creatures must be based on the idea of the game . . ." (p. 29). When F. buys the factory, he does not exploit it for commercial success, but turns it into a playground (p. 42). Games play a very large part in *The Favourite Game*, as the title would suggest: Breavman plays a game with Bertha which leads to her fall from the apple-tree (p. 14), he plays "The Soldier and the Whore" with Lisa (pp. 27 ff) and he wrestles with her in the snow (p. 34), he visualizes Krantz as "first figure of a follow-the-leader game through the woods" (p. 99), he watches a baseball-game at the boys' camp where he works for the summer (p. 209), and at the very end of the novel he remembers "the favourite game" of his childhood:

Jesus! I just remembered what Lisa's favourite game was. After a heavy snow we would go into a back yard with a few of our friends. The expanse of snow would be white and un-broken. Bertha was the spinner. You held her hands while she turned on her heels, you circled her until your feet left the ground. Then she let go and you flew over the snow. You re-mained still in whatever position you landed. When everyone had been flung in this fashion into the fresh snow, the beautiful part of the game began. You stood up carefully, taking great pains not to disturb the impression you had made. Now the comparisons. Of course you would have done your best to land in some crazy position, arms and legs sticking out. Then we walked away, leaving a lovely white field of blossom-like shapes with footprint stems.   (p. 223)

The dust-jacket of *The Favourite Game* declares that "the favourite game itself is love", but this seems to be a serious mis-reading of the novel. As I read it, and especially the final para-graph, the favourite game is to leave an impression on the snow, to leave behind one an interesting design, and by extension I take this to include the novel itself, which is Cohen's design of his own early life, and by further extension all artistic creation. The game is beautiful for Cohen because it is associated with the innocence of childhood and because it is a successful attempt of the human imagination to impose order upon reality. Two of F.'s ideas in *Beautiful Losers* are relevant here. At one point he declares "Prayer is translation. A man translates himself into a child asking for all there is in a language he has barely mastered" (p. 56). At another, we are told that F.'s "allegiance is to the notion that he is not bound to the world as given, that he can escape from the painful arrangement of things as they are" (p. 55). "Escapism", so long a derogatory term in twentieth-century literary circles, is for Cohen a desirable thing: movies, games, radio hit tunes, art and prayer are desirable things because they lift us out of the ruck of routine and above the rubble of time.

There are other ways in which *The Favourite Game* is premonitory of *Beautiful Losers*—the incidental comments on Canada, on Montreal, and on Jewish life and values; the humour; the alternation between tenderness and violence; the wavering between self-glorification and self-doubt; the hostile allusions to scientific achievement; the many ambivalent references to machinery; the stress on sexual ecstasy and especially upon the oral forms of it and upon masturbation; the contempt for conventional bourgeois behaviour and attitudes; recurrent images which give to the novel a poetic resonance; the emphasis upon loneliness and nostalgia—but rather than take time to develop them I feel I must point out how this first novel *differs* from its successor. It is a much more subjective novel, and a much more self-indulgent one. Whereas *Beautiful Losers* is about a cast of characters none of whom bear much resemblance to Cohen himself or to members of his family and his friends, *The Favourite Game* is quite obviously autobiographical. Like Joyce's *Portrait*, it is a novel in the lyrical mode, whereas *Beautiful Losers* is much closer to the dramatic mode of *Finnegans Wake*. Much of *The Favourite Game* is taken up with family history—the death of Breavman's father, the neurotic possessiveness and ultimate psychosis of his mother, the pathetic respectability of his uncles. These scenes, and those dealing with the author's own youthful memories, are the strongest part of the book: the author is still at the stage of recording rather than dominating and transforming reality. When, in the Shell-Gordon interlude, he tries to get into the minds of a young New England woman and her husband, most of the life and particularity goes out of the style.

Since *The Spice-Box of Earth* was also a very personal book, Cohen seems to have felt that he must break out of the prison of self and attempt a more objective art. The significance of his third book of poems, *Flowers for Hitler* (1964), at any rate in relation to *Beautiful Losers,* lies in its strenuous effort to broaden and deepen and objectify its author's interests and sympathies. In a rather too flamboyant but still basically honest note to the publisher, which is printed on the dust-jacket, Cohen declares of *Flowers for Hitler*:

This book moves me from the world of the golden-boy poet into the dung pile of the front-line writer. I didn't plan it this way. I loved the tender notices Spice-Box got but they embarrassed me a little. *Hitler* won't get the same hospitality from the papers. My sounds are too new, therefore people will say: this is derivative, this is slight, his power has failed. Well, I say that there has never been a book like this, prose or poetry, written in Canada. All I ask is that you put it in the hands of my generation and it will be recognized.

I have not read carefully the reviews of *Flowers for Hitler,* so I cannot say whether Cohen's fears were justified. I do know, however, that the charge of derivativeness has been levelled at *Beautiful Losers,* and that it has been compared (very vaguely, as is the safe way) to Sartre, Gênet, Burroughs, Thomas Pynchon, John Barth, and Allen Ginsberg. One important object of my present exercise is to show that *Beautiful Losers* can best be seen as the culmination of Cohen's own artistic development, not as the imitation of someone else.

Flowers for Hitler is not quite as different from its predecessors as Cohen's dust-jacket statement might lead us to believe. As the title suggests, there is still the juxtaposition of beauty and ugliness, tenderness and violence, which we have seen to have been a feature of his work from the beginning; there are still a number of love poems which combine wit, tenderness, and passion; there are still poems of humorous self-mockery and ironic ballads of everyday life. But the new element is there, and it predominates. It takes, largely, two forms: disgust at and revulsion from the greed, hypocrisy, and cruelty of twentieth-century politics, and a newly urgent longing for a religious transfiguration which will rid the poet of his self-absorption.

In the political poems, he expresses the idea that the horrors of our age make those of previous generations seem insignificant. Here, for example, is "Congratulations":

Here we are eating the sacred mushrooms
out of the Japanese heaven
eating the flower
in the sands of Nevada

Hey Marco Polo
and you Arthur Rimbaud
friends of the sailing craft
examine our time's adventure
the jewelled house of Dachau
Belsen's drunk fraternity

Don't your boats seem
like floating violins
playing Jack Benny tunes?
(p. 15)

Canadian political life is merely sordid and dull:

The gold roof of Parliament covered
with fingerprints and scratches.
And here are the elected, hunchbacked
from climbing on each other's heads.
(p. 18)

History he dismisses as an opiate:

History is a needle
for putting men asleep
anointed with the poison
of all they want to keep
(p. 25)

(This passage, incidentally, turns up again in *Beautiful Losers,* in slightly amended form, as "F.'s Invocation to History in the Middle Style," p. 188.) Canada is "a dying animal" to which he refuses (adapting a line from Yeats) to "be fastened" (p. 35). Everywhere he looks he sees guilt and corruption, and he feels his own involvement in it and revulsion from it.

This part of *Flowers for Hitler* points forward to F.'s political involvement in *Beautiful Losers*: F. is a French-Canadian nationalist, a Separatist, a Member of Parliament, a revolutionary leader, and his final political gesture is to blow up the statue of Queen Victoria on Sherbrooke Street. But F. himself recognizes that the sense of involvement with other men which leads to his kind of political activity is only a stage on the way to the final break-through which he hopes "I" will achieve. "I"'s final apotheosis transcends politics: it involves transfiguration, not an improvement of time but a leap into eternity. Cohen's inability to take politics seriously perhaps explains the rather artificial, laboured quality of the political poems in *Flowers for Hitler*. (Or perhaps it is that my own inability to take politics seriously inhibits my response to the poems.)

The final answer of *Beautiful Losers*, the loss of self in the pursuit of sainthood, is also adumbrated in *Flowers for Hitler*. The process begins in confession of guilt: in the very first poem, "What I'm Doing Here," Cohen confesses that he has lied, conspired against love, tortured, and hated, and he ends by calling upon "each one of you to confess" (p. 13). Confession leads to humility, as in "The Hearth" where he learns that his lust "was not so rare a masterpiece" (p. 14), and to self-abnegation in which he vows to forget his personal style and surrender to the mysterious silence, become a vessel for renewing grace:

> I will forget my style
> Perhaps a mind will open in this world
> perhaps a heart will catch rain
> Nothing will heal and nothing will freeze
> but perhaps a heart will catch rain . . .
>
> (p. 27)

He longs for purgation and discipline leading to a new life:

> There is a whitewashed hotel waiting for me
> somewhere, in which I will begin my fast and
> my new life.
> Oh to stand in the Ganges wielding a yard of
> intestine.   (p. 61)

> Let me renew myself
> in the midst of all the things of the world
> which cannot be connected.   (p. 70)

This idea is perhaps best expressed in "For Anyone Dressed in Marble," in a passage which also finds its way in *Beautiful Losers*:

> I see an orphan, lawless and serene,
> standing in a corner of the sky,
> body something like bodies that have been,
> but not the scar of naming in his eye.
> Bred close to the ovens, he's burnt inside.
> Light, wind, cold, dark—they use him like a bride.
>
> (p. 80)

The "saint" is a lawless orphan because he has detached himself from the claims of family and society; he stands in a corner of the sky because he has transcended earthly values; he has a body because he is still human, but he has overcome the human fault of missing the particular in the general by the use of "coarse names"; aware of human violence as expressed in the gas ovens of Nazi Germany, he has been purged by his closeness to it and has become a kind of empty vessel into which the eternal powers may pour themselves.

With all this as background and context, *Beautiful Losers* (1966) becomes relatively easy to appreciate and understand. I say *relatively* easy, because it remains a difficult and sometimes baffling book The first time I read it I only had a glimmer of its meaning; I have now read it eight times, and I still do not fully understand it. (It is ironical that Dennis Duffy, reviewing it in *Tamarack Review,* Summer, 1966, should have stated, "As it stands, it is a novel definitely to be read, but only once.") However, I think I understand it better than the authors of most of the reviews I have seen, and at the risk of being wrong I am going to make an attempt at elucidation.

First, the title. Beautiful Losers are those who achieve the beauty of "sainthood" (and it is necessary to put that word in quotes because Cohen uses it, as we shall see in a moment, in a special sense) by losing, or rather by voluntarily surrendering, their selves and the ordinary world. In the eyes of the world, they are "losers," for they are victims: Catherine dies in agony of slow starvation and self-torture; Edith is crushed by a descending elevator; Mary Voolnd is mauled by savage police dogs; F. dies in an asylum for the criminally insane; "I" is at the end of the novel a ragged, stinking, old "freak of the woods." But *sub specie aeternitatis*, or in the eyes of God, these characters are not losers at all: Catherine deliberately surrenders herself to be the Bride of Christ, is canonized, and becomes a miraculous healer; Edith commits voluntary suicide to teach "I" a lesson which at first he ignores but which ultimately leads him to his apotheosis; Mary Voolnd surrenders herself to the sexual pleasure of F. when he is at his unattractive worst and brings him the good news of his recognition as first president of the republic; F. deliberately casts himself in the subordinate role of teacher and guide of "I" and shows him the way to the Promised Land; "I" achieves final apotheosis and in the last paragraph of the novel is seen playing the role of Mediator between God and Man, or of the Suffering Servant who has gone through agony to achieve compassion:

> Poor men, poor men, such as we, they've gone and fled. I will plead from electrical tower. I will plead from turret of plane. He will uncover His face. He will not leave me alone. I will spread His name in Parliament. I will welcome His silence in pain. I have come through the fire of family and love. I smoke with my darling, I sleep with my friend. We talk of the poor men, broken and fled. Alone with my radio I lift up my hands. Welcome to you who read me today. Welcome to you who put my heart down. Welcome to you, darling and friend, who miss me forever in your trip to the end.   (p. 243)

Voluntary loss of self for some higher cause is, then, the main theme of *Beautiful Losers*, but it is developed in great complexity and intricacy against a background of mythological ecumenicity and is supplemented by a variety of secondary themes.

At a climactic moment of the novel, Edith breaks into Greek to declare "I am Isis, born of all things, both what is and what shall be, and no mortal has ever lifted my robe" (p. 183). We may recall here that on the first page of the novel "I" declares that he wants to "know what goes on under that rosy blanket" of Catherine Tekakwitha: so Catherine is also Isis. Indeed all the women of the novel are essentially the same woman, or the same goddess, just as Isis gradually took over all the other goddesses in the ancient world. The greatest significance of the Isis cult, which developed in Egypt in the seventeenth century B.C.

and gradually spread throughout the whole Mediterranean world, lay in her role of Universal Mother and her agency in effecting immortality of the soul and renewal of life. She included in herself the virtues of all other goddesses, and she offered to her devotees forgiveness, purgation, communion and regeneration. Her mythological role in piecing together the fragments of her husband Osiris symbolized her miraculous healing power. Once one becomes aware of Edith's role as Isis, many of the jigsaw pieces of the novel fall into significant patterns: it is in her Isis role of Universal Mother that Edith, with her phenomenally large nipples, gives herself to "I" and F., comforts the stranger on the beach at Old Orchard, Maine (p. 36), and even cradles the "famous head" of the presumably forgiven Hitler against her breasts (p. 183). By her voluntary suicide in the elevator shaft, Edith effects a restoration of her husband similar to Isis's restoration of Osiris. When we read the description of Edith's coating herself with "deep red greasy stuff" and saying to "I" "Let's be other people" (p. 14), we recall that one of Isis's roles was that of the bringer-forth of the indwelling self, of the agent of miraculous transfiguration. "I" notes that Edith's "kisses were loose, somehow unspecific, as if her mouth couldn't choose where to stay" (p. 23)—and this we can relate to the concept of the mouth of Isis as full of the breath of life, issuing forth to heal the soul and regenerate the dead. We recall also that Mary Voolnd, another Isis figure, is a nurse, and that Edith is several times referred to as a nurse.

The second major mythological framework of *Beautiful Losers* is that of Christianity. This is an apt juxtaposition since the cult of Isis rivalled the cult of Christ in the Mediterranean world, and sometimes blended with it. Isis herself was frequently identified with the Virgin Mary, and this identification is made anew in Cohen's novel. Catherine is the Iroquois Virgin, and models herself upon the Virgin Mary; by renouncing the ownership of her own flesh she achieves a mystic vision:

And as she thus disclaimed the ownership of her flesh she sensed a minute knowledge of his innocence, a tiny awareness of the beauty of all the faces circled round the crackling fires of the village. Ah, the pain eased, the torn flesh she finally did not own healed in its freedom, and a new description of herself, so brutally earned, forced itself into her heart: she was Virgin.

(pp. 50-1)

But since Edith and Catherine are obviously one person in different guises, Edith is also the Virgin Mary: although she is not physically a virgin, she plays the role of intercessor and comforter. So also does Mary Voolnd, although her way of expressing compassionate love may seem the very antithesis of virginity.

The men also are loosely associated with Christian figures. F. refers to himself on various occasions as Moses, who has led his friends within sight of the Promised Land but cannot take them there; at other times he speaks of his role in terms which recall John the Baptist. "I," on the other hand, develops eventually into a Christ-like figure. In the final paragraph, as we have seen, he becomes the compassionate mediator pleading from his tower. (In this connection, it is worth noting that in the poem "Suzanne" Cohen speaks of Christ on his "wooden tower", the Cross.) Previous to that, "I" has stayed for a prolonged period in a tree-house in the woods, paralleling Christ's sojourn in the wilderness. Even the body-builder Charles Axis is linked with Christ: "'Charles Axis is all compassion, he's our sacrifice!'" (p. 72), and his name suggests that he too is an axis or link between God and man.

A number of other mythologies are worked into *Beautiful Losers,* but there is space here only to glance at them. There are, as we might expect since "I" is a folk-lorist, anthropologist, and student of the North American Indians, many references to and indeed detailed descriptions of Red Indian myths and rites— Rainmaking (p. 31), mythical cosmogony (p. 85), the wrestling match between the White one and the Dark one (p. 88), Klooskap (p. 89), the Oscotarach or Head-Piercer's Hut (pp. 114, 133, 184), and the Andacwandet or Fuck-Cure (pp. 128-132). Greek mythology is represented, significantly, by Icarus (p. 212) and Prometheus (p. 237), both of whom fit the novel well since they sought to unite heaven and earth, God and man. There are apt references to Oriental Indian mythology and religious rites: to the mandala (p. 214), yoga (pp. 160, 236), Asoka's Circle, and Tantric love perfectionists. The Jewish Kabbala is mentioned, as is the Chinese "Holy mountain" and the wisdom of Kung.

These more or less ancient mythologists are supplemented with more recent myths and magical manifestations: the magic of Houdini (p. 38), the mythology of the comic strips and radio programmes, the magic rituals of the Masonic Order (p. 145), the myth of astrology (see, for example, the reference to the Virgo disease (p. 162)*, the magic of firecrackers and guns and rockets. But the contemporary mythology and magic which is most stressed is that of the movies. There are several references to the goddesses of the silver screen, Marilyn Monroe and Brigitte Bardot, and a host of references to the magic powers of the film to heighten reality, preserve the past, record the present, create imaginary worlds, expand the consciousness, enlarge the awareness, arouse the conscience, stimulate the passions, or excite the imagination. The System Theatre becomes the contemporary temple or cathedral, into which only initiates are allowed to pass after negotiating the barrier of the ticket collector in the outer courtyard or foyer.

All of these references to mythology and magic reach their culmination in the passage which announces the secondary (some might argue that it is the primary) theme of *Beautiful Losers*: that magic and religion *not* science and politics are the real powers in the world. In what F. describes as the "sweet burden of my argument," he proclaims:

God is alive. Magic is afoot. God is afoot. Magic is alive. Alice is afoot. Magic never died. God never sickened. Many poor men lied. Many sick men lied. Magic never weakened. Magic never hid. Magic always ruled. God is afoot. God never died. God was ruler though his funeral lengthened. Though his mourners thickened Magic never fled. . . . Though laws were carved in marble they could not shelter men. . . . Magic is afoot. . . . But Magic is no instrument. Magic is the end. . . . This I mean my mind to serve till service is but Magic moving through the world, and mind itself is Magic coursing through the flesh, and flesh itself is Magic dancing on a clock, and time itself the Magic Length of God. (pp. 157-8)

As I have said, there are several subsidiary themes running through *Beautiful Losers*. Perhaps the third most important is that which announces the close association of religion and sex. One of the apparent paradoxes of this novel is that its main

---

*This obscure allusion is indicative of the patient skill with which this novel has been worked out. It is F. who says he has the Virgo disease, as elsewhere he declares that he once was a woman and had a Swedish operation to change his sex. Virgo is the sixth sign of the Zodiac, and by the Egyptians was assigned to Isis. It was symbolic of hermaphroditism, and was the supreme expression of the dynamic consciousness.

characters, all of whom are "heroes" in the sense that they are to some degree at least being held up to our admiration, have such divergent attitudes towards sex. Catherine renounces the flesh altogether and remains a virgin; Edith, on the other hand, is a relatively compliant wife to "I" but without compunction commits adultery with F. on six or seven occasions. F. is completely promiscuous, admits that he has chased women wherever they have led him, glories in his sexual "scores" with both sexes, and even in his dying moments has his hand up the skirt of Mary Voolnd. "I" has had homosexual relations with F., has had a rather frustrating sexual life with Edith (she is not compliant enough for him—he has rather special tastes), and spends a great deal of time in masturbation. All the sexuality in the novel, of course, comes to a climax in the orgy which F. and Edith perform with the so-called Danish Vibrator or Sex Machine. What are we to make of all this? Is Cohen upholding virginity or promiscuity, sexual abstinence or sexual orgies?

I am not sure that I can satisfactorily answer these questions, but I think the clue to the resolution of the paradox is in Cohen's special conception of sainthood. Recalling F.'s advice to "go down on a saint," "I" speculates:

What is a saint? A saint is someone who has achieved a remote human possibility. It is impossible to say what that possibility is. I think it has something to do with the energy of love. Contact with this energy results in the exercise of a kind of balance in the chaos of existence (p. 95).

To "go down on a saint," then, is at second-hand to make contact with the energy of love, as well as to combine physical ecstasy with spiritual vision. Catherine is a saint because she has achieved the remote human possibility of making contact with the energy of love, that is God, through the renunciation of the flesh; Edith is a saint because she has made contact through her maternal role towards all men; F. is a saint because he has made contact with divine energy through sex and because he commits himself to the remote possibility of a revolution in Quebec; "I" becomes a saint at the end of the novel because by exiling himself to the wilderness he has purged himself of pride and selfishness and made of himself an empty vessel into which divine love can pour. A saint, if you like, is an extremist. For

Cohen, truth is not in the mean but in the extremes. F. declares "I was never drunk enough, never poor enough, never rich enough." Catherine in the extremity of her flagellations is closer to Edith and F. in the extremity of their orgy with the Danish Vibrator than she is to a member of the bourgeoisie leading a respectable and moderate life. Is it too fanciful to suggest that in referring to the sex machine by its initials, D.V., Cohen is suggesting that the surrender to it is not so very different from the surrender to God's will?

A closely related subsidiary theme is that of what we might call pan-orgasmic sex. F. declares that "all parts of the body are erotogenic. All flesh can come!" (p. 32) and he maintains that almost any contact can lead us into "the nourishing anonymity of the climax" (p. 33). (Here, incidentally, is another of the links between religion and sex—sex leads to anonymity, into that loss of self-consciousness which is the prerequisite of religious response.)

Rather than deal further with the minor themes of the novel, I should like now to say something about its technique. In structure it resembles a symbolic poem: it is divided into the traditional three parts, and its parts are woven together by recurrent thematic motifs and thematic images or symbols. Among the motifs are references to "I"'s constipation (a symbol of the self locked in upon itself), to his masturbation (a symbol of his lonely self-absorption and self-indulgence), to games (symbols of life as free choice), to radio music and radio serials (symbols of attempts to reach contact with some outside force or message), to baptism (symbol of purification and the entry into a new life), and above all to movies, films, cinemas and film-stars (symbols, as we have seen, of contemporary magic and escape from this world). Among the thematic images are the blanket or veil (symbol of mystery and the hoped-for apocalypse), birch and pine trees (symbols of natural growth, beauty, and the fragrance of natural things), rivers, springs and pools (symbols of purification and divine grace), birds (symbols of the ingression of the divine upon the human), altars and temples (symbols of worship, aspiration and sacrifice), stars (associated with Isis and symbols of divine perfection and protection), the elevator (an ambivalent symbol, suggesting both the ascent to heaven and the descent into hell), mountains (symbols of contemplation and detached wisdom), machinery (another ambivalent symbol, suggesting the "eternal machinery" of cosmic process and the destructive machinery of warfare and greed), the necklace (symbol of multiplicity in unity, the many in the one), crystals, snowflakes and the rainbow pictures seen through them (symbolic of divine order, intricacy and vision), soap and especially F.'s "soap collection" (symbols of purification through suffering), rockets, firecrackers, and "fiery journeys" (symbols of the attempt to penetrate the veil of heaven), fishes (symbols of Christ and of divine grace), candy (symbol of pleasure and perhaps of God's mercy), the factory which is converted into a playground (symbol of the transfiguration of labour into play, as in the last stanza of Yeats' "Among Schoolchildren.") Each of these motifs or images recurs frequently, and in each case the symbolic suggestion is intended: the result is a novel more intricately interwoven than any Canadian novel of my experience.

An associated feature of the technique of this novel is its clever manipulation of chronology. We move back and forth from the present to the near-past to the distant-past of Catherine Tekakwitha, the seventeenth-century Iroquois virgin, and yet the transitions, though often abrupt and frequent, are never misleading or confusing. Similarly, although we shuttle back and forth between various points of view, we never get confused between the different characters: each is consistent (if only in inconsistency), distinctive, and credible.

Beautiful Losers, the riches of which I have only touched upon, is certainly the chief accomplishment of Leonard Cohen thus far, and the culmination of all his previous work. But it is not likely to be the end of the phenomenon of Leonard Cohen. Already, since it was published less than a year ago, he has published another book of verse, *Parasites of Heaven* (1966), and he probably has another novel underway. Also, the deftness of his short play, "The New Step," contained in *Flowers for Hitler,* suggests that he may have the capacity to become a dramatist of the first rank, and his knowledge of movie technique is such that I feel sure he could be a successful film-maker. Floreat, Leonard Cohen!

The Outlook for Canadian Literature*

For over a quarter of a century now, I have been engaged intermittently in the task of publicly taking the pulse of Canadian literature. I am not quite so naive as to think that my activity in this regard has been of any particular help either to the patient or to the public, but it has been a source of innocent amusement for me, and at least I have the satisfaction of knowing that the patient is in rather better health than when my diagnosis began. This is a statement which not all doctors could make with equal assurance.

It was in December, 1938, that I made my first and very tentative examination. I had a few months before arrived in Cambridge, England, as a Research Student in English Literature. Although I had only lived in Canada seven years, I had conceived a deep love for the country and a considerable although by no means profound admiration for its literature. I was annoyed to find that my fellow-students at Cambridge were not only ignorant of a Canadian literature, but pretended to believe that it did not exist. I therefore wrote, and published in *The Cambridge Review*, an article optimistically entitled "At Last— A Canadian Literature."[1] There was no question mark after that title: it was an arrogant assertion, rather than a modest question, and the symptom, no doubt, of a youthful brashness which I have not even yet succeeded in eliminating from my personality.

The theme of that first article was that after a long period of derivativeness, Canadian literature was at last finding distinctive voices and distinctive modes of utterance. I based my case

*Published in *Canadian Literature*, Spring, 1968.
[1]See p. 1 above.

largely on the poetry of E. J. Pratt and the novels and stories of Morley Callaghan; both of these writers I had come to know personally during my student days at the University of Toronto. The case was certainly not argued very cogently, for there were virtually no Canadian books available to me in Cambridge, and I had to write almost entirely from memory.

The reception of that article was not so enthusiastic as to determine me to play permanently the role, recently attributed to me by *The Times Literary Supplement*, of "the distinguished apologist for Canadian literature," and I might well have lost all interest in the subject had it not been for an incident in my early teaching career at Brandon College. The University of Manitoba at that time had a series of province-wide radio programmes known as "The University on the Air," and Brandon College had been assigned a group of these programmes with the sub-title "Manitoba Sketches." I was asked to do a fifteen-minute talk on "Manitoba in Literature," and as the only Manitoba author I had ever read was Frederick Philip Grove, I devoted the whole programme to his novels. One thing led to another: the editor of the *Manitoba Arts Review* asked me to develop the radio talk into an article; Dr. Lorne Pierce of The Ryerson Press read the article and asked me to expand it into a book; and so my curious career as a Canadian literary critic of sorts was launched.

When I began my study of Canadian literature, two much more distinguished men were also—quite unknown to me—making their first systematic examinations of it. I refer to the late E. K. Brown and to A. J. M. Smith, both of whom published very important books on the subject in 1943. As far as the *study* of Canadian literature is concerned, the decisive turning point in my opinion was the publication in that year of Brown's *On Canadian Poetry* and of Smith's *Book of Canadian Poetry*. Neither of these men could be charged with parochialism, narrow nationalism, or special pleading, since both, although of Canadian origin, had received their postgraduate training at great overseas universities and had taken up important posts in American universities—Brown at the University of Chicago, and Smith at Michigan State.

At that time the study of Canadian literature was far from being academically respectable. A few universities included a small amount of Canadian writing in their literary courses, but there were no full-year undergraduate courses in the subject, still less any graduate courses, and still less any professors of English who made Canadian literature their specialty. The situation has changed radically in the past two decades, and it is changing so rapidly today that one begins to wonder whether the pendulum may not swing too far. The number of students taking courses in Canadian literature in our universities is already large, and shows no sign of abating. There are approximately two hundred and sixty such students this academic year at U.N.B., and I am told that there are four hundred and fifty at the University of Western Ontario, well over a hundred at the University of Alberta, and over two hundred at the University of British Columbia. Even the University of Toronto, which in my day allowed us about two weeks for a hasty glimpse of Canadian literature at the end of a course rather misleadingly called "American and Canadian Literature," has recently initiated, I understand, a full undergraduate course in the subject.

Furthermore, the Americans, who have so assiduously cultivated English and American literature, are now looking for fresh fields to conquer—and many of them are looking over our border. An Institute of Canadian Studies was recently set up at the University of Vermont, and Canadian literature is being studied, usually in the larger context of the literature of the Commonwealth, at several other American universities, notably Texas and Pennsylvania. Another symptom of this growing American interest in our literature is the recent establishment of a Commonwealth Literature group in the Modern Language Association of America. This trend is sure to continue and accelerate.

There are yet other signs that the study of Canadian literature has become academically respectable. One was the foundation in 1959 at the University of British Columbia of the magazine *Canadian Literature*, which, under the distinguished editorship of George Woodcock, has maintained a high standard of literary history, criticism and scholarship. Another was the publication in 1965 of *The Literary History of Canada*, a book of almost a thousand pages issued by the University of Toronto Press under the general editorship of Professor Carl F. Klinck. This book is important in itself, as it is the first truly comprehensive study of its subject; but it is perhaps even more important for the stimulus it is sure to provide for other, more specialized studies.

Now that at last we can all see how vast the field is, before very long a host of busy miners will be sinking their exploratory shafts all over it.

For although much has been accomplished in the scholarly study of Canadian literature during the past quarter of a century, much more remains to be done. There are still no definitive studies of the main genres of Canadian literature—of the Canadian novel, Canadian poetry, Canadian essays, Canadian short stories. And there are still almost no good biographical and critical studies of individual authors, of Lampman, Carman, Roberts, Scott, Pratt or Leacock.

Another virtually unexplored area is that of Canadian travel literature, which if traced in detail from its origins, would provide us with much more information about our social, economic and cultural history. Among the most exciting chapters in *The Literary History* are those by David Galloway and Victor Hopwood which deal with the literature of Canadian exploration. They have opened up for us a whole new dimension of our writing, and extended by almost two centuries the depth of our literary tradition.

One corner of this area is the study of the reactions to the Canadian scene of such distinguished literary visitors as Captain Marryat, Charles Dickens, Matthew Arnold, Oscar Wilde, Rudyard Kipling and Rupert Brooke, and more recently of English writers such as Wyndham Lewis and J. B. Priestley. A study of the records they left of their impressions of Canada would help us to understand not only this country, but the country from which they came. A little over two years ago, Mr. Geoffrey Keynes was kind enough to let me look through his collection of the manuscript letters of Rupert Brooke, and to read and make notes on those which Brooke wrote from Canada. Brooke's sardonic and often supercilious remarks undoubtedly reflect the cultural poverty of our country at that time, but even more clearly they reveal the kind of upper-class English snobbery which made Englishmen in those early years of this century so suspect among us.

Another fruitful area of research is the reception which Canadian literature enjoyed (or suffered) in Great Britain. We speak glibly of the international reputations established by Haliburton, Parker, Roberts, Carman and Leacock, but no one has yet made a close study of the precise nature and extent of their reputations. I spent the academic year 1962-63 in Cambridge making a beginning on this study, and although all the evidence is not yet available I can offer a few tentative conclusions.

Firstly, we tend to exaggerate the overseas vogue of these authors. Haliburton was widely and enthusiastically reviewed in the British press, but in this respect he was a solitary exception. Gilbert Parker was never taken seriously as a novelist, and was judged quite rightly to be an entertainer rather than a serious artist; Roberts had almost no British recognition as a poet, and only a brief and fairly perfunctory one as a writer of prose nature sketches; Bliss Carman was the only Canadian poet to have his books regularly reviewed in the best literary periodicals of England, but he was always described as a minor poet and his vogue (if that is not too strong a word) lasted only for slightly over a decade; Leacock was always reviewed, but not with any great discernment.

To illustrate the ironies that turn up in such a study, let me cite the first English review of a Leacock book—his *Elements of Political Science* (1906)—in the course of which the reviewer in the *Athenaeum* accused Leacock of being unable to see a joke. Or take these sentences from the *Times Literary Supplement*'s review of Leacock's *Literary Lapses* (1910):

These are slight American humorous sketches, on a great many subjects. . . . Mr. Leacock is not a subtle wit. He must be taken in small doses and hardly bears reperusal. But a little of him in the right mood is very comforting.

Do they not catch perfectly the smug complacency of the British intelligentsia in 1910—even to the failure, still only too prevalent in the United Kingdom, to differentiate between Canada and America? It is only fair to add, however, that by 1912, when *Sunshine Sketches of a Little Town* appeared, the *TLS* had discovered Mr. Leacock's Canadianism. The reviewer went to the other extreme: from patronizing Leacock as an American he switched to embracing him as a Britisher:

His real hard work . . . is distilling sunshine. This new book is full of it—the sunshine of humour, the thin keen sunshine of irony, the mellow evening sunshine of sentiment. Universal things like these are not intended merely to pamper the pride of Imperialism. Still, we cannot resist a secret joy in the fact that all the queer and crooked characters that flourish in maple-shaded Mariposa . . . are British-born.

Such little ironies are frequent. Early in 1929 two interesting but admittedly imperfect novels by Canadians appeared in England—Frederick Philip Grove's *Our Daily Bread* and Raymond Knister's *White Narcissus*. If they had been reviewed seriously and sympathetically in such an influential English weekly as *The New Statesman and Nation,* their authors might have been decisively encouraged and a basis might have been laid for their English reputations. Instead, it was their bad luck to fall into the hands of that supercilious and bad-tempered old Etonian, Cyril Connolly, who was given eleven novels to review *en masse* on the eve of leaving for a Spanish holiday. Blithely he dashed off a review of which these are the relevant portions:

Our Daily Bread and *White Narcissus* are Canadian novels. One is soft-boiled and the other hard. The publishers are to be congratulated on starting a line in colonial fiction with "a country which has produced remarkably few novelists of a thoughtful quality." One is a wistful little love-story, mildly sophisticated, the other a typical family epic in the American style. The idea is refreshing; there must surely be many more colonies in which the necessary condition, quoted above, will apply. Meanwhile Canada is behind Jamaica, which has quite a good novelist within it, and a coloured expatriate outside.
. . . These books have finished this reviewer—more than he could do for them—and tomorrow they will be left in a hotel or dropped in the equable Adour, while he makes his way still fleeing from simple people and those who write about them, towards the mountains of Aragon.

Three years later Raymond Knister was to die, possibly by suicide, certainly in despair.

The second conclusion I would draw from my study of the reception of Canadian literature in England is that our cultural image there is largely a function of our political reputation. When England was most Empire-conscious, in the period from 1890 to 1918, there were a good many favourable discussions of Canadian writers and of Canadian literature generally. As

Canada gradually asserted its independence in the nineteen-twenties and thirties, the English interest in us proportionately declined. Our contribution to the Allied effort in World War II again stimulated some interest in our literature, but as we have once again asserted our independent role the interest has waned. Only recently, when there has been some revival of imperial sentiment in the terms of a Commonwealth cultural entente, has there been a revival of interest on a modest and tentative scale. But in spite of all the improved systems of communication in our time, Englishmen as a whole are still ignorant of what Canada is really like. The supreme example of this is the *Times Literary Supplement* reviewer of Robert Davies' and Tyrone Guthrie's book about the Stratford Shakespearian Festival, *Twice Have the Trumpets Sounded*. Referring to that Ontario theatrical venture, the reviewer wrote, "Mr. Guthrie did not patronize his prairie public. . . ."

But I may seem to be in danger of confining the outlook for Canadian literature to the outlook for the academic study of Canadian literature. I do not mean to imply that the health of Canadian literature depends upon the amount of academic critical scrutiny it is given, but this is nevertheless symptomatic of a wider, more general interest in what our writers produce.

When he wrote *On Canadian Poetry* in 1943, E. K. Brown began with a chapter which is a classic statement of the difficulties which had traditionally plagued Canadian literature until that time. If we consider his statement, and see to what extent conditions have improved in the twenty-odd intervening years, I think you will agree that the outlook for Canadian literature is much more hopeful today than it was a generation ago.

Brown begins by asserting, somewhat defensively, that "there is a Canadian literature, often rising to effects of great beauty, but it has stirred little interest outside Canada. . . . Canadian books may occasionally have had a mild impact outside Canada; Canadian literature has had none." It would be idle to pretend that there has been a really radical improvement in this respect. To the authors of international reputation whom Brown mentions—Haliburton, Roberts, Parker, Connor, Montgomery, Service, Leacock, Mazo de la Roche and Morley Callaghan—we may now add the names of Ethel Wilson, Mordecai Richler, James Reaney, Norman Levine, Margaret Laurence and (somewhat dubiously, since they are not clearly Canadian) Brian Moore and Malcolm Lowry. But it still true to say that these writers are known rather as individuals than as parts of a specifically Canadian tradition. For reasons which I have mentioned, interest in our national literature, as a distinctive part of the literature of the Commonwealth, is growing and will continue to grow, but I do not believe that the growth will be as rapid or as far-reaching as we might like it to become. Why should the British or Americans—our most likely outside readers—devote much of their attention to our literature, when they already have so much of their own? Canada is simply not yet an important enough figure on the world's stage to command that kind of interest. The United States is now so powerful that the British feel they must seek to understand her, but an understanding of Canada is not, and is not in the foreseeable future likely to be, high on their list of priorities.

To put my conclusion on this point briefly, I believe that the growth of outside interest in Canadian literature over the next generation will be measurable but not large. This means that we Canadians must scrutinize our own literature, and learn to set and apply our own standards of judgment. We have been too prone in the past to await the verdict of London or New York; our verdicts for the foreseeable future will have to be largely our own.

This brings us to Brown's next point, which is that "even within the national borders the impact of Canadian books and of Canadian literature has been relatively superficial." Here I believe there has been a demonstrable improvement in the space of a generation. For a long time Canadian writers had to find their publishers and their public outside Canada; now a Canadian book can command a large enough audience at home to make its domestic publication economically viable, even on occasion profitable. Irving Layton is a good example of a Canadian writer who survives almost exclusively by virtue of his reputation within Canada, and the bulk of the sales of such accomplished writers as Ethel Wilson, Robertson Davies, Hugh MacLennan and Earle Birney are transacted in Canadian bookstores. There is a tremendous voluntary enthusiasm for Canadian books among Canadian students, and among a growing number of Canadian adults. I have some evidence that this conclusion is not merely the result of my own prejudices: Norman Levine, who served a year or two ago as Resident Writer at the

University of New Brunswick after sixteen years of voluntary exile in the United Kingdom, told me that he found an almost miraculous change for the better in the Canadian interest in books and writers.

Brown's third major obstacle to the development of a Canadian literature is what he calls "the colonial spirit." "A colony," he says, "lacks the spiritual energy to rise above routine" and "it lacks this energy because it does not adequately believe in itself." He goes on:

It applies to what it has standards which are imported, and therefore artificial and distorting. It sets the great good place not in its present, nor in its past nor in its future, but somewhere outside its own borders, somewhere beyond its own possibilities. . . . It is clear that those who are content with this attitude will seek the best in jam and toffee from beyond the ocean. That anything Canadian could be supremely good would never enter their heads. . . . Canada has no distinct flag, and no single distinct anthem although Mr. Mackenzie King paused on the very brink of asserting the latter; the relations between the Canadian Provinces and the federal government are subject to review in London; and the Judicial Committee of the Privy Council, also in London, is our highest court. But Canada has her own ministers in foreign countries, makes treaties without reference to Britain, and declares, or refuses to declare, war by the instrument of her own Parliament. Is it any wonder that Canadian thinking about Canada is confused . . .? The average English Canadian would still like to have it both ways and is irritated, or nonplussed, by the demand that he make a resolute choice; at heart he does not know whether Canada or the Empire is his supreme political value.

Our first reaction, on re-reading those words a scant generation after they were written, is to be heartened by the progress that we have made. We do have a flag, we shall soon have an anthem, and for better or for worse we have cut almost all the imperial ties. On second thought, however, we may wonder whether we have merely replaced one dependence with another: are we not now in danger of becoming a mere appendage of the United States? Temperamentally an optimist, I do not think so. Although we have yet far to go in fully defining and valuing our Canadian identity, I believe that we are on that road, and that as we clarify our national goals our literature will at once reflect and guide us towards those objectives. We are far more ready today than we were a generation ago to judge what we have by our own standards, to put, for example, our own *imprimatur* upon our writers rather than to await the judgment of critics beyond our borders. As *The Times Literary Supplement* noted of Canadian criticism in its recent Commonwealth issue, we are no longer on the defensive: we see our own strength and weakness and neither boast of the one nor grovel over the other. We are at least approaching that state of cultural maturity in which we are ready to see ourselves steadily and see ourselves whole.

The next obstacle to the development of good Canadian literature cited by Brown is the spirit of the frontier, or its afterglow. He explains this as follows:

Most Canadians live at some distance from anything that could even in the loosest terms be known as a material frontier; but the standards which the frontier-life applied are still current, if disguised. Books are a luxury on the frontier; and writers are an anomaly. On the frontier a man is mainly judged by what he can do to bring his immediate environment quickly and visibly under the control of society. No nation is more practical than ours. . . . The uneasiness in the presence of the contemplative or aesthetic is to be ascribed to the frontier feeling that these are luxuries which should not be sought at a time when there is a tacit contract that everyone should be doing his share in the common effort to build the material structure of a nation. That a poem or a statue or a metaphysic could contribute to the fabric of a nation is not believed.

This passage now has an even more old-fashioned ring than Brown's description of our political dependence upon Britain. Theatres, art galleries, and centres for the performing arts have sprung up all over the country; poets read their works to large and enthusiastic audiences in every major city from coast to coast; our writers and artists are generously provided with fellowships, medals and travel grants by the Canada Council; resident painters, sculptors, musicians and writers are becoming a commonplace feature of our universities. We have come to realize that the quality of our lives and the prestige of our nation depend just as much on our art and culture as upon our science and technology, and we manifest an almost frantic desire to make up for our long neglect of things of the mind and the spirit. The Canada of the post-Massey Report era is no longer content to be a frontier society.

We are not content to be—but there are certain senses in which we still are, for all frantic efforts to progress. The interest in literature in particular and the arts in general is still confined to a relatively small group of our population. The theatres and art galleries have been built, but by the great mass of the population they are regarded as exotic growths. In many cities the theatres have trouble maintaining themselves, and the art galleries either fail to draw many visitors or draw them for the wrong reasons—for such reasons as social prestige and the desire to display one's new dress or hat. Of more direct relevance to the welfare of Canadian literature is the generally low cultural and intellectual level of our newspapers, magazines, radio and television programmes. In a country like England, a serious writer can augment his income by writing occasional reviews or essays for such newspapers as *The Observer, The Sunday Times,* or *The Guardian,* or for such magazines as *The New Statesman and Nation, The Spectator,* or *The Listener.* We have no such newspapers or magazines in this country. The book pages of even our best newspapers are naive and clumsy in comparison, and the fees they pay for reviewing are ridiculously low. Although *Saturday Night* is making a real effort to play a role in Canada similar to that of *The New Statesman* and *The Spectator,* its circulation is still so relatively small that it cannot exercise the kind of influence or command the prestige which would encourage our best writers to contribute frequently to it. And of course when we look at radio and television we realize only too keenly that we have not fully outgrown the frontier mentality. Despite all the heroic efforts of the C.B.C., the intellectual level of ninety-five per cent of our television and radio programmes is moronic.

We have not yet, then, really outgrown the malign influence of the frontier spirit, although we have made some demonstrable progress. A more thorough-going transformation has occurred in the space of a single generation to the puritanism which Brown lists next among the obstacles to our literary development. Canadian Puritanism, says Brown, "allows to the artist no function except watering down moral ideas of an orthodox kind into a solution attractive to minds not keen enough to study the ideas in more abstract presentations." No one can deny that puritanism is still a force amongst us, but it has lost its power to control the media of communication. Books which were in trouble with the censors thirty or so years ago, such as Frederick Philip Grove's *Settlers of the Marsh* or Morley Callaghan's *Such Is My Beloved,* now seem innocuous, almost naive, beside some the poems of Irving Layton and Leonard Cohen or such recent Canadian novels as Hugh Hood's *White Figure, White Ground* and Stephen Vizinczey's *In Praise of Older Women.* There is virtually no subject that a Canadian writer cannot discuss frankly today.

The final obstacle which Brown mentions, regionalism, I have never been able to see as an obstacle. He admits that regionalist art may have its virtues, particularly that of accuracy, but he asserts:

In the end, however, regionalist art will fail because it stresses the superficial and the peculiar at the expense, at least, if not to the exclusion, of the fundamental and universal. The advent of regionalism may be welcomed with reservations as a stage through which it may be well for us to pass, as a discipline and a purgation. But if we are to pass through it, the coming of great books will be delayed beyond the lifetime of anyone now living.

What worries me about the logic of Brown's argument is his assumption that regional accuracy and universal validity are incompatible. Are they incompatible in the Irish poetry of Yeats, or the Wessex novels of Thomas Hardy, or the Russian plays of Chekhov? Rather than seeing the strong regional particularities of this country as an obstacle to great art, I see them as an advantage—an advantage which we only began to exploit in the poetry of Carman, Lampman, Roberts and Scott and the novels of Grove and MacLennan. A regional novel or poem may be merely a pretty idyll; and too many of ours have been only that. But it may also be a work which reveals the basic stuff of human nature by a penetrating study of the here and now, and that is what I hope much of our literature may become.

Brown summarized his account of the difficulties confronting

Canadian literature in 1943 with this sad sentence: "What I have been attempting to suggest with as little heat or bitterness as possible is that in this country the plight of literature is a painful one." I do not think that any honest writer could subscribe to this verdict today. The life of the artist is always a painful one, but the pain today in this country is the inner torment caused by the effort at creation, and the anxiety generated by the apparent drift of the world towards nuclear war. The specifically Canadian environment is *not* hostile to the writer, although it may in some areas still be indifferent to him. Gradually, all our traditional excuses for inaction and lethargy are being removed.

We have today a literature which is still not great by world standards, but which is lively and interesting. Poets such as Layton, Reaney, Mandel, Birney, Livesay, Souster and Nowlan are as productive and as skilful as any comparable group writing in the English-speaking world, and prose writers such as Mac-Lennan, Frye, McLuhan, Richler, Moore, Davies, Wilson, Laurence and Levine are for the first time in our history as plentiful and as dextrous as our poets. Every year sees the emergence of new talents, so that today, again for the first time in our history, we have productive writers in every age group. Only in drama is there still a dearth of activity. Our great distances and our scattered population have so far been almost insuperable barriers to the growth of an indigenous theatre and theatre literature, but the theatres which have been recently built in almost all our major cities are bound—since art like nature abhors a vacuum—to stimulate playwriting in the not too distant future. Already the inimitable James Reaney has made a promising start.

To return to my original metaphor, my diagnosis and prognosis must be that the patient is healthy and is likely so to continue for the foreseeable future. Canadian writers have a growingly eager audience, and the old obstacles to our literary development have virtually disappeared. Whether or not my optimism is justified will depend upon factors beyond our national control: upon the diligence and talent of writers who are born amongst us, and upon the survival of human civilization in this anxious atomic age.

Index

"A, B, and C—The Human
Element in Mathematics," 69
"Abel Cain," 119
Abraham, Heights of, 97
Absalom, 245f.
Acorn, Milton, 205, 217
Acrobats, The, 209
Acta Victoriana, 227
Adam, G. Mercer, 123
Addison, Joseph, 70, 75
Africa, 144, 212
Agassiz, Louis, 181, 185
Ainsworth, Harrison, 158
Alexander, W. J., 8
Algar, F., 155n
Allanburgh, Ont., 168
"Allegory of Sleep, An," 220
"All Our Edens Are Lost and Never
Regained," 220
Allworthy, Squire, 70
Alphabet, 211, 227
America, 2, 3, 6, 8, 11, 75, 135, 272
America, A Search for, 7ff, 14, 18, 26
American Tragedy, An, 13
American Wars, 61
Amherstburg, Ont., 164
"Among Schoolchildren," 267
Anacreon, 196
Anatomy of Criticism, 204
Anderson, Patrick, 103, 108f, 111,
129, 199f
Angled Road, The, 210
Anka, Paul, 213
Appraisals of Canadian Literature, 46
*Apprenticeship of Duddy Kravitz,
The*, 209
*Arcadian Adventures With the Idle
Rich*, 70f, 73f
Archives, Public, of Canada, 163,
164n
Argosy, The, 185
Aristotle, 60
Arlen, Michael, 226
Arnold, Matthew, 2, 50, 93, 181f,
193, 205, 214, 271
Arthur, Sir George, 162

As for Me and My House, 29, 128
Askin, Colonel John, 79, 151f
Askin, Madeleine, 151f
Askin Papers, The John, 151n, 151f
"Astarte," 119
As Ten, As Twenty, 109
Athenaeum, The, 123, 157, 159, 272
"At Gull Lake: August, 1810,"
41, 236
"At the Cedars," 41f
Atlantic Advocate, The, 176, 177n
Atlantic Monthly, 123
Atlantic Ocean, 82, 159
Atlantic Provinces, 177
"At Last—A Canadian Literature,"
268
Auden, W. H., 106, 109, 116, 131,
139, 217, 226
"Au nombre de mes joies sans
nombre," 216
Austen, Jane, 93, 231
Australia, 2, 6
Autobiography (of Oliver Goldsmith),
54, 56n
"Ave," 195
Avison, Margaret, 204, 217, 227, 237
Ayorama, 211

Bacon, Sir Francis, 229
Bailey, A. G., 63n, 80, 104, 107, 129,
176, 185, 201
Bailey, L. W., 178, 181, 185
Baird, Irene, 29, 208
Baker, R. P., 46, 48, 82
"Ballad of Me," 142
Balzac, Honoré de, 28
Barbados, 153f
Barbara Ladd, 190
Barbusse, Henri, 138
Barchester Towers, 94
Bardot, Brigitte, 264
Barker, George, 82
Barometer Rising, 128
Barr, Robert, 124f
Barth, John, 257
Bateman, Major, 155n

281